Don't read this book without preparing to be disturbed in all the right ways. If you love the local church, like so many of us do, you know there are days when you want to shout with joy, exhilarated by its beauty and power. And there are many other days when you wonder why God would ever choose the likes of us to usher in his kingdom because of how petty, divisive, shortsighted, judgmental, mediocre, and apathetic we can be. Mark Buchanan calls us out of our safe zones of comfort to a vision that is transformational—and somewhat terrifying. It's the only kind of church that can change the world. So dig in, wrestle with these biblical truths, and commit yourself to building a community that is anything but safe.

—Nancy Beach, author of *An Hour on Sunday* and *Gifted to Lead: The Art of Leading as a Woman in the Church*

Mark Buchanan has been in the foxhole of church ministry for more than twenty years! He knows the landscape of the church and the kingdom. His new book, *Your Church Is Too Safe*, is a clarion call for the rest of us to wake up before it's too late. Artistically written, beautifully told, arresting to the heart, jarring to the soul, yet filled with hope and promise. You'll love Mark's invitation to join him in the foxholes for kingdom causes.

—Stephen W. Smith, founder of Potter's Inn and author of *The Lazarus Life* and *The Jesus Life*

I don't think I want to go the church the Mark Buchanan writes about. It would be too unnerving (sort like being around Jesus). But Buchanan writes with such verve and is so steeped in biblical truth, I think he's convinced me to join that church, because in the end it's a place where the unsettling and merciful God is found.

—Mark Galli, Senior Managing Editor, *Christianity Today*

Other Books by Mark Buchanan

MARK BUCHANAN

AUTHOR OF *YOUR GOD IS TOO SAFE*

YOUR CHURCH IS TOO SAFE

WHY FOLLOWING CHRIST TURNS
THE WORLD UPSIDE-DOWN

ZONDERVAN®

ZONDERVAN.com/
AUTHORTRACKER
follow your favorite authors

We want to hear from you. Please send your comments about this book to us in care of zreview@zondervan.com. Thank you.

ZONDERVAN

Your Church Is Too Safe
Copyright © 2012 by Mark Buchanan

This title is also available as a Zondervan ebook. Visit www.zondervan.com/ebooks.

This title is also available in a Zondervan audio edition. Visit www.zondervan.fm.

Requests for information should be addressed to:

Zondervan, Grand Rapids, Michigan 49530

ISBN 978-0-310-33123-0

Published in association with the literary agency of Ann Spangler and Company, 1420 Pontiac Road S.E., Grand Rapids, MI 49506.

Cover design: Rob Monacelli
Cover photo: Getty Images / Robert Llewellyn
Interior design: Matthew Van Zomeren

Printed in the United States of America

12 13 14 15 16 17 18 /DCI/ 19 18 17 16 15 14 13 12 11 10 9 8 7 6 5 4 3 2 1

For Sarah,
my Princess,
full of laughter
and wisdom,
who daily brings joy
to the house
like you once brought bouquets
of the prettiest dandelions,
that bright,
that real:
may you be safe
and dangerous
always

CONTENTS

INTRODUCTION
WHAT ARE YOU ARGUING ABOUT?

I'M BORED.

As are many people in church.

Bored, and also apathetic, passive, testy, lonely, disheartened. We're wary and weary and cranky and sad.

It's a long list.

There's an enormous gap between the life Jesus offered and the life we're living. We feel it. We see it. We sense that whatever else Jesus came preaching, *this* can't be what he had in mind: a roomful of people nodding to old platitudes, nodding off to old lullabies, perking up to Jonah-like rants, jumping up to split hairs or break company at the smallest provocation. He can't have dreamed a church gorging itself on feeling good and allergic to self-denial. He can't have hoped for a church that was more concerned with itself than with the world it inhabits. When Jesus announced that the kingdom was at hand, this can't be what he meant.

What happened?

When did we start making it our priority to be safe instead of dangerous, nice instead of holy, cautious instead of bold, self-absorbed instead of counting everything loss in order to be found in Christ?

.   .   .

I've been a pastor—a Baptist one, if you must know—more than twenty-two years, and a traveling speaker for twelve of those years, and so I've had some front-row and hands-on exposure to much of this. I've kept at it for more than twenty-two years because it hasn't all been the way I'm describing it. There have been many beautiful moments: conversions so unforeseen and inside out they almost made God's outstretched arm tangible; restorations of lives so sweet and lasting they almost made the Holy Spirit's holy dance visible; worship services so thick with God's presence that, like the saints of old, I've almost begged God to stop lest I die for joy; spiritual friendships so enriching and joyous I've tasted heaven.

I've been up the mountain and seen the kingdom come in power.

But most of my twenty-two years I've spent on the downside of the mountain.

The story I'm thinking about here is in Mark 9. It is the story of Christ's transfiguration, and then the story that comes right after that. It begins with Jesus inviting Peter, James, and John to witness the kingdom "come with power" before they "taste death."[1] They go to a mountaintop with him and there behold a spectacle of staggering beauty and terror. Peter, as an old man, remembers it vividly—he was an eyewitness, he says, to the "Majestic Glory."[2] What he saw, what they saw, was virtually a reenactment of Moses on Sinai, except this time Moses and Elijah are only bit players. They have walk-on parts, cameos. Moses is not here to receive stone tablets graven with law, and then come thundering down the mountain's flank to confront wayward Israel with God's unbending decree; Moses is here to listen to Christ. Elijah is not here to call down fire from heaven, and then order the death of Baal's frenzied prophets; Elijah is here to behold Christ. They witness what later the writer of Hebrews describes: "In the past God spoke to our forefathers through the prophets at many times and in various ways, but in these last days he has spoken to us by his Son, whom he appointed heir of all things, and through whom he made the universe."[3]

Moses was a prophet. Elijah too. Both had much to say.

But now the last days are upon us, and when the Son—heir of all things, maker of the universe—speaks, then all who have ears, Moses and Elijah among them, strike one posture only: they listen and they behold.

Peter, James, and John witness the entire spectacle, with borderline comical results. Peter, rash, brash, scared spitless, offers to build tabernacles for the three holy men. The fisherman aspires to carpentry, which is its own kind of tribute. Various interpretations of this abound, but best to stick with Mark's gloss on it, inserted parenthetically: "He [Peter] did not know what to say, they were so frightened."[4]

The things we say when we don't know what to say. The things we say in fear and shame and ignorance. If every idle word is written down, as we're told they are, then somewhere in heaven there must be a book of sayings that compiles all this— *Ridiculous Things Holy Men Have Said through the Ages: A Compendium of Terrible Gaffes and Stupid Remarks at Sacred Moments*. Abraham and Sarah, Moses and Aaron, Saul and David, Jonah and Jeremiah, and countless others, would make the final edit. I'd read it, if only because I'm sure I'd be quoted extensively myself.

Back to Mark 9. I love this story, the whole thing, not least because it's a template for my own encounters with the Majestic Glory. It evokes the moments of encounter I've had with Christ, when I'm left speechless or else uttering gibberish, terrified, awestruck, renewed in my heart's longing for the King and his kingdom, willing to do something, anything, even a foolish thing, to honor and enshrine the moment. I love that, according to Hebrews, all who follow Christ get to go up the mountain, to behold for themselves the Majestic Glory.[5] It's not just for a few, not anymore.

But what I don't love is that, almost always, what awaits us on the downside of the mountain is similar to what awaited Jesus and Peter and James and John on the downside of their mountain — indeed, similar to what Moses met on the downside of his mountaintop encounter with God. Best to quote the story in full:

> When they came to the other disciples, they saw a large crowd around them and the teachers of the law arguing with them. As soon as all the people saw Jesus, they were overwhelmed with wonder and ran to greet him.
>
> "What are you arguing with them about?" he asked.
>
> A man in the crowd answered, "Teacher, I brought you my son, who is possessed by a spirit that has robbed him of speech. Whenever it seizes him, it throws him to the ground. He foams at the mouth, gnashes his teeth and becomes rigid. I asked your disciples to drive out the spirit, but they could not."

"O unbelieving generation," Jesus replied, "how long shall I stay with you? How long shall I put up with you? Bring the boy to me."

So they brought him. When the spirit saw Jesus, it immediately threw the boy into a convulsion. He fell to the ground and rolled around, foaming at the mouth.

Jesus asked the boy's father, "How long has he been like this?"

"From childhood," he answered. "It has often thrown him into fire or water to kill him. But if you can do anything, take pity on us and help us."

"'If you can'?" said Jesus. "Everything is possible for him who believes."

Immediately the boy's father exclaimed, "I do believe; help me overcome my unbelief!"

When Jesus saw that a crowd was running to the scene, he rebuked the evil spirit. "You deaf and mute spirit," he said, "I command you, come out of him and never enter him again."

The spirit shrieked, convulsed him violently and came out. The boy looked so much like a corpse that many said, "He's dead." But Jesus took him by the hand and lifted him to his feet, and he stood up.

After Jesus had gone indoors, his disciples asked him privately, "Why couldn't we drive it out?"

He replied, "This kind can come out only by prayer."

The downside of the mountain is church. The Majestic Glory, just revealed, is once again veiled (almost makes you wish Peter had built at least one of his huts), and the usual suspects are out in droves: disciples bickering with religionists in the face of the world's deep pain, both sides useless and prayerless; evil dancing on the bones of the vulnerable; fathers pleading, clinging to the remnants of their faith; the crowd bored with and cynical about the whole sorry sight, having lost wonder long ago.

It's all so tediously familiar.

Then Jesus shows up, and everything wakes up: the crowd, "overwhelmed with wonder," runs "to greet him." The father's faith, though wilted by Jesus' hapless followers, revives. The demon flips out, then clears out. In short order, the whole ordeal is resolved, once for all.

And once more the church learns a lesson we've needed to learn ever since: we don't pray enough. This kind comes out *only* through prayer.

We don't dwell in the presence of God long enough, deep enough, to operate out of the fullness of his power and presence. We wield heaven in dribs and drabs, in spits and spats, by fits and starts.

When all else fails, we argue.

Question: is it too late to find a more excellent way?

. . .

I've lived too long on the downside of the mountain. A few years ago, it got me irritated enough to try something else. I didn't leave the church where I'm pastor. I didn't make bold announcements couched in five-year plans, or denounce the idea of five-year plans. I had no real strategy at all.

I just tried something else. I had a definite yet fuzzy (stay with me) sense of where I was going. I wanted the church to look more like the kingdom. I had little idea what that meant, and still less idea about how to get it. But I was well entrenched in midlife, bored, and with nothing to lose but my reputation, my comfort, my paycheck, and maybe my sanity.

So I thought it worth the try.

The results are mixed: thrilling, depressing, brilliant, messy. Almost every week, often several times a week, people encounter someone from our church and, in the encounter, bow the knee to Jesus Christ. (Half an hour ago I got an email from one of our pastors who helped a young woman do this very thing this morning.) And almost every week, someone leaves. They get mad at us for some infraction or another — I never said hi to them in Walmart on Wednesday, or I commended a book by an author they disapprove of, or, more seriously, they were in the hospital, close to death, and no one came.

Marriages beyond all hope are being restored.

Marriages we thought exemplary are falling apart.

Addicts are being set free.

Addicts are lapsing, and stealing from us.

People are choosing to live lives of costly purity.

People are choosing to live lives of cheap thrills.

The results are mixed.

But the jury's in, and the verdict is: there's no going back.

. . .

This book is that story, at least bits and pieces of it. It's that story, plus here and there stories of other churches, most of which do not fit any of the nearly useless labels bandied about today. But this can be said about them: they seek the kingdom of God and his righteousness, day in, day out, as first priority.

But all those stories are told in relation to a bigger story, the story of God's way with us. This book is mostly about that bigger story. It's my attempt to hear and then relate Scripture in a way that releases the church to be more like the kingdom. In the simplest terms, the book is a biblical manifesto for that.

There are many Bible texts I've read and read and never *heard*. I'm starting to hear some of them better, less distorted or muffled. It took me two decades to really hear anything the Bible had to say, for example, about the nations. And for most of my life I missed the radical implications for the church of Christ's incarnation and the Holy Spirit's outpouring. And for many years I was nearly deaf to the Scripture's steady drumbeat about the kingdom of God, and largely blind to how that kingdom is among us—often hidden, stealthy and surprising, but present.

God speaks, and some will say it's just thunder.

But God still speaks.

This is a book for the bored and the curious and the bold—and the timid who want to be bold. It's a book for those who want more from the church and for the church, but not necessarily anything new.

It's a book for those who wish the church looked more like the kingdom.

CHAPTER ONE

SINGING HEAVEN'S LOVE SONG

SHOULD THE CHURCH BE RELEVANT TO THE WORLD?

We've spilled a lot of ink over that question.[1] We've exchanged many words, both exhortatory and accusatory, trying to resolve it. It vexes us sorely. There are those who decry the church's stodginess, its veneration of old wineskins, its adherence to outmoded cultural forms. They seek a church that nimbly adapts to the world's music and dress and causes. And there are those who lament the church's trendiness, its fetish for new wineskins, its pursuit of faddish cultural novelties. They seek a church gloriously indifferent to the world's latest fashions.

We tote out Jesus' warning to be *in* the world but not *of* it, but then have endless and exhausting debates about what constitutes which. We have those who think the kingdom's come because we've preserved ancient songs and starchy vestments and Latin-strewn liturgies, and we have those who think it's come because we smoke Cuban cigars and drink Belgian beer and treat Starbucks as sacred space. If I wear torn jeans and a ratty T-shirt to church, am I *of* the world or *in* it? If our church worships to hip-hop music, which preposition are we falling under, *in* or *of*? If our liturgy hasn't changed since 1633 or 1952, or 1979, is that because we refuse to be *of* this world, or because we're failing to be *in* it?

And now I will resolve the matter for all time.

It doesn't matter. The kingdom is not about any of this. The kingdom of God is not about eating or drinking or music styles or how up-to-date or out-of-date we are.

The kingdom of God is a republic of love. Not the sentimental or sensual thing the world calls love, but the 1 Corinthians 13 kind: fierce, wild, huge, feisty, pure. The unbounded extravagance at the heart of the heart of God. This love is the song God sings over us, and calls us to sing loudly. What makes the church both a mystery and a magnet to the world is when we love in this way, God's way.

This love makes us relevant. Its absence makes us irrelevant, regardless of whatever else we're doing.

Question: is the love in your church such that people *in* the world and *of* the world would be willing to forsake all other loves just to know this love? Would they give up their addictions, their diversions, their compromises, their resentments, because the love your church has is better and truer and deeper than anything they've found anywhere else?

If yes, your church is relevant to the world.

If no, it's irrelevant.

It's not that God can't override our poor examples. He does all the time. It's not that God's love can't bleed through our pallor, can't burn through our coldness, can't subvert our wariness, can't multiply the meagerness of what we have. If he couldn't, if he didn't, woe to us, for we sometimes give God little else to work with. It's just that God seeks embodiments of his love. It's what he designed his church, in whole and in part, to be. It's tragic when our churches become, in whole and in part, mostly obstacles to divine love.

. . .

My favorite podcast is *Quirks and Quarks*, a science program from CBC Radio. In the course of an hour, Bob MacDonald, the show's host, interviews four or five people, usually researchers, on sundry topics related to the broad field of science. I glean all manner of cocktail party information from it: the current state of research in space-based energy supplies, the condition of ice floes in Antarctica, the design of prehistoric fish tails or crocodile teeth, the tales core samples from lake bottoms tell, the molecular structure of toxins in Arctic shrews, the pigmentation shifts of mating frogs in the Amazon, the olfactory powers of leaping spiders in East Africa. Fill me with an hour or two of Bob and his endlessly fascinating parade of field and laboratory experts, and I can sound, for small stretches, like a scientific know-it-all.

On November 21, 2009, Bob interviewed Dr. Kathleen Wermke, Director of the Center for Pre-Speech Development and Developmental Disorders at the University of Wurzburg in Germany. She was flush with a new discovery. She'd recently published results from a research project comparing the cries of newborns in Germany with those of newborns in France. The research involved extensive and precise recordings in maternity wards of infants, still swaddled, mewling and wailing. Dr. Wermke digitally graphed the pitch and cadence of those cries, and then painstakingly compared, baby for baby, those cries along ethnic lines.

What they discovered stunned them: babies cry *with an accent*. In France, babies consistently inflect from a low to a high pitch. It's a *wah-ayyy!* In Germany, it's the opposite, high to low. It's an *ayyy! wah*. The revolutionary element in this discovery is that the intonation pattern exactly mimics the "melody" of the mother—or, more precisely, the patterns of speech characteristic of the mother's national language. The French language tends to have an intonational rise at the end of a sentence; the German language an intonational fall at the end. The womb-bound baby hears this, and copies it at birth.

A baby eavesdrops on its mother for nine months. It puts its ear to the rail of her bones and listens to the train of her sorrow and gladness coming for miles. The child emerges from its mother's insides with her voice ringing in its ears, her music echoing in its own bones. Like an opera singer's understudy, the child is formed in the presence of a mighty voice. Sprawling naked into daylight, its first instinct is to sing its mother's song.

This got me wondering. If earth is heaven's womb, if time is eternity's belly, what song do we overhear from heaven that we try to sing on earth? We may sing it poorly, squalling and squawking, but we sing it instinctually. It's in our bones. So what's the music of heaven? What's the voice of the Father that every human's heard, at least in muffled form, and every human can copy, at least in mangled form?

Love.

Love is the music of heaven. When we love, no matter how awkwardly, we hum an anthem sung perfectly, all day, every day, in heaven.

Our humming might be nearly tuneless. It might be fragmentary, staccato, uneven. It might be croaky, jangly, warbly. It may be hard for others to identify the melody. It might be hard on the ears. But there it is, the Father's voice thinly echoed in our own.

. . .

A lot has been handed to me by way of love. Still, I'm slow to learn, slow to sing. At the least, I rarely sing heaven's song with the operatic gusto, the soaring and booming, the passion and pathos that the music calls forth. I grew up in a family with its commonplace share of problems, but I never lacked love. Indeed, I remember from early childhood the distinct feeling of being adored, which may have bred its own nest of problems. But I did not struggle, then or now, with feeling unloved. I learned love's song early, while I was still being formed in my mother's womb, and I've heard good renditions of the song nearly daily since.

I should be a great lover. But somewhere, somehow, the tune glitched in me. There was a copy error. It was like cat claws had been raked across the grooves of my LP, and every time the turntable spun the record, the needle skipped and the song garbled.

Here I am at fifty. I've been loved well all my days, and yet still I love poorly. Oh, don't misunderstand: I express, from the heart, deep affection for my wife, my children, my friends, my church. If you asked any of the above, "Does he love you?" I think, I hope, all or most would say, unhesitatingly, "Oh, yes!"

But the song I sing still seems thin to me — a sweet-enough but untrained voice, unaccompanied for the most part, muttering a simple folk song that charms but fails to inspire.

What's lacking is extravagance. What's missing is a bigness of heart that seeks the other out, even the unlovely, even the unlovable, to lavish love on them. What's missing is a pouring out, an overflowing, a scattering far and wide.

This, after all, is the love the Father has shown me, and you. This is his song.

God began singing that song before the creation of all things. Jesus in his high-priestly prayer says, "Father, I want those you have given me to be with me where I am, and to see my glory, the glory you have given me *because you loved me before the creation of the world.*"[2] Before sea, sky, tree, bird, serpent, there was love: the eternal, infinite, pure love that flowed in and from Father to Son, Son to Spirit, and then back again, round and round, unhindered, unbroken, undiminished, wild and unbridled. The old theologians called this *perichoresis*, the self-giving dance of the Three-in-One God. God *in himself* is an entire community of radical love. God in himself is a city on a hill. And the pulse of that city, its lifeblood, is love.

What God does in creation is share the love. God creates, but not out of boredom or loneliness or the need to find his creative edge. God has all God needs in the company of the Godhead. God created because God is extravagant and, above all and in all, desired to share with that which he created the love he has been from all eternity.

But God's creation went awry (in case this is news to you). We wanted power more than love, and so rejected love. That's why within minutes of the fall of humanity, Adam and Eve are in a blistering row of accusation and avoidance, and why in the next generation brother turns on brother. We're in exile from the love we were invited to dwell in.

Jesus came to heal that. The pure, infinite, eternal love of Father, Son, and Holy Spirit did not end with the fall. Our catastrophe in no way impaired or depleted God's love. As then, so now: his love continues unabated. But a way needed to be reopened for us to participate in that love. And a deep ongoing healing needs to happen for any of us to truly dwell in it.

That's what Jesus is up to. Just listen to some of the things he says.

As the Father has loved me, so have I loved you. Now remain in my love. If you obey my commands, you will remain in my love, just as I have obeyed my Father's commands and remain in his love. I have told you this so that my joy may be in you and that your joy may be complete. My command is this: Love each other as I have loved you. Greater love has no one than this, that he lay down his life for his friends. You are my friends if you do what I command. I no longer call you servants, because a servant does not know his master's business. Instead, I have called you friends, for everything that I learned from my Father I have made known to you. You did not choose me, but I chose you and appointed you to go and bear fruit—fruit that will last. Then the Father will give you whatever you ask in my name. This is my command: Love each other.[3]

May they be brought to complete unity to let the world know that you sent me and have loved them even as you have loved me.

Father, I want those you have given me to be with me where I am, and to see my glory, the glory you have given me because you loved me before the creation of the world. Righteous Father, though the world does not know you, I know you, and they know that you have sent me. I have made you known to them, and will continue to make you known in order that the love you have for me may be in them and that I myself may be in them.[4]

It's no wonder the apostle Paul, who was overtaken by this love when he was still an enemy of God, never recovered from his amazement that this love sought him or his thanksgiving that this love won him. No wonder he prays that God "out of his glorious riches ... may strengthen you with power through his Spirit in your inner being, so that Christ may dwell in your hearts through faith. And I pray that you, being rooted and established in love, may have power, together with all the saints, to grasp how wide and long and high and deep is the love of Christ, and to know this love that surpasses knowledge—that you may be filled to the measure of all the fullness of God."[5]

If we get this—how deeply, completely, unreservedly we are loved—we get it all: "filled to the measure of all the fullness of God," as Paul puts it. That's a lot of God.

And so no wonder, then, that the apostle Paul writes 1 Corinthians 13, the justly famous Love Chapter. It is read at most weddings, with scarcely a hunch about what it means. "If I speak in the tongues of men and of angels," it begins, "but have not love, I am only a resounding gong or a clanging cymbal. If I have the gift of prophecy and can fathom all mysteries and all knowledge, and if I have a faith that can move mountains, but have not love, I am nothing. If I give all I possess to the poor and surrender my body to the flames, but have not love, I gain nothing."[6] If I am Seneca or Gabriel, if I am Isaiah or Daniel, if I am John the Baptist, Mother Teresa, Hugh Latimer, Billy Graham, Toby Mac, but something besides love moves me, it doesn't matter. I give nothing. I receive nothing. I am nothing.

This love is no mild, tepid thing. It is no flight of fancy, no frisson of giddiness, no mere ruffle of sensation. This love is neither nice nor prissy nor fragile nor coy. This love is fierce and wild and dangerous and unbreakable. It is sublime and subversive. It is indefatigable and undefeatable. It is nothing less than the love God has for you, to bind you and to loose you, to take you captive and then set you free.

This love is extravagant.

How extravagant? "How great is the love the Father has lavished on us, that we should be called children of God! And that is what we are!"[7] When this love really takes deep and lasting hold, we find we are free to love not just the lovely but the unlovely. We find at work in us a love that compels us to love the most of these (those who are more than we are), the least of these (those who are less than we are), and the worst of these (those who are against who we are).

Winners.

Losers.

Enemies.

Love for the most of these, the winners: with this kind of love, Saul could have loved David, and Cain Abel. Love for the least of these, the losers: with this kind of love, wealthy Dives could have loved beggarly Lazarus, and the priest the leper. Love for the worst of these, our enemies: with this kind of love, Paul loved the Philippian jailer, and Stephen his accusers.

This love is the revolution Jesus loosed on the earth. This love is the fire he kindled. This love is the song he came singing. He loved wary, cowardly Nicodemus with such love. He loved fiery, reckless Simon the Zealot with it, and loved runty, conniving Zacchaeus as well. He loved his mother, and Mary Magdalene, and demon-afflicted Legion, and the rich young ruler who spurned his invitation, and Peter who denied his name, and Judas who betrayed him unto death, and the priests who condemned him, and the thieves who mocked him, and the soldiers who nailed him to a tree — he loved all with such love.

> Sing, Daughter Zion;
>> shout aloud, Israel!
> Be glad and rejoice with all your heart,
>> Daughter Jerusalem!
> The LORD has taken away your punishment,
>> he has turned back your enemy.
> The LORD, the King of Israel, is with you;
>> never again will you fear any harm.
> On that day
>> they will say to Jerusalem,
> "Do not fear, Zion;
>> do not let your hands hang limp.

The LORD your God is with you,
   the Mighty Warrior who saves.
He will take great delight in you;
   in his love he will no longer rebuke you,
   but will rejoice over you with singing."[8]

God sings over you with rejoicing, and then calls you to sing aloud with the same joy. "Sing lustily," Wesley sometimes wrote over certain of his hymns when he wanted them sung robustly, nothing held back. That's God's cue. "That song I sing over you," he says. "You know, my love song for you? It's my favorite song. We three Kings, the trinity of Father, Son, and Holy Spirit, have been belting it out for eons now. Never gets tired. Every refrain better than the one before. That's the song I want you to sing too. And sing it loud, like you mean it."

Sing lustily.

"That the world may know."

.   .   .

I already told you that I sing this song poorly, not lustily.

But I'm getting better. I see, almost every day, promising signs that this love, in all its wild extravagance, is taking hold of me more and more and is flowing through me less hindered, less dammed, less diverted, less diluted, flowing through me to the most of these, the least of these, the worst of these. To all of these. Sometimes a hopeful sign that this is so appears one moment and is squelched the next. But the distance between such squelchings is getting longer, and the duration of them shorter, and so I know God is loosing and binding in me what he wants me loosing and binding on earth.

And this is important. It's important for its own sake, because it's tragic whenever God's love goes astray in any of us, gets lost in translation. It's tragic whenever love's Niagara Falls, poured into our hearts, trickles out Cripple Creek. It's maybe more damaging to know the love of God and not share it than never to know it in the first place; isn't that what Jesus found so damnable in so many of Israel's religious leaders, men upon whom God had lavished his inheritance but who became older brothers, not squandering it but hoarding it, complaining about its scarcity?

But it's also important because without extravagant love, the church will never turn the world on its head. It won't even turn the world's head. Without love, the church will leave the world exactly how we found it. We'll be no better than a priest or a Levite walking past a man in a ditch, leaving him to die. Again, I don't mean that God cannot and does not overrule our sometimes lackluster performance. He always has a Good Samaritan or two in the wings, should the church fail. And sometimes he just goes direct. His love often intersects human hearts apart from any human agency; it is a love "shed abroad in our hearts by the Holy Ghost,"[9] as Paul puts it, and he would know. It's just that God has designed his church to be both locus and channel for divine love. Everyone loses when we fail at this, we maybe most of all.

"What the world needs now is love, sweet love. It's the only thing that there's just too little of." Those are a couple of lines out of a song from my parents' era.

It's true. And God put the church on the earth to meet that need, to make up what's lacking. He put the church here to sing, and sing lustily, the song God's sung since before the creation of the world. The song God's sung for the sake of the world.

. . .

I've seen our church sing that song over many people. Like Mandy.

Mandy's family is a mash-up. Her parents have been through so many marriages and divorces, so many flings and one-night stands, that Mandy can't keep track of all her half sisters and half brothers, stepmothers and stepfathers. She's been raped by many of the men her mother dated. She developed a habit of promiscuity in grade school. And around that time began to resort to an exotic cocktail of drink and drugs, legal and street, to numb the pain. When she showed up, she was angry, depressed, and stuck.

And sick of life. Most days, she thought seriously about ways to end it.

A lady who worked at a boutique where Mandy shopped invited her to a ladies' retreat our church was hosting. Mandy was wary but hungry. Her home life, chaotic and scattershot as it was, did manage to establish in Mandy a deep prejudice against religion, and especially Christianity. Her dad was a belligerent atheist. Her mom, with whom she mostly lived growing up, embraced an exotic amalgam of New Agism, Eastern mysticism, and good old sexual promiscuity. Mandy absorbed from all that both a rigorous skepticism and a softheaded gullibility. She didn't know what to make of a churchy event like a ladies' retreat.

But in the end, Mandy's intrigue trumped her suspicion, and she came. The speaker talked about the love of God—this vast ocean, deep and wide, purifying and intoxicating, unfathomable yet right here, inviting you to dive in. Mandy had never heard this. She could scarcely believe this. She wept and wept at the news of this.

And then she dove.

What *convinced* her to dive in was the sheer beauty of divine love. But what *drew* her to that divine love was the very real demonstration of it in the women she met at the retreat. These women heard Mandy's story and didn't pull back. They didn't judge. They didn't withhold their love from her.

They just showed her greater love. They laughed with her, cried with her, prayed for her. They offered her good counsel to deal with a struggle she was having with Burt, her live-in. One woman offered to come with her on Sunday night, after the retreat, and help Mandy explain to Burt what had happened at the retreat.

That was several years ago. Mandy is now married—to Glenn (Burt didn't take the news of her conversion well)—and they have three beautiful children. She is involved in a ministry in our church. She's led many women, including a few of her siblings, to know the love of Christ that's bound and loosed her.

. . .

Every time I see Mandy, I think of the Samaritan woman Jesus met at a well. That story is told in John 4. Jesus and his disciples are traveling through Samaria, heading to Jerusalem. Jesus is exhausted and hungry and thirsty. Especially thirsty. He sits at the edge of the well while his disciples go to town to buy food. His thoughts turn to the water deep beneath him, cold and dark and fresh. His mouth is dry as a potsherd. His tongue sticks to the roof of his mouth.

I thirst.

A shadow falls across him. He looks up. A woman is there, alone. She tries to ignore him. A sideways glance, a pose of aloofness. She acts like he's not there, moves around him like he's some innate physical obstacle, immovable.

"Will you give me a drink?" Jesus asks.

The voice, the question, the man: they startle her. They startle her out of her silence and avoidance.

"You are a Jew and I am a Samaritan woman. How can you ask me for a drink?"

And then unfolds a remarkable encounter, a life-turning exchange. But not at first. At first, her speech is as cagey as her silence, a series of diversions and evasions. Jesus offers her living water, "the gift of God." She's puzzled and intrigued, but when Jesus exposes her condition, she scurries down a rabbit trail. She wants to talk about worship. That might be a good thing, but as so often happens with talk of worship, it bogs down quickly into hairsplitting and argument baiting. Is this style better than that style? Is old better than new? Is tradition better than innovation?

Jesus cuts through all that with a clear word about the heart of worship: it's about the heart *in* worship. It's about a heart that longs for God and seeks him wherever he might be found. It's about a heart that wants truth in the inmost parts, and opens itself wide as a bird's mouth to receive it, and steeps in it until it works its way to the outermost parts. Worship is not about a style or a form or a place. That's not what God's seeking. He's seeking not a kind of music or liturgy or architecture but a kind of person: humble, hungry, wide awake, who comes in spirit and truth, bold and beseeching both, ready to live toward God out of their depths.

Which is all fine and well. But the woman, either overwhelmed or underwhelmed, tries her last dodge: "I know that the Messiah (called Christ) is coming. When he comes, he will explain everything to us."

And then Jesus pulls out his showstopper (with a kind of Yoda syntax): "I who speak to you am he."[10]

That changes everything. She runs back to town, "leaving her water jar" (a lovely and revealing detail: she's distracted in all the right ways now), and does something that, in the telling, flies by so swiftly we could easily miss the revolution at hand: she goes back to her town and says to the people, "Come, see a man who told me everything I ever did. Could this be the Christ?"

And they heed her.

She "said to the people." That's the revolutionary detail. That's the shock wave of the story. We have little background to this encounter. We know, from the text at hand as well as from other places, biblical and historical, about the mutual hostility and suspicion between Jews and Samaritans. We know — John tells us straight up — that Jews don't talk with Samaritans, and at the story's close he tells us again, less directly, that her gender is a cultural problem as well.

But we can also, with a bit of sleuthing, shade in a few more details about this particular story. We know that in general women in the ancient Near East never went to the well at "the sixth hour" — high noon. It's too hot. And we know in general that women in this culture never went to the well alone. The trip to the well was done in the cool of the day and in the company of others. There must always have been exceptions to these customs. But the fact that this woman has lost at love so often — five ex-husbands — and has become so cynical about or damaged by that that she's given up on matrimony altogether — the man she's with now is not her husband — is a significant clue about why she's at the well by herself at noon: she's ashamed. She's estranged. She's probably outcast — scorned by her community, distrusted by the women especially. Villages have names for women like this. *Tramp* is one of the nicer ones, and it just gets worse from there — home wrecker, whore, hussy, slut.

She "said to the people."

"They came out of the town."

The encounter with Christ has healed the rift. Whatever's kept her apart from the rest of the town, Christ has mended. Whatever authority she's lacked, Christ has restored. Whatever shame's kept in the shadows, Christ has removed.

"Come, see a man who told me everything I ever did." All we know for sure that Jesus told her is that she's had five husbands and she's shacking up with her current guy. That she describes this as "everything I ever did" says a lot about how these things weigh on her, how completely they define her.

But it also says a lot about Jesus. It tells us the tone with which he spoke. There couldn't have been a single note of condemnation in it. There couldn't have been even a shadow of scolding or shaming. She heard the voice of love. She heard the voice of acceptance. She does the math: the Messiah reveals himself to me, teaches me about God's heart for worship, and offers to me the gift of God — and he does it knowing full well everything I've ever done. My past doesn't disqualify me. My past has not forfeited my future. He doesn't hold my past against me.

. . .

I was speaking in a town near Toronto a few years ago, and one of the singers on the worship team told a story about the Man who knows everything we do and still invites us to know him, still imparts to us the gift of God. The singer was part of a church-plant on the east side of town — lots of drug addicts, drug dealers, gang leaders, prostitutes, the usual suspects — and so often the services were filled with a wild assortment of God evaders and God chasers. Every Sunday, the church served communion — mostly because every Sunday, people needed the Bread of Life and Living Water. They needed to know that Jesus did for them what they could never do for themselves.

One Sunday, a streetwalker who'd never been to the church before came in. She was in rough shape: bruised, shaking, bedraggled. When the pastor stood up to serve communion, he explained what it is: taking Christ himself, his forgiving, redeeming, healing life, into the very blood and bones of ourselves. It is feasting on Christ's forgiveness and love and promise of newness.

Then they passed the plate of bread around. The streetwalker took a handful of bread and piled it on the lap of her short skirt. When invited, she ate it all, licking crumbs off her fingers. Then the cup came around, and the streetwalker did likewise: took six or seven little thimblefuls and downed them all, tipping each cup back to drain the dregs. All the time, she wept.

She wasn't physically hungry. She wasn't physically thirsty.

She was starved for love. She was parched for grace. She could not get enough of Christ.

"Come, see a man." Come and see the man who knows everything I've ever done and still offers me everything he's ever done. Come, meet the man who knows me through and through and loves me all the same.

Come, meet the man.

CHAPTER TWO

SONS OF THUNDER
(OR HOW THE SON MAKES ALL THINGS NEW)

JESUS CALLED THEM SONS OF THUNDER, and that named them well. Those boys, James and John, were hotheads. They were heel grabbers. They were thin skinned. They were hair triggered. They were light fingered. Quick to take offense, nurse a grudge, exploit a weakness, steal a birthright, pilfer a blessing. They were momma's boys and chips off the old block. They were in it for themselves. They were ready, at the least provocation, real or imagined, to bust chops. They were prepared, at the slightest opportunity, real or imagined, to seize advantage. They'd happily, to defend their own honor, loose weapons of mass destruction on tiny Middle Eastern villages. They'd happily, to advance their own honor, make a land grab for the best real estate in heaven. They thought being in Jesus' camp gave them a monopoly on power and clout.

I picture them. John has a rash of acne, bright as war paint, along his jawline. James has narrow eyes and a sullen downturn to his mouth. Both are chronically tensed up. They bristle with personal grievance. Just spoiling for a fight. They instinctively divide life into two categories: threats to be countered, and advantages to be taken.

And then they changed. Not all in a rush; it happened by inches, in a slow roundabout way. But John's epithet wasn't Son of Thunder. It was Apostle of Love. Likely, James's life took a similar turn. The Sons of Thunder became Sons of God.

It's a story worth telling, and reflecting on, not the least because it says something to the church. As then, so now: anger never gets us very far. Another James, the brother of Jesus, says as much: "My dear brothers and sisters, take note of this: Everyone should be quick to listen, slow to speak and slow to become angry, because our anger does not produce the righteousness that God desires."[1]

"Our anger does not produce the righteousness that God desires." Anger actually makes us too safe. It's a posture we strike to avoid the more costly, risky, messy way of dealing with strangers and enemies, which is to love them. The Sons of Thunder learned this; they learned that it takes more courage to love your enemy than to attack him.

. . .

Imagine Jesus choosing his disciples. He spent all night in prayer, in a hidden place, and then called them to himself "that they might be with him, and that he might send them out."[2] "These are the twelve he appointed: Simon (to whom he gave the name Peter), James son of Zebedee and his brother John (to them he gave the name Boanerges, which means 'sons of thunder'), Andrew, Philip, Bartholomew, Matthew, Thomas, James son of Alphaeus, Thaddaeus, Simon the Zealot and Judas Iscariot, who betrayed him."[3]

That's the story in broad outline. For some of these men, we're given close-ups in other parts of the Gospels: Matthew, the tax collector, sitting at his booth. Peter, the fisherman, hauling in his nets. Andrew, Peter's brother, introducing Peter to Jesus, then slipping beneath Peter's bulky shadow. Philip. Nathaniel. Bartholomew. All have a story, long or short, detailed or vague.

And then there's James and John. It's those two, plus Peter, we have the most footage for. Often their stories — Peter, Andrew, James, John — crisscross, since they were business partners. And Peter, James, and John were Jesus' "favorites," his inner circle.

And here's how it started. Jesus walked by a lake one day, saw James and John fishing with their father, Zebedee, and he called them. Without blinking, they followed. According to Mark, Jesus called James and John Sons of Thunder, though whether this was soon or late, when he first met them or after he got to know them, we don't know. Maybe it was late, after this event: "As the time approached for him to be taken up to heaven, Jesus resolutely set out for Jerusalem. And he sent messengers on ahead, who went into a Samaritan village to get things ready for him; but the people there did not welcome him, because he was heading for Jerusalem. When the disciples James and John saw this, they asked, 'Lord, do you want us to call fire down from heaven to destroy them?' But Jesus turned and rebuked them. Then he and his disciples went to another village."4

Maybe it's here Jesus hangs the moniker on them: Sons of Thunder. Noisy menaces. Cloudy threats. Bombastic loudmouths. Jesus had advised, when a town turns you back, just to kick its dust off your feet. That's violence enough. But these two would rather hurl lightning bolts. Their hands itch to pull the "Annihilate" switch. They've got Jonah's disposition toward Nineveh, savoring the thought of a mushroom cloud blooming over the place's head. "That will teach them not to mess with us."

There's a second incident that happens around this time. Jesus tells his disciples the reason they're going to Jerusalem. It's not what they're thinking. They're thinking conquest. They're thinking Romans crushed beneath Messiah's feet. They're thinking big men groveling for mercy. They're thinking holy war on a Psalm 2 scale: "Kiss the Son, lest he be angry, and ye perish from the way, when his wrath is kindled but a little."5

Jesus tells them the terms of engagement are much different: " 'We are going up to Jerusalem,' he said, 'and the Son of Man will be delivered over to the chief priests and the teachers of the law. They will condemn him to death and will hand him over to the Gentiles, who will mock him and spit on him, flog him and kill him. Three days later he will rise.' "6

That's got to stop them in their tracks. The biblical record shows that the disciples had no category for even hearing this kind of talk, let alone comprehending it. It was blather to them. If it didn't come across as heresy—Peter's indignant response treats it as such7—it came across as gibberish, which is to say not at all.

But James and John do grasp *something* of Jesus' meaning. Here's the second incident: "Then James and John, the sons of Zebedee, came to him. 'Teacher,' they said, 'we want you to do for us whatever we ask.'

" 'What do you want me to do for you?' he asked.

"They replied, 'Let one of us sit at your right and the other at your left in your glory.'

" 'You don't know what you are asking,' Jesus said."[8]

I'm guessing they latch onto Jesus' final comment—"three days later he will rise." And I imagine they scale that to a size that's human, earthly, political: three days in, Jesus gets his war boots. He hits his stride. He turns the tables. The rest, I'm thinking, they chalk up to some kind of apocalyptic hyperbole—the first few days of battle don't go well, is all he's saying, right? Well, never mind all that: the third day, it all comes together.

They don't miss the implications: there's glory to be had here. There is, in good Roman tradition now turned on its head, a big victory parade to follow. An ascending of the Praetorian steps. A laying of wreaths. An imperial honoring.

"You don't know what you are asking."

It's maybe after one or both of these incidents that Jesus named them Sons of Thunder.

But this can't be the first time they've behaved this way. This can't be, even in an environment crackling with fear and astonishment, the first time these character traits have surfaced. These stories are representative anecdotes of pattern behavior. These stories are cases in point, forensic evidence to establish an overall verdict. This stuff is bred in their bones. It's in so far and so deep, so fused with their guts, that they can't even help it. Hit them—you will not get another shot. Take their tunics—well, don't even try.

And then they change. And change dramatically. They turn inside out. At first they are new creations merely by virtue of Jesus' saying so, with no real evidence to back it (which is typical for most of us). But they actually become these new creations in the flesh, in real time, for all to see. You could take before-and-after portraits of these guys and be astonished. Is the miserly, miserable, ornery little scrapper in that picture the wise, gentle, generous love-dispenser in this one? Wow. Whoever did his makeover is good.

We know how that happens. They learn Christ. Jesus speaks into them—he *breathes* into them—long and deep enough that a long and deep altering happens within, bone and gut and muscle. He woos them to break them to make them new. The anger that bristles up in them at the least sign of contention is drawn out of them like poison and replaced by supernatural patience. The self-aggrandizing schemes that preoccupy their waking hours and linger in their sleep wither and die, and in their place dreams of sacrifice and servanthood grow. The self-pity that twists and sours their bellies washes away, and a thankfulness and almost giddy kidlike joy floods in.

They become as he is.

And then they do as he does.

Being as he is and doing as he does distills to one main thing: loving as he loves. John and James, such unlikely candidates for this, learn to love with a love that prevails. Christ loves the world in order to overcome the world. He loves the world and us within it, in all our folly and rebellion and brokenness. He loves it, and us, until we surrender and become whole. And then he loves us still.

This is the shape of discipleship. It may not be anger and coveting that mark us out when Jesus first finds us. It may be cowardice or laziness or aloofness or lewdness, or any number of sundry ways our character misrepresents the kingdom. But as we walk with Jesus, learning his ways, empowered by his Spirit, we "are being transformed into his likeness with ever-increasing glory."[9] Sons of Thunder, and Daughters of Gossip, and Stepchildren of Avarice, and Adoptees of Impurity, and all the rest, in Christ's hands become, in word and deed, new creations.

Apostles of Love.

. . .

The Bible has another way of describing this: overcoming evil with good.

God never flinches from naming evil or sin. Christians ought not to flinch either. I appreciate the recent emphasis on the "missional church." This rediscovery of the heartbeat of the early church has been long overdue. But I do have a growing misgiving about some of it: in our eagerness to make up for lost time and regain lost ground, and to reach lost people, we're running a risk of calling evil good, or at least of not naming evil.

I'm fully aware that many churches are boldly naming evil, and often boldly confronting it. I don't think the church since the time of Wilberforce has been as awake to systemic evil, and as ready to do battle with it, as it is today. It's heartening. When I think of the work of, say, International Justice Mission—their rescue of modern-day slaves, their intervention on behalf of girls forced into the sex trade, and their strategy for restorative justice, for both the victims and the perpetrators of evil—I'm happy to be in ministry at such a time as this.

But there are also troubling signs all about. Sometimes we're so eager to win the world we compromise with it. I think of a church I know that allowed a practicing witch on the worship team because they saw it as an evangelistic opportunity. I think of many churches I'm aware of that, not wanting to fall into the prudish, tongue-clucking, finger-wagging posture that for so long marked out our stance on sexual issues, straight or gay, have overaccommodated, overcompensated, and stopped calling people, regardless of their sexual orientation, to a biblical standard of holiness and purity.

I say all this to make a simple point: we can't overcome evil (or sin, for that matter) if we dare not name it.

The age we live in is more confused than ever. This is not the moment to become vague and apologetic about the truths, both doctrinal and ethical, we've received once for all. Our age may not need heavy-handed dogmatism, but it's desperate for steady-handed clarity. There is a growing need to name, truly, accurately, faithfully, the evil that is all around, and to call, insistently, patiently, lovingly, men and women to a more excellent way.

Not long ago, an unmarried couple—not from the church, not Christians—came to see one of the pastors at our church. Their lives were in shambles. They argued nonstop, and their arguing was turning violent. They were in a holding pattern of anger and accusation that was destroying both of them. The pastor, after a mere fifteen minutes, looked at them and said, "Well, you both need to realign your lives with God and with God's ways. You need Christ. And you need a whole new way of living." He told them how to come into a relationship with Christ, but neither of them were ready for that. "Okay," he said. "But even now you can start doing things God's way. Clearly your way is crap. For a start, you need to stop pretending you're husband and wife. You need to tear this whole relationship down to the ground and start over. So," and here the pastor looked at the man, "you need to move out by this evening."

The couple were stunned. They left, silent and indignant.

The next week the man phoned back. "Okay. I did as you said. I moved out that night. Things are already a hundred percent better. What's the next step?"

This is not the age for being unclear.

All the same, naming evil is at most and at best half our job. In fact, if all we do is name evil, we won't even be doing half our job. We'll be undoing it as much as doing it. Naming evil, period, is a posture the church in certain places and during certain eras has perfected. It's too easy to become a connoisseur of wrongdoing. Professional denouncers. When the church *en masse* adopts this position, it's not our finest hour. We've denounced abortion, but not always shown hospitality to the single mothers in our midst. We've signed petitions against same-sex marriages, but not always loved our wives "just as Christ loved the church and gave himself up for her."[10] We've spoken out publicly against pornography, and privately indulged it.

By itself, naming evil is as close to useless as an activity gets.

The other half of our job is to overcome evil, the evil we've dared to name, with deep enduring good. This is the church's real calling. This is the deeper and harder half of our job. This is what makes the church different from everything else in the world, or is supposed to. We open ourselves to the Holy Spirit's power and creativity to discover a third way between revenge and capitulation, between attacking evil and succumbing to it. That third way is overcoming. It is naming and facing evil head-on, and defeating it not with petitions and lawsuits, not with guns and tanks, but with goodness.

With love.

The movie *Gran Torino*, which Clint Eastwood directs and stars in, is a potent dramatization of this very principle. It's not for the faint of heart; the language turns the air a smoky blue and is strong enough to blister paint. But I know of few mainstream movies (*To End All Wars* comes to mind) that portray so compellingly the overcoming of evil with good. Eastwood plays Walt Kowalski, a bigoted, surly, stubborn old veteran of the Korean War who lives in a permanent state of disgust over how his middle-American neighborhood has become a colony of Asian immigrants. The family who moves in next door to him is, of course, Asian, three generations of them. Walt wants nothing to do with them.

But circumstances conspire against that. He ends up involved in their lives, they in his. Beyond all reckoning, he becomes a kind of father to Bee Vang and his sister Ahney Her. Ahney is brutally gang-raped by her own cousin and his gang, who have become an increasing threat to both Walt and his Asian neighbors. Walt decides there and then to take action. Enough is enough is enough. He's a guerrilla fighter from way back, a shotgun-toting Dirty Harry in an old man's dyspeptic rage, and he starts plotting revenge. Bee Vang is right there with him, ready to kill or die to defend his sister's honor. But Walt tricks him and locks him in his cellar.

This job is all his.

What happens next is shocking. Walt goes to the gang's house and calls them out from the front lawn. They come bristling with weaponry. Walt reaches inside his coat as though to draw a gun, and they open fire. They riddle him with bullets. He flops on the ground and dies.

He's unarmed. He was reaching for his lighter.

Turns out, he never intended to fight the thugs at all. He intended to overcome them. He intended to absorb their evil in order to defeat it.

As I said, that dramatizes the principle of overcoming evil with good. But for most of us, it overdramatizes it. Few of us will ever be called upon to overcome evil by laying down our lives. But all of us are called upon, usually daily, to overcome it by laying down our rights. Jesus alone carries the full weight of atonement. But sometimes, as Paul says, we "fill up in [our] flesh what is still lacking in regard to Christ's afflictions."[11] We are all called to perform what might be called "mini-atonements": acts that, though they don't deal with the root of evil in the way that Christ's once-for-all atonement does, do overcome the effects of evil, at least in the moment. We're called to meet cowardice with courage, anger with gentleness, bitterness with tenderness, stinginess with generosity, and a thousand other ploys of evil with counter-ploys of good. When we are cursed, we praise. When we are mistreated, we rejoice. When we are attacked, we bless.

The apostle Paul, who was himself a Son of Thunder in his young-gun days, learned this well. In 2 Corinthians, he describes carrying the death of Jesus in his own body so that the life of Jesus is made available to others. And he lists all the ways he's had to overcome evil with good: "We are hard pressed on every side, but not crushed; perplexed, but not in despair; persecuted, but not abandoned; struck down, but not destroyed."[12]

He sums it up this way: "Therefore we do not lose heart. Though outwardly we are wasting away, yet inwardly we are being renewed day by day."[13] The phrase Paul uses for "we do not lose heart" means he is not overlorded by such things, not mastered by them. But literally, it means he is not "out-eviled" by them. The evil embedded in the hurt aimed against him can assault him but not destroy him. Something else, something greater, some deep enduring good, is going on inside the man. It's that deep enduring good that triumphs over all the badness.

That would be God. That would be the heart of the Father who overcame the world's worst evil with the cross. He overcame it by giving his Son, Jesus, to lay down his life, when other options were readily available.[14] No wonder Jesus announced, "You have heard that it was said, 'Love your neighbor and hate your enemy.' But I tell you: Love your enemies and pray for those who persecute you, *that you may be sons of your Father in heaven.* He causes his sun to rise on the evil and the good, and sends rain on the righteous and the unrighteous. If you love those who love you, what reward will you get? Are not even the tax collectors doing that? And if you greet only your brothers, what are you doing more than others? Do not even pagans do that? Be perfect, therefore, as your heavenly Father is perfect."[15]

Except that God invades us, that he woos us to break us to make us new, we can't do this.

But because God has, we can. Now that God has, all that's needed is for you and me to go and do likewise.

. . .

Let's return to the Sons of Thunder, those angry young men with whom we began this chapter.

John, late in life, received a new name, not from Jesus but from the community formed around Jesus. They called him the Apostle of Love. Whatever Jesus saw in the man, and in his brother, that prompted the moniker he hung on them had faded to oblivion. All that rage and entitlement hadn't even left a faint stain. They are named anew, and that renaming inscribes a change so vast and so deep, it becomes the story of the gospel itself: that Christ Jesus can take a man, any man, any woman, and change them from what they are into what Jesus himself is, in very nature.

Sons of Thunder into Apostles of Love.

Behold, he makes all things new.

There's a legend about John that, if not true, rings true. He lived — we do know this — to a very old age. The story is that as he lay dying, his beloved community gathered around him, grieving. They longed for one last word from the man who had shown them Christ in word and deed. So he gave them his last word: "Love one another."

He fell silent. He closed his eyes.

"Is there more?" someone asked.

"No," he said. "That is enough."[16]

CHAPTER THREE

WHAT LURKS ON THE EAST SIDE

I DID AN INTERVIEW SEVERAL YEARS AGO with a radio station in Detroit. Every eight minutes, we took a break and I was switched off the air for three minutes of commercials. I listened while I waited for the host to fetch me back. It was clear from the commercials that the show's main listening audience was Christians in suburbia: ads for new cars, house renovations, elite schools, investment planning, vacation agents, all done, run, sold, brokered by "Christians just like you."

The most striking ad was for a ministry called Joy for Jesus. Joy for Jesus was raising funds for a program that helped poor children on Detroit's East Side. The inner city. The urban wasteland. The commercial began: "Street gangs. Prostitution. Drugs. Rising crime rates. Violence. This is what those who live on the East Side face every day. If these people *are left to themselves*, many of them will turn to these things. But you can help. How? Well, *you don't even need to go to the East Side*. For a mere twenty dollars a month, you can bring a miracle to someone who, without you, has no future."

Let me confess something: I'm a sissy and a coward. I love comfort. So I understand altogether too well the appeal of this: I don't even need to go to the East Side. I don't have to leave my safety, my comfort, my clean streets, my smiling, well-bred, well-behaved—and very quiet—

neighbors. I don't have to get my own hands dirty or blistered. I don't have to dodge bullets, rats, cockroaches, viruses. I don't have to come face to face with people's despair and anger. I don't have to look at their ugliness or messiness or sickness. I don't have to be surprised and humbled by their wisdom and thankfulness and beauty. I don't have to go to the East Side! I can be heroic, a bestower of miracles, a guardian and herald of hope, with no real interruption to my life.

I like that. And—let me hasten to add—it's not a bad thing, sending my money but not myself. If I insisted that I had to show up personally every time I wanted to do good on this earth, I would leave most of that good undone and, when I did show up, be mostly a burden and a nuisance to those who are getting it done. God accomplishes great things through ordinary people's twenty-dollar donations. But it makes me wonder: If I make a habit of avoiding the East Side, if I seize every little last excuse not to go there, in the end am I gaining or am I losing? Do I not risk, with all my deft avoidance, avoiding Jesus himself? "I came to you," Jesus says, "hungry, naked, thirsty. I was in prison. And you came to me." Maybe if "these people are left to themselves," the worst consequence is that so are we.

Jesus, it seems, spends a lot of time on the East Side.

Mother Teresa found Jesus on the streets of Calcutta, touching open sores. Henri Nouwen found Jesus in the L'Arche community of Montreal, caring for handicapped adults. Dietrich Bonhoeffer found Jesus in Flosenberg, a Nazi death camp. Harvard graduate Jonathan Kozol found Jesus in New York's inner city.

Kozol in 1964 moved to a poverty-stricken, crime-ridden neighborhood in the South Bronx and became a fourth-grade teacher in the public school. He's written ten moving books on his experience there. One of them, *Ordinary Resurrections*, tells the story of a remarkable church, St. Ann's in the South Bronx:

> St. Ann's [is] a small Episcopal church, extremely poor, run by one of the most astonishing preachers I've ever met. Mother Martha was a high-powered corporate lawyer who gave it up in the '80s to become a priest. She has a remarkable after-school program for children—about 80 children come to the church every day for intensive tutoring, supper, and prayer.
>
> ... My affluent friends often misunderstand why I [moved] to the South Bronx. Affluent white people ... essentially pat me on

the head and say, "It's nice that you ... spend time with those children." ... the implication ... is that I ... have a bag of colonial blessings straight from Harvard Yard and [I] ... sprinkle them among the children of the poor. It's not like that at all. I go in search of blessings, and I find them every time. The children give far more than they receive.

America underestimates its poorest children. The tragedy of grossly segregated and unequal education is not ... that these children are cheated of the riches that America could give them, but that we [are] cheated of the treasures these children could [give] us.[1]

"You don't need to go to the East Side." The South Bronx. Sudan. The local Rez.[2] You can spend your whole life avoiding those places, staying clean, playing safe, avoiding trouble.

And missing Jesus.

.   .   .

That was basically Jonah's motto: I don't have to go to the East Side.

And then guess where God called him?

That's a story to be told. Jonah was no hero and no martyr. If anything, his example serves as a string of warnings, a litany of what not to do. Jonah was a God evader. A coward and a bully with a wide streak of vindictiveness. He cringed at mercy, bristled with anger, relished retribution. His emotions worked in a narrow range: boasting, blaming, gloating, sulking, avenging.

Let me say, by way of confession, that I feel a kinship with him. In part, because God uses the foolish things of this world to shame the wise: God used Jonah in spite of himself, just as he's often used me that way. But I also confess a kinship with him because there is some of his churlishness and wariness and self-pity and self-righteousness churning in my blood too, and unless I make clear and daily resolve to move in the opposite direction, I could quickly be the man's doppelganger, his spiritual double. And, besides which, I'm bald like him, and almost hold him blameworthy for it.

Jesus sometimes named the demons before he cast them out. I'm trying to do the same.

Here's an additional reason I admit my kinship to the man: because Jonah represents a way of doing church that sometimes I'm sorely tempted to resort to. The Jonah model of doing church is, in fact, so tempting that wide swaths of churches have adopted it, at least by default.

But as I said, that's a story to be told, so let me retell the story first.

Jonah lived in the Northern Kingdom of Israel in the eighth century BC. This was long past the glory days of David, when the kingdom was fearsome and good, expansive and generous. This was long past the splendor days of Solomon, when no king in his right mind would pick a fight with Israel. You kept your distance. If you came near at all, it was to pay homage to Israel's king, to bow at his feet or sit at his feet.

Jonah lived long past all that. Israel in those days had become insular and afraid. The kingdom had divided into two halves shortly after Solomon's death, and the two halves lived in a rickety truce punctuated by frequent rivalries. The Northern kings, Jonah's half, had a penchant for idols and vanities and treacherous alliances.

But recent events had restored some of Israel's former glory: an archrival, the Arameans, had been crushed by a mutual enemy, the Assyrians. Israel's king, Jeroboam II, had made the most of that and had expanded his northern borders.

Life was good.

But complacency had set in. This is the same Israel that the prophet denounces with stinging insult: "Hear this word, you cows of Bashan on Mount Samaria, you women who oppress the poor and crush the needy and say to your husbands, 'Bring us some drinks!'"[3]

The Assyrians, east of Israel, had grown quiet in recent years, preoccupied with their own problems. But they hadn't gone away. And when they were around, they were ruthless and warring. Gluttons for land and blood. They relished brutality and were just as happy to destroy a town as loot it. They had little interest in tributaries. They liked total annihilation or complete subjugation. They wanted corpses or slaves. The nations around Assyria hated and feared them, and worked out whatever combination of military resistance, political alliance, and groveling appeasement kept them at bay. But they just kept coming. Poet Lord Byron famously described them in his poem "The Destruction of Sennacherib," a retelling of the Isaiah 37 prophecy:

> The Assyrian came down like the wolf on the fold,
> And his cohorts were gleaming in purple and gold;

And the sheen of their spears was like stars on the sea,
When the blue wave rolls nightly on deep Galilee.

Assyrian kings were known to send, like Russian mafia, human body parts, neatly dissected, through the mail as a tactic of intimidation. An inscription found in the ruins of Assyria, attributed to ninth-century-BC King Asshurizirpal after he laid waste to an unnamed city, contains this boast: "Their men, young and old, I took as prisoners. Of some I cut off the feet and hands; of others I cut off the noses, ears, and lips; of the young men's ears I made a heap; of the old men's heads I built a minaret."

Quaint.

And one more thing: their capital was Nineveh. That was the epicenter of their evil.

Nineveh is the city God wants Jonah to visit, to preach there. It's first stop in the evangelistic crusade. In fact, it's the only stop.

The analogy's been made before, but it's worth repeating: dispatching a Hebrew to Nineveh in the eighth century BC is like God sending a Jew to Berlin in 1944 with a personal message for Hitler and his henchmen. It's an assignment bound to be met with revulsion and loathing, stunned disbelief, bitter indignation. Besides all that, it was a journey of grueling proportions: desert, mountain, swamp. It was an affliction of miles, a trudging through merciless heat and cruel cold, amid bandits and wild prowling things, across deep swift rivers and up high steep mountains.

So Jonah heads the opposite direction. He flees as far from Nineveh as a boat ticket will take him: Tarshish, in Spain. The outer bounds of the known world. As westerly as Nineveh is easterly.

I understand this. I understand the illogic of investing exorbitant time and energy and expense in trying to escape an undesirable task. Though I've found over and over what Jonah discovers — in the end, it's quicker, saner, safer, cheaper to buckle down and do the thing God's asking — I try anyhow. I know that evading God's call is never a means of evading God's call. I know that it's only a means of twisting and prolonging the route to getting there. I know I could go straight at the thing the Lord requires of me and do the thing cleanly. Or I could bolt, dodge, delay, and merely make a waste and a mess.

Often enough, I make the waste and the mess all the same.

An example: all the times I've avoided a hard conversation with someone because I'd hoped benign neglect would make the problem vanish. Yet in almost every instance, it's made the problem bigger, many headed, unwieldy.

But Jonah isn't just fleeing the task. In fact, according to the story, he's not fleeing the task at all. He's fleeing God. "Jonah ran away from the LORD" is the way the story puts it, twice.[4] He's hightailing it from Yahweh, tripping the light fantastic to evade the great I AM.

This detail is more than incidental. It's at the heart of what's wrong. Jonah is not quibbling over God's itinerary for the mission trip. His conflict is not over means and ways. As far as that goes, Jonah would be in good company: Moses, Naomi, Samuel, Hosea, Jeremiah, Habakkuk, Jesus. All were asked to do things they'd rather not and had a complaint or two with God about it. Moses, stammer-mouthed and crumble-boned, argued with God about his orders to confront Pharaoh. Naomi, with death and poverty at every turn, loudly and bitterly accused God of harsh treatment. Samuel, forced by God to anoint Saul as king then forced by God to depose him, complained to God vigorously. Hosea must have balked—though we have no record of it—at God's command to woo and love his extravagantly unfaithful wife. Jeremiah and Habakkuk, hard pressed on every side, openly lodged complaints against God; Jeremiah went so far as to accuse God of deceiving him. Jesus, in agony of soul, begged God to take the cup of suffering from him. None of them wanted to do what God asked. But in each instance, their disagreement with God was an expression of their intimacy with him.

Jonah might have stood in this hallowed tradition. But he didn't. He stands in another tradition, less hallowed: the company of the God evaders. Adam and Eve started the tradition, with their camouflage of fig leaves, their bumbling game of Hide and Seek. Cain, the brother slayer, the restless wanderer, laid it into the foundations of the city he built. From there on, the rest of the story includes spectacular sinners like the Herods and the Prodigal Son, but less likely candidates as well, like the High Priest and the Older Brother. The story is as ancient as days and as recent as this morning's news. Every day, in every way, people everywhere use religion and irreligion, theology and blasphemy, God talk and devil worship to dodge an encounter with the living God.

Jonah stands in this tradition.

He runs away from the Lord. Of course, he doesn't get far. That story's well known: a wild storm, a near drowning, a big fish, a desperate (but strangely mannered) prayer, a spewing up, a starting over from the beginning. Jonah lands rump up and rumpled, reeking, on a beach somewhere, glazed with fish bile, marinated in whale innards.

Jonah, chastened, goes to Nineveh and does what he's told.

. . .

But does he? Jonah preaches in Nineveh a message of impending doom: "Forty more days and Nineveh will be overturned." To deliver this message, Jonah travels the breadth and width of the "great city of Nineveh" and keeps at it three days. We don't know what tone he used to declaim the message, but given his defiance at the start of the story and his sourness at the end, we might guess it wasn't heartbreak. More likely petulance, gloating, loathing. Relishing the idea of Nineveh reduced to charred remains.

"Forty more days and Nineveh will be overturned."

At the least, Jonah is faithful. God's entrusted him with a message, and he bears it with unwavering fidelity.[5] And after all, sin warrants divine judgment. Wickedness invites holy retribution. As Proverbs says, "Whoever remains stiff-necked after many rebukes will suddenly be destroyed—without remedy."[6]

But judgment doesn't come, not suddenly, not belatedly, not at all. Mercy falls.

The Ninevites "believe God." They repent. They *turn* (an important word, as we'll see in a moment). God relents.

And Jonah gets blistering mad.

I think Jonah knew what would happen all along. It was implicit in the message God gave him to proclaim: "Forty more days and Nineveh will be overturned." It's hidden in that word *overturned*. There's a perfectly good Hebrew word for "destroy" or "overturn" in the sense of complete obliteration: *samad*. It's not the word God puts in Jonah's mouth (though I imagine it's the word he longs to speak). The word God puts in Jonah's mouth is *haphak*. Some Bible translations render *haphak* as "overthrown" (KJV) or "destroyed" (CEV), but that misses its subtle ambiguity. *Haphak* can mean that. But just as often, it means "turned around, converted, transformed."

Annihilated, or converted.

Extinguished, or made new.

Obliterated, or blessed.

Crushed, or transformed.

It could go either way for Nineveh.

God embedded a promise in his message of doom. Jonah knew it and begrudged it. The Ninevites knew it and thrilled to it. For Jonah, the possibility of Nineveh's turning was a grievous disappointment. For the people of Nineveh, it was their last best hope.

. . .

The story tells us four things about Nineveh: it's great, it's wicked, it's very important, and it's clueless.[7]

These four things are true about all world cities. New York. London. Bangkok. Amsterdam. La Paz. Rio de Janeiro. Johannesburg. Cairo. Lima. Istanbul. Reykjavik. Kathmandu. Great, wicked, important, clueless cities all.

And to a lesser degree, but in the exact same way, are all cities. I live in Duncan, with a population between five thousand and seventy thousand, depending on how wide or narrow you draw the catchment. If you don't live near it, chances are you've never heard of it. If you do live near it, but not in it, chances are you don't think much of it. Drunken Duncan is our nickname, or was, and we're having a hard time living it down.

I've been here long enough to see both the town's plume and its underbelly. I've seen its greatness — last year, a flood devastated several homes, and the entire community mobilized, with little or no prompting, to assist those displaced. I've seen its wickedness — our area's statistics for domestic violence, for instance, are nearly double the provincial average, which themselves are depressing. I've seen its importance — we hosted the North American Indigenous Games in 2008, the "Olympics" for First Nations athletes, and set the new gold standard for the event. I've seen its cluelessness — we have thirty-two independent agencies in town trying to address the problem of "youth at risk"; most don't know the others exist or, if they do, have little inclination to work with one another, and some are openly disdainful toward the others.

It's been a long apprenticeship, learning to see this city as God does. For the first half dozen years, I pretty much kept to myself. I had an idea, though skewed and built on a lot of urban legends, of the city's wickedness and cluelessness. But I had little perception of or appreciation for its greatness and importance.

And I wasn't dreaming of *haphak*, of the place being overturned, turned around, transformed at the hands of a just and merciful God. I just wanted to preach sermons and build the church. We'd all pile in there like Noah's animals and sail away to Tarshish together, to happily mix my biblical metaphors.

Then it changed. Here's how.

I have a friend, Graham, who was high up in provincial politics until he wasn't — he was right hand to the premier (think governor plus senator if you're American), then turfed out, May of 2005, at the hands of voters, a stiff majority of whom didn't like his tough line with unions. That was the best thing, getting fired. He was logging fourteen- and sixteen-hour days at the legislative office, finessing bills, outmaneuvering protesters, stickhandling lobbyists, schmoozing dignitaries. Then, overnight, he was unemployed.

Graham had just become a Christian a few months before he became a government cabinet minister. The timing was great and terrible: great, because for the first time in his life he was looking beyond himself for strength and wisdom; terrible, because he had little time to cultivate a relationship with the source of that strength and wisdom. It was easy during those years at a cabinet post to simply resort to business as usual: Graham as driver, smooth talker, one-man wrecking crew. It was easy to forget about the strength and wisdom beyond himself.

Losing his job (with a nice fat severance package) meant he had no more weighty issues to manage, no more political messes to sort through. And it meant he had several months to be still. He used it to walk. To pray. To read. To worship. To build spiritual friendships. The results were dramatic. Graham went from a sincere but superficial Christian to a man wholly devoted to the kingdom of God.

And he got a burning. He got fire in the bones. He heard the voice of God, and the voice called him to a tricky and risky undertaking: Graham, hell or high water, was to be an ambassador of reconciliation between the First Nations people in our area and the wider, mostly white community. He hadn't a clue how or where to start, only that he had to.

I was there when the unction, so to speak, fell. We were at a conference together. Graham and his wife, Anneke, were wrecked. They knew what they must do. And I had an urge to pray for them. I wanted to bless and release them into God's call on their lives. So I asked several people to lay hands on them, and I prayed. I prayed that God would reveal what their next step was.

And that's when it happened. The next step, it turns out, was me. I was called into this too. God was asking me to join what he was doing. Graham and I had to venture out together.

That began a long and convoluted journey. I'll tell more of it in another chapter. But the upshot is that it's given me and our church eyes to see—eyes to see not only our city's wickedness and cluelessness but its greatness and importance. We've fallen in love.

About a year after this, our church adopted what has ever since been our unofficial mission statement: "to win the heart of the Cowichan Valley." (The Cowichan Valley is the wider region that our church and town are located within.) We've tried to win that heart in many ways. Mostly, we've asked God to break our hearts and open them. We've asked him to fill our days with divine appointments. We've sought to be the hands and feet of Jesus all over the place, with the aroma of Christ. We've allowed God's love to overflow us and to compel us. We've allowed it to burn and to cut us. We've allowed it to shape us and to root us. We've allowed it in to do its deep, stinging, scouring work so that less and less we look at others from a worldly point of view, and more and more others look at us as good news.[8]

Somewhere along the way, God opened my eyes to this city's greatness and importance.

. . .

God doesn't act toward Nineveh according to its wickedness. God has compassion on their cluelessness. He sees their importance. He seeks to salvage their greatness. And he finds a way to redeem their wickedness. Mercy triumphs over judgment, grace overwhelms vengeance, love trumps fear. Evil is overcome by good.

And Jonah is angry enough to die. God overturns the city in all the wrong ways, and Jonah's bitter on account of it. He wanted a mushroom cloud pluming bright and muscular over Nineveh's ziggurats. He wanted its greatness reduced to rubble. He wanted its importance lain in ruins. He wanted its cluelessness severely rebuked. He wanted its wickedness punished all the way down to hell.

Instead, God comes with healing in his wings.

The story ends with a conversation. At the least, Jonah is on speaking terms with God, which is an improvement, slightly, over the story's beginning, when Jonah didn't want to hear or to answer God. But he's testy, Jonah. He's surly and sullen and quarrelsome. He feels insulted and entitled, and he says as much. Here's the scene and the conversation:

> But Jonah was greatly displeased and became angry. He prayed to the LORD, "O LORD, is this not what I said when I was still at home? That is why I was so quick to flee to Tarshish. I knew that you are a gracious and compassionate God, slow to anger and abounding in love, a God who relents from sending calamity. Now, O LORD, take away my life, for it is better for me to die than to live."
>
> But the LORD replied, "Have you any right to be angry?"
>
> Jonah went out and sat down at a place east of the city. There he made himself a shelter, sat in its shade and waited to see what would happen to the city. Then the LORD God provided a vine and made it grow up over Jonah to give shade for his head to ease his discomfort, and Jonah was very happy about the vine. But at dawn the next day God provided a worm, which chewed the vine so that it withered. When the sun rose, God provided a scorching east wind, and the sun blazed on Jonah's head so that he grew faint. He wanted to die, and said, "It would be better for me to die than to live."
>
> But God said to Jonah, "Do you have a right to be angry about the vine?"
>
> "I do," he said. "I am angry enough to die."
>
> But the LORD said, "You have been concerned about this vine, though you did not tend it or make it grow. It sprang up overnight and died overnight. But Nineveh has more than a hundred and twenty thousand people who cannot tell their right hand from their left, and many cattle as well. Should I not be concerned about that great city?"[9]

What startles anyone familiar with the New Testament is that we've seen and heard a version of this elsewhere. It's not unknown to us. It's echoed in the Father's conversation with his older son in the parable of the prodigal son. Here's that:

> Meanwhile, the older son was in the field. When he came near the house, he heard music and dancing. So he called one of the servants and asked him what was going on. "Your brother has come," he

replied, "and your father has killed the fattened calf because he has him back safe and sound."

The older brother became angry and refused to go in. So his father went out and pleaded with him. But he answered his father, "Look! All these years I've been slaving for you and never disobeyed your orders. Yet you never gave me even a young goat so I could celebrate with my friends. But when this son of yours who has squandered your property with prostitutes comes home, you kill the fattened calf for him!"

"My son," the father said, "you are always with me, and everything I have is yours. But we had to celebrate and be glad, because this brother of yours was dead and is alive again; he was lost and is found."[10]

Two angry sons, both embittered toward their father's mercy, both preoccupied with what they have or don't have, both resenting the father's careless, boundless affection for riffraff and bad boys and whatever else the cat dragged in.

Both stories are open-ended. Jonah is asked a question: "Should I not be concerned?" The older brother is presented with an imperative: "But we had to celebrate and be glad."

We don't know, in either case, what happens next. Does Jonah concede God's point? Does he go further and embrace the Father's concern, feel the Father's compassion for the stranger and the enemy? Does the older brother join the party, go in to feast on a juice-dripping slab of prime rib slathered in horseradish, a mound of roast potatoes seasoned with herbs, a chunk of thick bread, a pint of mead to wash it all down, laughing with his head tipped back in thankful wonder, dancing till his legs go wobbly?

Who knows?

I think the detail is left out on purpose. And not so that we're left guessing: so that we're left to decide, What will I do?

When the Father stands begging you to join his audacious, extravagant initiative of mercy toward a broken world, with all its wasteful sons and clueless cities, will you say yes, or no?

.   .   .

At the writing of this, a video has gone viral on the internet that features an unnamed girl, lispy and bespectacled, maybe eight or nine years old, retelling the story of Jonah. It clocks out at almost eight minutes. The pastor sits behind her and to her right, looking slightly anxious and increasingly amused. Three older children sit directly behind her, fidgeting, oblivious to her, nervous about the recitations they must be preparing to give.

Our little storyteller looks like Shirley Temple. She's animated in the telling. She gestures and inflects brilliantly. She adopts different voices to convey the drama of the story: she renders Jonah testy and thin-voiced, God stern and deep-voiced, the ship's crew earnest and suspicious, the Ninevites haughty and then stricken. The whole thing's funny and convicting.

She embellishes the story a little. Jonah has a collection of farm animals. The ship's captain makes a few cynical asides to his crew. She weaves in a subtext of Jonah's inner dialogue. My favorite add-on, though, is how she ends it: Jonah returning home, walking the dusty lonely miles. With every step, the man is seared, cleansed, enlarged by divine love. Well, that's not how she puts it. This is: "And so Jonah made his long journey home, trying to love as God had taught him. The end."

I hope it is. And the beginning.

CHAPTER FOUR

PUT THIS TO WORK

Again, it will be like a man going on a journey, who called his servants and entrusted his wealth to them. To one he gave five bags of gold, to another two bags, and to another one bag, each according to his ability. Then he went on his journey. The man who had received five bags of gold went at once and put his money to work and gained five bags more. So also, the one with two bags of gold gained two more. But the man who had received one bag went off, dug a hole in the ground and hid his master's money.

After a long time the master of those servants returned and settled accounts with them. The man who had received five bags of gold brought the other five. "Master," he said, "you entrusted me with five bags of gold. See, I have gained five more."

His master replied, "Well done, good and faithful servant! You have been faithful with a few things; I will put you in charge of many things. Come and share your master's happiness!"

The man with two bags of gold also came. "Master," he said, "you entrusted me with two bags of gold; see, I have gained two more."

His master replied, "Well done, good and faithful servant! You have been faithful with a few things; I will put you in charge of many things. Come and share your master's happiness!"

Then the man who had received one bag of gold came. "Master," he said, "I knew that you are a hard man, harvesting where you have not sown and gathering where you have not scattered seed. So I was afraid and went out and hid your gold in the ground. See, here is what belongs to you."

His master replied, "You wicked, lazy servant! So you knew that I harvest where I have not sown and gather where I have not scattered seed? Well then, you should have put my money on deposit with the bankers, so that when I returned I would have received it back with interest.

"Take the bag of gold from him and give it to the one who has ten bags. For those who have will be given more, and they will have an abundance. As for those who do not have, even what they have will be taken from them. And throw that worthless servant outside, into the darkness, where there will be weeping and gnashing of teeth."[1]

Here's how I understand this story: there's no way to be a faithful servant of God and God's kingdom without taking some hell-bent-for-leather risks.

This parable in Matthew is about the kingdom of God. Jesus is in a round of such stories, telling us what the kingdom looks like, tastes like, feels like. How it surprises us. How it disrupts us. How to get in on it. How not to lose out on it.

The getting in or losing out has a lot to do with the kind of risks we take, or not. We're well schooled, from the writings of Paul and others, that certain kinds of people do not inherit the kingdom of God: the wicked, the impure, the deceitful, the rage fiends, and such. What we're less prepared for, though we've had ample warning, is the kind of person Jesus adds to that list: the cautious.

This parable, I know, is usually cast as a story about stewardship, good and bad. It certainly is that. But just as much, it subverts some of the usual ways we think about stewardship. Stewardship evokes images of prudence, frugality, caution. Tithing off the top. Not buying on credit. Living within my means. Reducing my carbon footprint. These are all excellent things. But the stewardship commended in this story takes us in a whole other direction: it's rough and tumble, wild and woolly. Good and faithful servants are those who shoot the moon. They run with scissors. They leap before looking.

The bad servant—the wicked, lazy servant—is the cautious one.

The bad servant receives something from the master—not as much as the others but part of the master's possession, just like the others. The purpose of the master's entrusting all these stewards is one thing: "increase my wealth." In Luke's similar parable, the master says to his servants, "Put this money to work until I return." Do something with what I've given you so that my net wealth grows because you're on the job.

At least two servants heed that. One servant doesn't.

Why? It's not because he doesn't have enough. That may seem the root issue—he's got only one talent. He likely resents those given more. Resentment is its own form of entitlement: since I've been shortchanged, I owe nothing, and I am owed much. I am exempted from further duty. He may feel he has too little to lose, like the Monopoly player down to his last few pieces of paper money. But a talent is still an extraordinary sum of money. It was roughly twenty years' wages. And anyway, this man is not expected to make a return on more than he's been given. His master would be happy if he went down to the bank and opened a starter account that accrued two percent interest.

The root issue is not the amount. The root issue is this servant's view of the master. Put bluntly, he sees the master as cheap, so he's cheap. He sees the master as stingy and hoarding and mean-spirited, so he goes and does likewise.

In a word, this man has bad theology.

Which is the real point of the story: how you see God affects how you live. Our theology determines our destiny. All our problems, as well as all the solutions to our problems, are at base theological. How we see God affects how we live. Is God good, generous, loving, kind, gracious? If you believe that, you will more and more live that. As you worship and follow and serve that God, more and more you'll be like him. You'll go and do likewise. But if lurking in the back of your mind—or maybe not so far back—is a view of God that sees him as angry, miserly, demanding, mean and demeaning, more and more you'll be like the god of your understanding. You'll go and do likewise.

We've seen what the bad servant's bad theology produces. Not wild living. Not extravagant self-indulgence. Not wanton wastefulness. He's no prodigal son. His bad theology produces extreme caution. Utter passivity. He won't trust anyone or risk anything. It's not that he misuses what the master entrusts. Prodigals do that, and God has a soft spot for them. No, it's that he never uses it at all. The master has no soft spot for that. In fact, when we set this story side by side with Jesus' story of the prodigal son, the conclusion is startling: God would rather we waste his possessions than preserve them intact.

What's the man's punishment? His world closes on him. His world of scarcity becomes the only world there is. In fact, it's impossible for him to live anywhere else. His view that God's mean and stingy becomes self-fulfilling prophecy. His God is too small, so his heart is too small, so his life is too small, so his world is too small. I love the way Eugene Peterson translates Proverbs 11:24: "The world of the generous gets larger and larger; the world of the stingy gets smaller and smaller" (MSG). This man's world has shrunk to the size of a windowless prison cell.

Very dark. Very lonely. Very cramped.

The world he's made is the world he dwells in.

. . .

Well that's depressing.

But here's good news: there are at least two good and faithful servants, likely many more. This is a church of people who get it right at least 2 to 1.

And we can figure out, by comparison and contrast with the one bad servant, what's going on in the heads of those good and faithful servants. They have good theology. They see and love the heart of the master. What they see is a master who himself isn't cautious; he entrusts his possessions, without any micromanaging, to his servants. And these are big chunks of coin — the largest amount represents a hundred years of wages. He's a risk-taker supreme.

And they see a master who's very generous. When the servants get it right, he gives them more. In fact, even though the money is all his, the story ends with the servants getting to keep what they were originally given and keep what they made, and then getting more besides. He's prodigal, this master.

And they see a master who's very happy. In his generosity, he invites them to share his greatest possession: his own happiness. They get to partake in the hilarity, the levity, his love for a party.

But they also see one more thing. They see what the bad servant also sees but doesn't understand. The bad servant levels a diatribe against the master—you reap what you haven't sown, gather what you haven't scattered. I used to read that as part of this servant's bad theology: his thinking's so warped, he sees things that aren't there and misses things that are. Partly that's true. But in this case, he's right. The master does exactly what the bad servant accuses him of: he reaps what he hasn't sown and gathers what he has not scattered. The master says so himself.

And that's the whole point of the story.

The bad servant has observed correctly and concluded wrongly. The very fact that this master operates this way is amazing. It's great good news. It means that the Master actually invites us and entrusts us to grow his kingdom for him. You and I actually get, by direct invitation from God, to make the kingdom of God bigger. We do it with the Master's wealth, all that he provides. But we get to create something for God that's more than just what God handed to us. God looks for that, rewards us for that, and invites us to share his joy in that.

The Master says, *That car and house and those relationships and that money—make more of those. Multiply their effect. Accrue interest on them, at the least. When I show up, have more to show for the things I've given. The last thing I want here is for you to keep the thing all shiny and new. You don't give your children bicycles hoping they never get scratched, never lose a spoke, never pop a tire. Well, I don't give things either without the expectation that they'll get well used.*

God trusts you with his stuff. Now you need to trust God with the stuff he trusted you with, putting it to work until he returns. God invites you to expand the borders of his kingdom and increase its wealth. Your town should look different because you used what God put in your hand for the kingdom. How much kingdom any of us actually gets to see and enjoy here on earth in large measure depends on how good and faithful servants we are.

A friend of mine recently pointed out the alternate translation of Romans 8:28. The usual rendering goes something like this: "For we know that God works all things together for those who love him and are called to his purposes." Which is great. God has got our back. God is looking after us. But most Bibles also have a little asterisk beside that verse pointing to an alternate rendering. It goes like this: "For we know that God works together with those who love him *to bring about what is good."* That says something that is missing from the first rendering. It says God is looking for some good and faithful men and women to help him bring the kingdom on earth as it is in heaven.

. . .

E. V. Hill was a great African-American preacher who his whole life served an inner-city church. But he was preaching once in an upscale white suburban church, and he said something like this:

> As I drove to your church building this morning, through your neighborhood, I noticed you folk have a lot of fine things. You have big houses, and very pretty. You have lovely gardens. You have new shiny cars. You have schools that got no barbwire around them. It's very nice.
>
> But something's missing, and at first I couldn't figure out what. Then it hit me. You ain't got no graffiti. None. You can't have a hood without that. I tell you what, I'll go get some of my boys, we fix that for you. And I'll even suggest what word we write in our graffiti. We write it on your schools, on your homes, on your cars and your boats, even here on your church. The word I'd like to write is this: "Temporary." All this stuff one day goin' up in smoke.
>
> Now, here's the deal. You could give up a little bit of all that temporary stuff and get yourself something that'll last forever.

And I would add this: while you bank toward forever, use some of that capital to grow the kingdom here on earth.

Whatever he's given, put it to work.

CHAPTER FIVE

GOING TO MORDOR

Historian Daniel Boorstin documents a momentous shift that occurred in North America in the nineteenth century: we stopped calling people who went on trips travelers and started calling them tourists.[1]

Traveler literally means "one who travails." He labors, suffers, endures. A traveler—a travailer—gets impregnated with a new and strange reality, grows huge and awkward trying to carry it, and finally, in agony, births something new and beautiful. To get there, he immerses himself in a culture, learns the language and customs, lives with the locals, imitates the dress, eats what's set before him. He takes risks, some enormous, and makes sacrifices, some extravagant. He has tight scrapes and narrow escapes. He is gone a long time. If ever he returns, he returns forever altered.

In a sense, he never goes back.

A tourist, not so. *Tourist* means, literally, "one who goes in circles." He's just taking an exotic detour home. He's only passing through, sampling wares, acquiring souvenirs. He tastes more than eats what's put before him. He retreats each night to what's safe and familiar. He picks up a word here, a phrase there, but the language, and the world it's embedded in, remains opaque and cryptic, and vaguely menacing. He spectates and consumes. He returns to where he's come from with an album of photos, a few mementos, a cheap hat. He's happy to be back. He declares there's no place like home.

We've made a similar shift in the church. At some point we stopped calling Christians disciples and started calling them believers. A disciple is one who follows and imitates Jesus. She loses her life in order to find it. She steeps in the language and culture of Christ until his Word and his world reshape hers, redefine her, change inside out how she sees and thinks and dreams and, finally, lives. Whatever values she brought into his realm are reordered, ofttimes laid waste, and kingdom values take their place. Friends who knew her before scarcely recognize her now.

A believer, not so. She holds certain beliefs, but how deep down these go depends on the weather or her mood. She can get defensive, sometimes bristlingly so, about her beliefs, but in her honest moments she wonders why they've made such scant difference. She still feels alone, afraid, sad, self-protective, dissatisfied. She still wants what she's always wanted and fears what she's always feared, sometimes more so. Friends who knew her before find her pretty much the same, just angrier.

You can't be a disciple without being a believer. But — here's the rub — you can be a believer and not a disciple. You can say all the right things, think all the right things, believe all the right things, do all the right things, and still not follow and imitate Jesus.

The kingdom of God is made up of travailers, but our churches are largely populated with tourists. The kingdom is full of disciples, but our churches are filled with believers. It's no wonder we often feel like we're just going in circles.

.   .   .

I first read J. R. R. Tolkien's Lord of the Rings trilogy when I was fifteen. That was 1975, more than twenty-five years before Peter Jackson's vivid screen adaptation of the trilogy. For me, the books were vivid enough. They wracked and tumbled me like some elemental thing, a windstorm, a landslide, a flash flood. Every night for several hours, I inhabited Middle Earth tangibly. I stood in its grassy meadows, on its rocky heights, under its canopy of stars. I bathed in its rain and basked in its sun. I lolled in the idyllic peace of Hobbiton, but fretted over the shadow moving toward it. I traveled — travailed — with Sam and Frodo on their way to Bree, pursued by dark riders. Together, we wended through the treacherous forest of Mirkwood, enjoyed the Falstaffian hospitality of Tom Bombadil, traversed the haunted barrenness of the Barrow Downs. We picked up Merry and Pippin and Aragorn along the way, then travailed on to Rivendell, arriving in the nick of time and barely breathing.

Rivendell was such a relief. Rivendell, the Elfin kingdom high in the craggy folds of the Misty Mountains, is a paradise. A place safe and serene, immune, it felt, from the shadow stretching over all Middle Earth. I wanted to stay there for good, with Frodo and Sam and all the rest. To sleep in warm beds and wake in light-soaked rooms. To eat delicious, plentiful, nourishing meals. To wander through ordered gardens, and pass over stone bridges under which rush waterfalls as they sluice from great heights to great depths. I wanted the story to end there, the drama to resolve there. Rivendell is a place of unbroken tranquility, and I wanted to dwell there for good.

It was not to be. Soon after arriving, the Fellowship of the Ring is formed, a rickety alliance of nine mismatched pilgrims—a dwarf and an elf, two men, four hobbits, and a grizzled and elusive wizard—who venture into wonders and dangers, battles and betrayals, wrong turns and detours, all with a singular mission, though no real sense how to accomplish it: they must get to Mordor and destroy the ring. The ring is a thing of hypnotic seduction and despotic power. If it falls into the hands of its maker, Sauron, his power will become boundless and his evil all-consuming. The shadow will become all there is. The ring can be unmade only in the place it was made, melted in the fire it was forged with: the bowels of Mount Doom in the heart of Mordor.

Mordor is as close to hell as any place short of hell gets.

It's a dangerous mission. It's a hopeless mission, but their only hope. It's a mission that can be accomplished not by armies, treaties, even strategies but only by a total and vulnerable incarnation: the smallest, weakest creatures, Frodo and his ever-loyal but none-too-bright companion, Sam, must don the disguise of evil and walk into the very heart of darkness, climb its Golgotha, and face its evil head-on. They must face it personally. Only then can that evil be broken and defeated, for them and for everyone. They are willing to lose their lives for the life of the world.

Which sounds like another mission we're well acquainted with.

The point here: no one accomplishes such a mission, or joins it, or heralds it, as a mere tourist. Only a travailer can. Only a fellowship of travailers can.

But there is a subplot here. That fellowship is a fellowship in name only when it is formed back in Rivendell. In the place where life is easy, where good things abound, where no threat encroaches, it's impossible to get a dwarf and an elf to trust each other — even to be civil with one another — if their lives depended on it, precisely because in a place like that their lives will never depend on it. They can live forever there in their prideful independence. They need rely on no one. They need not trust anyone. They can simply become more entrenched in their belief that they are superior, all else are fools.

But you have to give up those illusions when you go on a dangerous mission together. There, each needs what the other brings. Each must learn to trust and rely on everyone else. Each must be humbled and stretched and burdened. Each must be willing to sacrifice the things that they cling to — their stuff, their status, their comfort, their dreams. And out of that willingness, deep cries to deep. Iron sharpens iron. Enemies, sworn enemies with personal and historic resentments, become friends, willing to lay down their lives for the other. There is no request too great, or need too perilous, that each won't turn heaven and earth for the sake of the other.

Tourists make poor companions. Those who dwell in Rivendell form frail and shallow community. Only travailers — only those who venture out together on a dangerous mission — form community, community with sinews and sturdy bones. Travailers discover how hard and needed and beautiful and life-giving community like that is. Together, they risk much and give much and suffer much and love much.

Meanwhile, back in Rivendell, everyone's doing just fine on their own.

. . .

I love that the church of late has discovered the power of life together. Or at least we talk about it a lot. It's deeply right that we seek to nurture that life together over lingering meals, rambling conversations, leisurely walks, dropping in on one another unannounced.

But if we're not careful, we'll have a perfect life in Rivendell and forget about Mordor. We'll prefer fellowship to mission. We won't ride up to the gates of hell and demand they give way. We won't invade the heart of darkness and overthrow it. And in the end, the depth of our life together will show it: we'll be acquaintances but not soul mates; buddies and girlfriends but not brothers and sisters; willing to help each other out in a pinch with a meal or two, a little housework, the loan of a car for a few days, but not "sharing all things in common,"[2] not "considering others better than ourselves."[3]

Any church too safe became that way because somewhere, somehow, they started wanting to dwell in Rivendell more than travel to Mordor. They started caring about fellowship more than mission, and in the end lost both.

I often hear talk that pits fellowship and mission against one another, treats them as competing imperatives. "Why are we caring for all *those* people when we're not caring for our own?" The logic here is that pursuing mission means neglecting fellowship. But the opposite is true: to neglect mission is to destroy fellowship. Mission enhances fellowship, and fellowship strengthens mission. This isn't to say that our fellowship becomes easier when we take seriously our mission. In significant ways, it becomes more difficult. It just becomes *necessary*. It changes from a middle-class luxury to a working-class necessity. We stop being picky and get desperate. We probably argue with one another even more when we're on a dangerous mission together—after all, the stakes are so high—but we usually argue about things that matter. We laugh harder, cry more often, fight more fiercely, and endure greater hardship. We risk much and give much and suffer much and love much.

Has your church lost its mission? I can guarantee that, if it has, it's also lost, or soon will, any meaningful fellowship. It might look like Rivendell around the place, but each will keep increasingly to his own. No one really needs anyone else, and if they did, they'd never say. After losing your mission, it's only a matter of time before your fellowship becomes that in name only.

. . .

There's a fairly easy way to measure whether your church has a dangerous mission: do you desperately need God and one another to accomplish it? I don't simply mean praying before you work and needing a sufficient handful of volunteers to run your programs. I mean that, aside from God showing up and showing the way, and aside from people laying down their lives with you (or for you), what you're trying to do won't get done. I cannot do it without you, and we cannot do it together without God. True mission requires leadership, volunteers, resources, and strategies. It calls for brainstorming and troubleshooting sessions. But above all, it requires a fellowship in which God works mysteriously, continuously, providentially to do more than we ask or imagine. To the extent that we can look at anything we're accomplishing and account for it on purely empirical grounds—anyone with the same team and resources could pull this off—it may be a good thing, but it's not a true mission. A true mission is eleven men, terrified, bickering, huddling in a hidey-hole, who turn the world on its head within a generation. A true mission is a solitary man, gathering with other men and women, and spending his life and health to abolish slavery in England.[4]

Or less historically monumental, but just as significant: it's a church that decides the best protest they could mount against abortion is for its members to open the spare rooms in their homes to pregnant teens, or the church that chooses to do the same to end the plight of the homeless in their community. Anyone who's attempted even a little bit of this finds out soon enough that, except we're in this together and God be our helper, it is not just hard: it's impossible.

. . .

I love the scene near the end of *The Return of the King*, the third installment in the movie version of The Lord of the Rings. The fellowship is now physically scattered but forever bound together. Frodo and Sam are somewhere in Mordor—alive, but for how long? The city of Gondor, the last bastion withholding Mordor's forces from overrunning all Middle Earth, has won a costly victory: they've temporarily driven the enemy back, but much of its fortifications lie in ruins and its armies are decimated.

A war council is drawn. They are reduced to a desperate measure: the last remaining fighters could storm the gates of Mordor. It's a crazy suicide tactic, bound to fail. The only good it will do is distract the eye of Sauron momentarily, and so buy Sam and Frodo, wherever they are, some time to accomplish the mission. The argument on one side is not to attempt it. For it likely won't succeed, and everyone will die trying.

Gimli, the dwarf, speaks and sums up the council so far. "Har-rumph. Vastly outnumbered. Zero chance of success. Certainty of death."

Then he pauses. He bunches up his bristly eyebrows and skewers everyone with his fierce unflinching gaze. And then he delivers the resolve: "Well," he demands, "what are we waiting for?"[5]

Jesus said that he himself builds his church on the foundation of our total allegiance. That church, his church, the gates of hell cannot stand against. We will storm those gates, crash them, trample them, and raid the kingdom of darkness inside.

Vastly outnumbered? No, greater is he who is in us than he who is in the world.

Zero chance of success? No, through him we are more than conquerors.

Certainty of death? No, though we die, yet shall we live.

Well, what *are* we waiting for?

CHAPTER SIX

WE BELIEVE
AND WE KNOW

I'VE USED ALMOST EVERY MODERN PROGRAM and technique for evangelism. I've exploded, become contagious, just walked across the room, gotten out of the saltshaker, invoked four spiritual laws, drawn chasms and crosses, handed out tracts, distributed free *Jesus* videos, counseled at crusades. All that, and more. All of it has had real value: It's given me boldness and conciseness in sharing the gospel. It heightened my sense of urgency about declaring good news. It's kept my heart tender toward the lost.

Sometimes, it's reached people.

But for years, for centuries, the church had none of this. No program. No curriculum. No manuals. No DVDs. No outreach pastors. No budgets for evangelism. All and the same, they pulled off a spectacular coup: subverted the most powerful empire on earth, turned wild men and rich men, slaves and warriors, paupers and emperors, girls gone bad and women of a certain age into saints.

The early church suffered a poverty of means. It was riven by heresy. It was filled with mobs of messed-up people. It was harassed and oppressed by neighbors and governments. Despite all this, the early church was exponentially effective in spreading the gospel.

Then there's us. The modern church has an embarrassment of

riches. It's a watchdog for doctrine. It is filled with people who, though messed up often enough, do not lack for therapies and therapists, spiritual directors and wise teachers. Despite all this, the modern church is glaringly impotent in spreading the gospel. Mostly, we grow our churches, when we do, with migrants from other churches.

Often we impute the blame for this on a lack of spiritual power. They, the early church, had the Holy Spirit. We, the modern church, have computers, sound systems, Sermon Spice, pretty buildings.

But I believe we also have the Holy Spirit.

The problem isn't quite that simple. It likely has more to do with an erosion of our confidence than with the absence of the Spirit. To put it simply, we are not gripped and astonished by the good news in the same way the early church was. We're more than doubtful, worse than skeptical: we're ambivalent. We're divided in the church's basic conviction: Jesus is enough.

I wrestle with this. Why, after more than thirty years of walking with Christ, do I still bristle with irritation at minor inconveniences or affronts—a slow driver, a long lineup, a barb of sarcasm? Why are so many of my reactions disproportionate to the event I'm reacting to—apathy in the face of global tragedy, grief or rage in the face of mere personal disappointment? Why do I secretly hope when I get on a plane that the seat beside me will be empty or, failing that, occupied by someone who wants to keep to themselves?

Part of the answer is that I'm me: introverted, driven, overextended. But some of it—a larger part than I'd like to admit—is the gap, variously wide or narrow, between what I say I believe and what actually shapes my life. Not all that I believe has become conviction. I hold some of my beliefs the way I hold ski poles and chain saws—happy to use them when they're useful, quick to fling them away when I feel imperiled.

A belief is something we hold. A conviction is something that holds us. A belief adorns our life. A conviction defines it. A belief helps us live better. A conviction does that also, but it's also what we'd die for.

Let me explain with a story.

I live in a valley between two steep escarpments—Mount Tzouhalem (zoo-*hay*-lum) eastward, Mount Prevost (*pre*-voh) westward. My back windows look east, toward Tzouhalem, my front windows west, toward Prevost. Both escarpments end in bluffs of sheer rock, steep faces that fall hundreds of feet to forest floor. But Prevost's bluff has an open geography—it's buffeted by winds that roll off the ocean and sweep all the way to our island's wilderness backbone. And Prevost also has a flank beneath the bluff that slopes down toward open fields.

All this makes Prevost perfect for paragliders. Beginning in early spring, continuing until late fall, I can stand most days in front of my living room window and watch bird men, bird women: half-crazy people who leap off the high point of the bluff with only a kite harnessed to them, a thin wide swath of bright silk tethered to their bodies by roughly a million thin vinyl cords. It's beautiful to watch. They loft and buoy in drafts of air. They turn slow circles. They arc along a stream of thermal current.

"How I'd love to do that," I said one day.

My wife, Cheryl, heard me and took me at my word.

So on my forty-fourth birthday, she presented me with a certificate, to be redeemed within the year, to go jump off a cliff.

And, actually, I could hardly wait. I called Claudio, the instructor, that very week, and the next week he and his girlfriend drove up from Victoria, an hour away, and together we drove up the switchback logging roads to the back side of Prevost. The road ends about a half mile from the pinnacle. Here, we parked the truck and pulled out a massive duffel bag, big enough to stuff a small elephant in. Claudio informed me that the bag contained the paraglider and two harnesses, one for him, one for me. The three of us, he, his girlfriend, and me, had to haul this to the top.

This was no easy task. The trail was steep and narrow and overgrown. The bag was heavy and cumbersome. We needed all three of us to manage it. We stopped often to catch our breath.

But we made it. There, while I looked on stupidly, Claudio and his girlfriend went quickly and expertly to work. They unfolded and laid out the silky canopy, disentangled and stretched taut the cords, attached the whole rig to the harnesses. His girlfriend would soon take the bag, light and empty and folded small, back down to the truck and meet us at the valley floor. But first, she had to help me get into my harness, a cross-strapping of belts and buckles, much like the kind climbers wear. We rigged up with me in front, Claudio behind. He explained that, at the count of three, I was to hightail for the cliff's edge. He'd be right on my heels. As we ran, he explained, the canopy would lift up, billow out with air, and put a massive drag on our forward motion. We just needed to keep running. If all worked according to plan, we'd barrel right over the edge, cantilever over empty space, and start soaring.

Right.

He started to count.

"Wait," I said. "So, you count to three, and on the count of three, I start to run and you start to run. And we run over the cliff?"

"Yes."

"And all will be well?"

"Yes."

"And this is for sure?"

"Well, nothing's for sure."

"But pretty for sure."

"Yes."

Claudio started to count.

"Wait," I said. "So that's it? That's all I need to know?"

"For now. The rest I'll tell you when we're in the air.

"One.

"Two.

"Three."

And so I ran, with all my might. Claudio kept up with me, step for step. That cliff edge came at us stupendously fast. Ten feet away, the canopy lifted and filled, and—just like Claudio said—it exerted a powerful backward pull on us so that our running became slow motion. "Keep running," he yelled, and I did.

And then all at once we were off the edge. My feet kept churning, like the whirlwind Coyote makes chasing Roadrunner when he misses a corner at the edge of a canyon wall and runs out into empty space. But unlike him, I didn't plummet when I looked down.

"You can quit running now," Claudio said.

Because we were flying.

The rest of the trip was pure adrenaline. The silence of our motion, the ground slipping away under our feet, the valley opening wide and bright beneath us. Claudio instructed me to move the cords up or down, and the smallest motion sent us wheeling in a new direction. As we curved off the flank of the mountain toward a grass field, Claudio asked if I wanted to come straight in for our landing or "do some tricks." I was in for a pound as for a penny by this point, so I chose the tricks. Claudio began doing hair-raising, stomach-fluttering things — spiraling and swooping, seesawing and plummeting. It was a rollercoaster without the rails.

In a few minutes, we lofted down soft and smooth, and the ride was over. Claudio's girlfriend was waiting with the truck. My wife and children had driven to the landing site and were waiting too. Claudio and his girlfriend, with me stupidly watching again, folded up the equipment, put it back in the elephant sack, and we parted company.

That was that.

But ever after, that experience has stood for me as a vivid illustration of the distinction between a belief and a conviction. Belief, I said before, is a thing we hold; conviction is a thing that holds us. The paraglider was one thing and then became the other. When I was helping heft the equipment up the mountain trail, it was a thing I held. I could have (and a few times did) put it down at any time. If the trail had been much longer or steeper, I might have abandoned the thing altogether as too unwieldy, too inconvenient. Requiring too much work. To walk away would have been embarrassing, but not catastrophic. It would have meant a loss of face and a hundred dollars, but little else.

But after I stepped off the cliff, the paraglider held me. I'd have abandoned the rigging only under the worst delusion. To unhitch myself from it would have been disastrous. It would have been fatal.

I've spent the last thirty years trying to move my faith from belief to conviction, from something I hold to something that holds me. My test for when I've crossed that line, stepped over that edge, is simple: if I unhook myself from this now, would it simply be embarrassing, or ruinous?

When it's the latter, I know belief has become conviction.

. . .

This is what I think we lack most in our evangelism. This is where our ambivalence is wasting us. When I was in the air, held aloft by a hundred pounds of silk and rope and strapping, I had no ambivalence. I wasn't waffling about whether I should stay connected. I could afford ambivalence on the ground; I couldn't afford a second of it in the air. Up there, I was totally dependent and totally committed. I was all in. A true believer.

And this, I say, is what's lacking in our evangelism.

John 6 is instructive. That chapter contains John's version of Jesus' feeding the five thousand. Except for the delightful detail that a boy provides the elements for the miracle — "five small barley loaves and two small fish" — John's account of things pretty much follows the story from the other three gospels. John even includes the story that follows in Matthew and Mark — Jesus' walking on water.

But after that, John parts company with the Synoptics.[1] John takes us to a place the Synoptics seem to know nothing about: the next day, that well-fed crowd, now hungry again, piles into a great flotilla of boats and sets out after Jesus. They catch up with him on the other side of the lake.

And the famous compassion of Jesus evaporates. His concern for the physical well-being of pilgrims must have dissipated midstep across the windswept lake. Just yesterday, "when Jesus looked up and saw a great crowd coming toward him, he said to Philip, 'Where shall we buy bread for these people to eat?' "[2] But just one day later Jesus meets the crowd with a gruff rebuke: "I tell you the truth, you are looking for me, not because you saw miraculous signs but because you ate the loaves and had your fill."[3]

What follows is a famous Johanine[4] diatribe from Jesus. He scolds the crowd. He accuses them of lowly motives. He challenges them to seek "food that endures." And to leave no one guessing, he spells out just exactly what kind of food he has in mind: "I tell you the truth, unless you eat the flesh of the Son of Man and drink his blood, you have no life in you. Whoever eats my flesh and drinks my blood has eternal life, and I will raise him up at the last day. For my flesh is real food and my blood is real drink. Whoever eats my flesh and drinks my blood remains in me, and I in him. Just as the living Father sent me and I live because of the Father, so the one who feeds on me will live because of me. This is the bread that came down from heaven. Your forefathers ate manna and died, but he who feeds on this bread will live forever."[5]

That does it. Jesus, in a single swoop, effectively sabotages his popularity. "From this time many of his disciples turned back and no longer followed him."[6] Jesus has a reverse church-growth strategy. In one sermon, he decimates his numbers. He knocks himself back from megachurch status to storefront start-up. There's not a pastor or an elder or a church consultant in the land who would endorse his approach. If the first banquet was a hit, we'd all reason, let's give 'em another one. If they're just warming up, let's hold off on the "hard teaching" until we've established a deeper relationship.

Jesus apparently hasn't read the books. He doesn't have a copy of *Just Walk across the Lake* in his knapsack. So he goes ahead and does this outlandish thing, offending the very people he wooed, and whittles his following from five thousand back down to the original gang. And then he gives them the option of packing it in: "You do not want to leave too, do you?" Jesus asks the Twelve.[7]

Peter, as usual, has the answer: "Lord, to whom shall we go? You have the words of eternal life. We believe and know that you are the Holy One of God."[8]

I'm guessing that the many disciples who picked up and left were believers. They held beliefs, some strongly. But when those beliefs became heavy and unwieldy, they dropped them and walked away.

The Twelve who stayed, however, were held by convictions.[9] When those convictions got hard, they still had no option but to remain harnessed because the alternative was harder still.

"To whom shall we go?"

The conviction of the Twelve was trussed up hard and tight to Jesus — his words, his identity. Specifically, their conviction was tied to Christ's lordship — his saving messianic identity, his eternal-life-giving words. "Lord, to whom shall we go? You have the words of eternal life. We believe and know that you are the Holy One of God." When Peter says "we believe," he's speaking about something more than fine points of doctrine to which he gives his assent. He's speaking about a truth that grips him hard and holds him tight and lifts him high. He's speaking about a singular source of hope and life. "We believe." But beliefs like this hold us more than we hold them. We believe *and know*.

This is the point where some of us have gotten fuzzy. Ambivalent. We believe well enough. That's not the problem. Indeed, given a moment to gather our thoughts, we might articulate a more comprehensive Christology than Peter did. We might add a remark or two about the divinity of Jesus or his atoning work or the example he sets for us and the power he imparts to us.

We believe.

It's just sometimes we lack conviction. We believe, but we don't always *know*. So even Peter, on a dark night among the interrogation of strangers, found his beliefs too costly, too cumbersome, and abruptly set them down, though only for a brief spell.

We believe *and* we know. That's the place I aim to be. That is the place of conviction, and it's out of conviction—not fanaticism (which, as Carl Jung said, is overcompensation for doubt) but deep abiding conviction—that our most authentic and most effective evangelism flows.

Evangelism does not reduce to tidy formulas. It does not distill down to a single strategy. It is as varied and surprising as the people who engage it, and as the people they engage. My own stumbling journey toward the kingdom involved the influence of a movie and soundtrack that, I found out much later, most Christians boycotted in its day: *Jesus Christ Superstar.* While churches were denouncing it as heretical, even blasphemous, at least one young teenager was being irresistibly drawn to Jesus by it.

So, no, there is no preferred or prescribed methodology for evangelism. But there are a few common denominators. The most basic is this: good news is always show-and-tell. Good news is *both* spoken and lived, declared and demonstrated. Biblically, there is no such thing as a disembodied gospel—a gospel that floats down to us as pure idea, words alone, philosophical proposition, bereft of flesh, blood, breath, touch, body.

This isn't to say a man or woman can't come to trust in Jesus from, say, reading a tract, or listening to a radio preacher, hearing a voice from heaven, encountering Christ in a dream. It's just to say that good news always—*always*—gets filled out *in situ*, in a real face-to-face encounter with living and breathing people; the tract reader must meet, somewhere, a Philip on his desert road.[10] The radio listener must *see* the reality of the truth he's heard, even if he only sees it, like many Muslim converts to Christianity do in remote Islamic villages, bear fruit in his own life. The one who hears the voice from heaven must also experience that voice afresh in the healing touch of an Ananias, the welcoming gesture of a Barnabas, the haunting memory of a Stephen, as the apostle Paul did after his vision and the voice from heaven.[11]

The Word becomes flesh. From the beginning, the bent of God's speaking has always been toward incarnation: the thing said becoming the thing done, the word uttered becoming the reality created, awakened, alive. He said, "Mountains," and there they were—Rockies and

Pyrenees, Alps and Andes, snow crowned and shadow bellied, alluring and warning. He said, "Horse," and there they were, gleaming and blowing, thundering hard across wide windy plains. He said, "Lazarus, come out," and there he was, bewildered and amazed, muscle and will and astonishment and friends unraveling his grave clothes. He said, "It is done," and it was, then, now, forever.

The Word becomes flesh.

The biggest complaint those who don't follow Christ level against those who do is that our words aren't fleshy enough. They're carnal, maybe, but not "now in flesh appearing." Too much of our proclamation lacks incarnation. Our words speak louder than our deeds, and so they come out funny, tinny, thin.

"Believe me when I say that I am in the Father and the Father is in me," Jesus said, "*or at least believe on the evidence of the miracles themselves.*"[12] Jesus' claims about himself and God are backed by visible demonstration. In his followers, though we seldom produce the miracles Christ did, it's miracle enough to see in us the Word become flesh, to see truth lived out, to see the command to "love one another" embodied. Jesus said that the difference between a sage and a fool is whether you "put into practice these words of mine."[13]

The early church testified about Jesus by what they said, but mostly by how they lived; their truth claims were continuously validated by their lifestyle. James, the brother of Jesus, warned Bible readers not just to listen to the Word (and he would add, I think, not just to speak it either) but to do what it says.[14] The apostle Paul preached not with "eloquence or superior wisdom," not with "wise and persuasive words," but with a "demonstration of the Spirit's power."[15] Something happened that was visible, tangible, irrefutable in people's lives when they heard and believed the good news. After, Paul instructed his churches that their every "word and deed" should be spoken and lived in the name of Jesus — in Jesus' authority, with Jesus' Spirit.[16] He promised his churches that if they simply followed his own example, just put into practice what they heard from him and saw in him, the "God of peace" would be with them.[17] The apostle Peter tells us to "live such good lives among the pagans that, though they accuse you of doing wrong, they may *see your good deeds* and glorify God on the day he visits us."[18] The apostle John says the test for knowing that a spirit is from God is that such a spirit will acknowledge "that Jesus Christ has come in the flesh." If any spirit does not acknowledge this, it's not from God; it is, rather, "the spirit of the antichrist."[19] I think, given the main thrust of John's first letter—that we can't merely say things but must live them—that John has in mind here more than creedal formula. Acknowledging that Jesus has come in the flesh is done "not with words or tongue but with actions and in truth."[20] In the book of Revelation, also from the hand of John, the primary way Jesus knows his churches is by their deeds, not their words. "I know your deeds," Jesus tells the churches.[21]

All of this is to say that the repeated refrain of the Bible is that just as the Word became flesh, so too our words must become flesh. "As the Father has sent me," Jesus said, "I am sending you."[22] There is no such thing as a disembodied gospel. It's when pagans "see our good deeds," not just hear our good words, that the good news becomes truly good news. The dimension of reality is added to the power of declaration. The good news, of course, is always a word from beyond us, independent of us. Its truth does not rise or fall on our faithfulness. But people want to know not just is the good news true but is it real? Does it work? Does it set captives free? Does it change sorrow into joy? What human faithfulness adds to God's good news is anecdotal proof of its realness. Just as it's hard to trust a dentist who has gum rot, or a mechanic who drives a jalopy, so it's hard to believe a gospel that seems to have left its bearers unaltered. But the opposite is also true: just as it's easy to trust a dentist who has a million-watt smile, and a mechanic who has an old car that still purrs, so it's easy to believe a gospel that appears to have turned its bearers' lives inside out.

The Word must become flesh and dwell among us.

Now in Jesus, preeminently, uniquely, the Word became flesh. He is the icon of God: God's radiance, his fullness, his presence. Jesus is in very nature God.[23] All that God is becomes tangible and visible, without diminishment or distortion, in Jesus of Nazareth. This is the basic theology of the incarnation: in Jesus, the Word became flesh and lived among us. This claim is the lifeblood of our faith. It is the touchstone of our orthodoxy. "The Son is the radiance of God's glory and the exact representation of his being."[24] "He is the image of the invisible God, the firstborn over all creation. For by him all things were created: things in heaven and on earth, visible and invisible, whether thrones or powers or rulers or authorities; all things were created by him and for him. He is before all things, and in him all things hold together.... For God was pleased to have all his fullness dwell in him."[25]

Jesus is the icon of God.

He does this brilliantly. He does this uniquely.

But the corollary is equally true, and just as vital: the church is the icon of Jesus. Christ's radiance, his fullness, his presence—all are to be tangible and visible, without diminishment or distortion, in the people of God. We are a royal priesthood. We are a holy nation. The way the Bible puts this: God's "intent was that now, *through the church,* the manifold wisdom of God should be made known to the rulers and authorities in the heavenly realms, according to his eternal purpose which he accomplished in Christ Jesus our Lord."[26]

And this: "Now I rejoice in what was suffered for you ... for the sake of his body, which is the church. I have become its servant by the commission God gave me to present to you the word of God in its fullness—the mystery that has been kept hidden for ages and generations, but is now disclosed to the saints. *To them God has chosen to make known among the Gentiles the glorious riches of this mystery, which is Christ in you, the hope of glory.*"[27]

The church is the icon of Jesus.

Or let me put that less starkly. Jesus is the "radiance of God's glory," and the church is (or should be) the reflection of that radiance; Jesus is the "exact representation of God's being," and the church is (or should be) a reasonable facsimile of Jesus' character. The church is not the source of anything divine, but we are (or should be) a faithful witness and an accurate reflection of things divine.

What is God like? Jesus.

What is Jesus like? The church.

We do this haltingly. But do it we must.

The next chapter shows how.

CHAPTER SEVEN

IT TAKES A VILLAGE

MY FAVORITE SCRIPTURE about God's method of evangelism is in the Old Testament: Zechariah 8.

Here's how it ends: "This is what the LORD Almighty says: 'In those days ten men from all languages and nations will take firm hold of one Jew by the hem of his robe and say, "Let us go with you, because we have heard that God is with you."'"[1]

This is evangelism Bible-style. It takes a village. It takes a church living as though Truth is true. The good news is not simply spoken; it's embodied as a way of life. The good news—that God has acted decisively, unilaterally, to break the power of sin and death and to turn captives and rebels into sons and daughters, and those into a kingdom of priests—gets lived out in such a way that people break roofs and grab coattails to get in on it. The evangelized, not the evangelists, do all the talking: "Let us go with you." They've heard "that God is with you." But they've heard that not from any insider. They've heard it from those wanting in. People are talking. There's a buzz, a *Godsib*:[2] "Many peoples and the inhabitants of many cities will yet come, and the inhabitants of one city will go to another and say, 'Let us go at once to entreat the LORD and seek the LORD Almighty. I myself am going.'"[3]

This is the dream of every church: that God's life among us is so obvious, so magnetic, so contagious, that people clamor for the privilege of joining. Rather than having to teach our members how to "grab hold of people," people are grabbing hold of us. Rather than telling our neighbors, "Come to our church; God is with us," they're telling one another that.

All these things happen "in those days." "In those days" refers to a time God promises at the beginning of Zechariah 8: "This is what the LORD says: 'I will return to Zion and dwell in Jerusalem'" (v. 3). In other words, "those days" describes a time when God returns and dwells in a specific community. It's a description of what happens in, to, and through a people when God is at the center of them. The entire chapter comprises a series of stunning acts God initiates for us, among us, through us. This is God's activity into which God's people are swept up and invited to joyfully steward.

There are several things.

A renaming. "This is what the LORD says: '... Then Jerusalem will be called the City of Truth, and the mountain of the LORD Almighty will be called the Holy Mountain'" (v. 3). The very land is named anew. *City* of Truth. Holy *Mountain*. Both the man-made and the God-made, civilization and creation, society and nature, world and earth, are caught up and brought into the saving and healing work of God.

This has deep resonance where I live. The land is under dispute. When the British came in the 1850s, they intended—indeed, their own laws required them—to pay for any land they possessed. This never happened, not in my region. It's a long and ignoble story, but the upshot is that today our city and its surrounding region rest on land never purchased. The real word for that: stolen. The feelings on all sides of this issue run deep.

Throughout our region, throughout our province, throughout our country, names of cities and towns, rivers and regions, mountains and coves tell an alternative history to the official version. One mountain bears the name of a Coast Salish chief, another the name of some English lord. The islands scattered down our coastline are named for Indian princesses, Spanish conquistadors, English explorers, Dutch settlers. The town I live in, Duncan, bears the name of a Scottish farmer, whereas the town next to us, Chemainus, is named after the tribal people who first lived there, whereas the city down the road, Victoria, carries the moniker of a British queen.

All these names tell stories, and many are stories of violence, betrayal, rivalry, deceit, greed.

We're due for a renaming.

City of God. Holy Mountain. This isn't a new imperialism. It's not a modern colonialism. As the last verse of Zechariah 8 makes clear, this mountain, this city, is a place of irresistible attraction for people from every tribe and tongue and nation. No one is coerced. Everyone is drawn.

And it's their idea to rename the place. "Jerusalem *will be called....* The mountain *will be called.*" The new names arise naturally. They are not imposed by decree; they are birthed out of the people's experience of God. That experience is so fresh, so real, so sweet, so good, so chastening, so refining, so renewing, it begs for new language, language that does not invoke the names of settlers and conquerors and chiefs and tribes, language that doesn't participate in our painful human history of claims and counterclaims, of domination and subjugation, but rather evokes the qualities of God himself—truth, holiness. Language that awakens us every time we speak it to the God who makes all things new. Language that overlays our rent-asunder story with God's work-it-all-together-for-good one. Names that redeem our blood-soaked rivalries with his blood-soaked sacrifice.

We are due for a renaming.

A breaking of generational walls. "This is what the LORD Almighty says: 'Once again men and women of ripe old age will sit in the streets of Jerusalem, each with cane in hand because of his age. The city streets will be filled with boys and girls playing there'" (vv. 4 – 5).

Churches are doing better than ever before at gathering the nations. I love this. I believe it is a sign of the kingdom in our midst. Zechariah 8 ends with a vision of multiethnic diversity and unity.

But a curious pattern is emerging in churches of multiethnic richness: it tends to come at the expense of multigenerational richness. The wealth of color has created a poverty of ages. The breadth that churches have attained on the ethnic front has produced a narrowness on the generational front. We're exchanging one homogeneity for another, and losing one diversity as we gain another.

Jesus loves the little children, be they red or yellow, black or white. But Jesus also loves the old man and old woman, and even a few of us who are middle-aged.

It's worth noting that the first division that God heals when he moves to town is not between classes nor races nor genders but between generations. Old and young. Under God's watchcare, each blesses the other. The old people sit in the streets. The children play at their feet. The old do not scold the young, and the young do not mock the old. Each basks in the presence of the other. Each makes the world safe for the other. Each lives in the shelter of the other.

When I first came to the church where I am pastor, sixteen years ago now, there were not many old people. At the time—fairly young myself—it didn't seem to me a problem. I paid it scarce attention. Then this text, Zechariah 8, started doing its work on me. When God shows up, I saw, the first social evidence of that is young and old together.

I started noticing the value that Scripture places on the generations, and especially on the very old and the very young. Psalm 22, that great cry of desolation that Jesus uttered from the cross, begins bleakly ("My God, my God, why have you forsaken me?") but ends in glorious hope—the rich and poor seeking and worshiping the Lord, all the ends of the earth and the families of the nations turning to him, bowing to him. But the last verse crowns it:

Posterity will serve him;
  future generations will be told about the Lord.
They will proclaim his righteousness
  to a people yet unborn—
  for he has done it.[4]

There's a similar emphasis in the giving of the covenant. Always, the generations are not far from God's pressing concern. "I will establish my covenant with him as an everlasting covenant," God says to Abraham about his "yet unborn" son Isaac, "for his descendants after him."[5] Father Abraham is given the covenant for the sake of his son Isaac, who has yet to see the light of day, who then receives it for the sake of his descendants, who have yet to see the light of day. When Moses teaches the covenant commandments to Israel, it is with explicit instructions to "impress them on your children."[6]

The Bible speaks of the wisdom and the folly of both old and young. In the story of King Rehoboam, King Solomon's son and successor, we see the folly of youth and the wisdom of age. The story is found in 1 Kings 12 and 2 Chronicles 10. Rehoboam ascends to the throne, and straightaway a delegation is dispatched from the people of Israel to make a request—that he lighten the "heavy yoke" of forced labor that his father, King Solomon, put on the people.

Rehoboam has to think about it. He needs three days. He consults first with the "elders" who had advised his father. These would be old men by now, papery skinned, rheumy eyed, sour breathed, an uncontained shaking in their hands. They've seen a lot. They stood alongside Solomon as he barked his decrees, amassed his wealth, bedded his women, indulged his lusts. They watched him drive the people harder and harder to build bigger and bigger monuments, all to the glory of his name. They watched Solomon go from a humble youth seeking the wisdom of the Lord to a pompous old tyrant and lecher turning "his heart after other gods."[7] In their day, they must have cheered him on. They must have helped organize and strategize all the exorbitant effort.

They're thinking otherwise now. They've had a front-row seat on a disturbing phenomenon: the "wisest man on earth" becoming the greatest fool in the universe. They've beheld wisdom in youth becoming folly in dotage. And my guess: they want to reverse that trend in their own lives. They want a shot of some earthly redemption. They glimpse their chance in Rehoboam.

So they have an answer instantly for the new king, and it's this: "If today you will be a servant to these people and serve them and give them a favorable answer, they will always be your servants."[8]

Rehoboam doesn't like this. It seems weak. It uses dirty words— *servant, serve*—words describing acts and attitudes beneath his dignity. The old men have spoken, and the old men think he should be in very nature a servant. Rehoboam can't imagine anything farther from his ambitions.

So he spurns their counsel and goes looking elsewhere. "Rehoboam rejected the advice the elders gave him and consulted the young men who had grown up with him and *were serving him*."[9] And, of course, they have different ideas: "Tell these people who have said to you, 'Your father put a heavy yoke on us, but make our yoke lighter'—tell them, 'My little finger is thicker than my father's waist. My father laid on you a heavy yoke; I will make it even heavier. My father scourged you with whips; I will scourge you with scorpions.'"[10]

That's what he wants to hear. That's advice that recognizes his authority (and compensates for his deep feelings of inadequacy). This makes him feel like a man. Forget all this wimp's talk of serving and servants.

This is the language of a god-king: master-slave, ruler-ruled, czar-serf. This is Pharaoh resurrected. The many serve the one, end of story.

"Rejecting the advice given him by the elders, he followed the advice of the young men." It doesn't go well. The move splits the kingdom in two, a wound that never heals.

Old men. Young men. Wisdom. Folly. The story plays all the notes in that key. We have Solomon, a young man supremely wise who becomes an old man supremely foolish. We have the elders, the men who grew up with him, advising him, growing foolish with him, who, too little, too late, choose the way of wisdom. We have Rehoboam and his gang, a young man and his toadies, reared in a culture of greed and power, who don't know wisdom when it kisses them on the lips.

Our own culture is well acquainted with these dynamics. Folly too often embraced. Wisdom too soon rejected. Wisdom descending into folly. Folly arising into wisdom, but often only after the damage is done. Pride and anger on both sides. Hurt and suspicion all around.

But when God steps into the center, the periphery shifts. A realignment happens at every level, but first it happens between the generations, maybe because here it's needed most and produces the most. Maybe because this is not just a symptom of health but health's very core, its necessary rootwork. Young and old love each other. Young and old seek out each other. Young and old learn from each other. Young and old live in the shelter of each other.

I have made Hebrews 11:21 an icon for my own journey: "By faith Jacob, *when he was dying*, blessed each of Joseph's sons, and worshiped as he leaned on the top of his staff." That's the faith I want to live and die by. In Jacob, the sign of that faith is a man who, though doddering and muttering, spends his last breath, his last strength, in worship and in blessing. And the ones he blesses are the children. He does not spend his meager breath and failing strength complaining about how loud the music is, how unruly and ungrateful the youth of today are, how poorly designed the facilities are for people with disabilities. He worships and he blesses. And the young ones receive his blessing as gift and as treasure. The children have his example to guide their own lives by. They have his legacy of faith passed down.

It's how I want to finish.

I think of the wisdom of the Cowichan people, the First Nations tribe in the region where I live. One of the former chiefs of the

Cowichans told me, "Every time we gather as a people, the purpose of our gathering is to make the world better and safer for our children." "Men and women of ripe old age will sit in the streets, each with cane in hand because of his age. The city streets will be filled with boys and girls playing there."

May our churches be the epicenter of this, a healing of the generations.

A homecoming of the prodigals and the restless wanderers. "This is what the LORD Almighty says: 'I will save my people from the countries of the east and the west. I will bring them back to live in Jerusalem; they will be my people, and I will be faithful and righteous to them as their God.'"[11]

Before the "stranger and the alien" are drawn to a community with God at the center, the estranged and the alienated come home. The scattered ones, the children of exile, those living in the far country, are brought back. The prodigals return.

This is religion at its best, religion in its truest sense. *Re-ligio*: to rejoin the ligaments. To reconnect the severed, shattered, scattered pieces. To restore to wholeness and fullness that which has been rent asunder.

When God returns to and dwells in our city, true religion comes with him. The prodigals know that there is food to spare in the Father's house. The exiles undertake their long journey home. The Cains, those restless wanderers living alone in their crowded and dangerous cities, start seeking the City of God.

The primary gift God gives to those who trust in him is reconciliation with him. But the primary gift the people of God give to those who are reconciled to God is a community of reconciled people. We give them the gift of our own wholeness and oneness. We give the gift of community. We invite them to be part of a people where everyone makes "every effort to keep the unity of the Spirit through the bond of peace."[12]

God calls us out of darkness and into marvelous light.[13] But his intent is that "if we walk in the light, as he is in the light, we have fellowship with one another."[14] So God prepares us to be a people who draw and who welcome every tribe and tongue and nation into the light by first making us light. And he does that, in part, by bringing those who are far away near. He does that by making the community of the converted also the community of the reconciled.

I'm a pastor, so I see up close the local migration of Christians from one church to another. Bill and Betty are mad at me, so off they go to the One, True, Pure, and Sacred Church of the Holy Apostolic Disciples of the Remnant. But Sally and Sam are mad at the children's director there, and they've come here. When both couples get mad about something in their new locations, they'll be off to the next place. This happens with such frequency, with so many high-sounding pious rationalizations, that it would be comical if it weren't a travesty.

Those not yet in the church see this, when they pay it any mind at all, and find it ridiculous and lamentable. They see right through it. They openly wonder, when they wonder about it at all, how the gospel, the central message of which is forgiveness and reconciliation, can be true when so many Christians live unforgiving, rent-asunder lives.

I've yet to find a good answer to that.

One sign that God has returned to dwell in the center of our lives and of our churches is that we become a living testimony of what we promise. We promise that in Christ all become new creations, no longer seeing others according to the flesh. We promise that in Christ we have the peace of God and the God of peace. We promise that we through Christ receive God's love and forgiveness, and then extend it — with authority — to the whole world. We promise all this, but then claim exemption for ourselves in some petty matter or another.

When God steps into the center, those who once were part of us, and now are not, come home. They come back. God's personal faithfulness to them and righteousness for them become their daily portion. What before was rumor becomes reality.

We become living testimony of the new life we promise to others.

May our churches be the gathering places for this reconciled community.

A restoring of commerce, religion, the land, and favor among the nations. "This is what the LORD Almighty says: 'You who now hear these words spoken by the prophets who were there when the foundation was laid for the house of the LORD Almighty, let your hands be strong so that the temple may be built. Before that time there were no wages for man or beast. No one could go about his business safely because of his enemy, for I had turned every man against his neighbor. But now I will not deal with the remnant of this people as I did in the past,' declares the LORD Almighty.

"'The seed will grow well, the vine will yield its fruit, the ground will produce its crops, and the heavens will drop their dew. I will give all these things as an inheritance to the remnant of this people. As you have been an object of cursing among the nations, O Judah and Israel, so will I save you, and you will be a blessing. Do not be afraid, but let your hands be strong.'"[15]

In Zechariah's vision, four restorations—religion, commerce, the land, and the favor of nations—tie together. (All four come under the phrase "This is what the LORD Almighty says," which works as a refrain in Zechariah 8 and signals, each time, a single promise from God.) That these four promises interweave—in a sense function together as one promise—is worth long reflection. Can any community or nation be deeply broken in one of these areas without it affecting all the others? In his book *Collapse: How Societies Choose to Fail or Succeed*, Jared Diamond documents the factors that lead to societal collapse. Among the key factors are corrupt or rigid religion, incompetent or greed-driven business, land exploitation and degradation, and enmity with surrounding nations.[16]

These are also Zechariah's four areas of restoration. They all rise together. Renewed commerce does not mean resorting to ecologically damaging ways of extracting resources from the earth; this isn't a strip-mining, ozone-thinning, habitat-destroying, rain-forest-razing way of generating wealth. Here, money is green in the best sense of the word. Heaven and earth, soil and root and rain and sun, work in shalom with commerce, with buying and selling, trading and innovating. It's an environment where fair wages are paid, free trade flows, and earthkeeping flourishes. All this works hand in hand with a rebuilt temple—with worship alive and abundant—which is all conducted under a covenant of mutual blessing among the nations.

Beautiful.

When God returns to and dwells with us, not only will lions and lambs lie down together, not only will swords be beaten into plowshares, but tycoons and tradesmen, loggers and tree huggers, oil barons and environmentalists, priests and politicians, worship leaders and senior pastors will lie down together too.

All will flourish under the restoring hand of God.

May our churches be the heartbeat of this.

A restoring of justice and integrity. "This is what the LORD

Almighty says: 'Just as I had determined to bring disaster upon you and showed no pity when your fathers angered me,' says the LORD Almighty, 'so now I have determined to do good again to Jerusalem and Judah. Do not be afraid. These are the things you are to do: Speak the truth to each other, and render true and sound judgment in your courts; do not plot evil against your neighbor, and do not love to swear falsely. I hate all this,' declares the LORD."[17]

A crucial shift happens here. It's announced by the phrase "These are the things you are to do." Up until this moment, this announcement, Zechariah 8 has been a litany of promises from God about what he will do. Right after this section, it resumes that tone, right through to the end. But inserted a little past midway is an imperative. There's something God requires of us. Up until now, everything God promises certainly requires our full participation. We won't benefit unless we embrace what God is doing. But it's all God's initiative. He declares, he acts, he brings things to us: our role, simply, is to receive.

But now God requires something of us.

My favorite YouTube video is a five-minute clip from an episode of *The Bob Newhart Show*. Bob, as you may know, is a psychologist in the show. In the scene, a woman comes for her first visit. Bob begins by explaining how he bills—five dollars for the first five minutes, and then nothing after that. The woman is thrilled. Bob assures her the session won't go over five minutes.

He asks her to start. She explains that she fears being buried alive in a box. He asks her to say more. The fear, she tells him, extends to other things—being in tunnels, elevators, houses, cars, "anything boxy."

"So basically you're saying you're claustrophobic?"

"Yes, that's what I'm saying."

This exchange takes about two minutes. Bob takes another ten seconds or so to empathize with her—how awful it must be to live with this fear.

"It's horrible," the woman says.

"All right," Bob says, "I'm going to give you two words that I think will clear up everything. Just take these two words and integrate them into your daily life, and you should be fine."

The woman is excited. She asks if she should write them down.

"Oh, you can if you like," Bob says. "But most people have no trouble remembering them."

"Okay," she says, leaning forward.

"You ready?" he asks.

"Yes," she says.

"Okay, here are the two words." Bob leans across his desk to put his face close to hers. "Stop it!"

There are some things God hates, and he simply says, "Stop it!" One thing God hates is injustice. He hates deceit. Unless we deal fairly and honestly with one another, unless we have a bone-deep commitment to do justly and speak truthfully, much of the good God intends to do gets undone. As I've said before, it's not that God cannot or does not override our poor representations of his character. God does this all the time, as his prerogative, out of sheer necessity. Indeed, a ground principle of good theology is that God is *always* the initiator and finisher—the author and perfecter—of his own saving and redeeming work. But he intends to get us in on the action. Like the servants whom Jesus enlists in his miracle of changing water into wine, Jesus invites us—no, commands us—to play a part. He reserves the miracle of transformation for himself, but he often gives us a significant stagehand role. Doing justly and speaking truthfully is one of our most crucial stagehand roles. And our performance enhances or mars his drama of redemption.

This has painful implications for me. As I've already said, I live on stolen ground: the first settlers in our region took the land from the Cowichan people and never paid for it, even though British law required from the beginning that "title must be extinguished"—legalese meaning that fair recompense had to be paid for all lands. The history here is a study in bad faith: not speaking "the truth to each other," not rendering "true and sound judgment in [our] courts," "plotting evil against [our] neighbor," loving "to swear falsely." All that's been done are all the things the Lord hates.

He asks us to do justly now.

I spoke recently at an event called The Gathering, a conference for First Nations Christians. A few of us white folk were invited to come along. It was good, for once, to be part of a white minority.[18] It was refreshing to worship the Lord God alongside Cowichan and Cree, Sioux and Lakota, Pennelekut and Squamish, Ojibwa and Carrier, and many more, but to do so in a style that incorporated the dances and drums, the chants and war whoops, the regalia and headdresses, of Indigenous people. It was, in a word, beautiful.

I spoke on Zechariah 8, and particularly on these verses. I confessed that I was part of a people who have done that which God hates. I said I was prayerfully struggling to know what to do next, how to undo what had been done, but I was committed to finding out.

Right after I spoke, a First Nations woman from the Cowichan tribe (*my tribe*, I like to call them now) told her story of being physically and sexually abused as a child in a nearby Residential School.[19] She spoke without bitterness or accusation. In fact, she told the story of her pain only so that she could tell the story of her joy: how Christ was redeeming and reclaiming and healing her in body, mind, and spirit.

But the room was heavy when she finished. Lisa, the white pastor, got up. She was overcome with emotion and said she was sorry. "I'm not apologizing because I was involved in what happened to you," she said. "I'm apologizing because I wasn't involved. Because, even when I knew terrible things were happening in those schools, I still did nothing."

That hit me hard. I spent most of my life blithely ignorant of what has been termed the Canadian Holocaust—the forced reeducation of several generations of First Nations children in conditions under which thousands died of disease, malnutrition, and abuse, and through which their Native culture, language, and heritage were systematically and brutally eradicated. And when I did become aware of it, and the ongoing fallout from it, I spent many years blaming "others" for it and wishing "others" would do something about it. Christian prayers of confession include both sins of commission and sins of omission—the evil we've done, and the good we've left undone. Toward First Nations people, I have few if any sins of commission to confess. Toward them, I have a lifetime of sins of omission to confess. This is part of the general malaise of our churches: this evasion of knowing about injustices, past and present, and then this apathy in the face of knowing. At our church, we have two kinds of movie nights. One is Family Movie Night, featuring a mainstream big-studio animation—*Up!*, *Megamind*, and the like—and the other is a Social Justice Movie Night, featuring a local or mainstream documentary—*Food, Inc.*, *Hope for the Sold*, and the like. The first draws hundreds. The second draws about a dozen.

So I welcomed what Pastor Lisa said next: "If you are white and you want to join me in apologizing, I ask simply that you stand." I stood. All the white people stood.

But we were completely unprepared, or at least I was, for what happened next: all the First Nations people began to weep. And then their weeping turned to sobbing. And then their sobbing turned to wailing. It pierced me. I felt the shame of all the wrong that my forebears had committed. I felt the shame of all the ways I, though not involved personally, had been personally uninvolved. Indifferent. Not wanting to know and, once knowing, just wishing they'd "get over it."

The wailing continued, got deeper, got louder. Just when I could not bear it another second, an older First Nations woman (I later found out she was chief of her tribe) came up to the front, asked for the microphone from the pastor, and said, "I do not want those of you who are standing to carry the weight of this. I forgive you. On behalf of my people, we forgive you."

The way all those people embraced me afterward, I knew they meant it.

I have learned something in the past six years as I have walked alongside my First Nations friends. I have learned why God hates injustice. It kills, steals, and destroys. These are all the works of the "thief." It's the devil's own, according to Jesus.[20] And so injustice cannot coexist with God.

It's the one thing he asks us to clean up.

May our churches have the courage to do this.

A recovering of spiritual vitality. "This is what the LORD Almighty says: 'The fasts of the fourth, fifth, seventh and tenth months will become joyful and glad occasions and happy festivals for Judah. Therefore love truth and peace.'"[21]

Fasts become festivals. Wearisome regimens turn to gladsome delights. Duty becomes privilege. The act of denying oneself, once a burdensome requirement, is now eagerly anticipated and joyously engaged.

And why not? When God is at the center, spiritual disciplines become all the more meaningful and rewarding. When we see the joy set before us, we're all the more eager to run with perseverance the race marked out for us, to throw off anything that hinders and the sin that so easily entangles, to endure hardship as discipline, to produce a harvest of righteousness and peace by discipline's steady hand of training.[22]

Surely this passage in Zechariah—fasts become festivals—was in Jesus' thoughts when he said, "When you fast, do not look somber as the hypocrites do, for they disfigure their faces to show men they are fasting. I tell you the truth, they have received their reward in full. But when you fast, put oil on your head and wash your face, so that it will not be obvious to men that you are fasting, but only to your Father, who is unseen; and your Father, who sees what is done in secret, will reward you."[23] Jesus connects fasting, as he does other spiritual disciplines, explicitly with intimacy with God, implicitly with service to people. That's the whole point.

We fast, we give, we pray, we do all this and more, not in order to be better people, though that tends to be a wholesome by-product of such efforts. We certainly ought not to do any of this to try to *look* better than other people, to impress or intimidate them. That sometimes is an unfortunate by-product of spiritual disciplines. But if it's our intent, if it's our motive and our goal, then the disciplines are decidedly not working. Indeed, they're carrying us in the opposite direction of where we should be heading.

Spiritual disciplines have one purpose only: to help us fulfill the greatest commandment—to love God with all we have and all we are, and to love others as ourselves. That's it. That's the sole value of alms, fasts, prayers, pilgrimages. That outcome alone is the measure of whether a discipline is working.

Only one thing, then, can make fasting—the most overtly self-denying of the disciplines short of celibacy—festive rather than gloomy: it must move us closer and closer into the circle of God's own life, closer into the epicenter of his truth and peace. Zechariah thus ends this section: "Therefore love truth and peace."

Loving truth and peace is a necessary condition for fully engaging spiritual disciplines, and loving truth and peace is also an inevitable consequence of fully engaging spiritual disciplines. In other words, love is both cause and consequence of the disciplines. Just as only the pure in heart see God, and only those who see God become pure in heart—heart purity is both cause and consequence of beholding God—so only those who love truth and peace fast with joy, and only those who fast with joy love truth and peace.

The simple conclusion is that God at the center revives us spiritually. Hard things become easy. Long roads shorten. Mountains bow down. What once was mournful, sad, and gloomy turns joyful, glad, and happy.

Fasts become festivals.

May our churches lead the way in this.

A breaking of ethnic, cultural, and political divides through an in-breaking of the gospel. "This is what the LORD Almighty says: 'Many peoples and the inhabitants of many cities will yet come, and the inhabitants of one city will go to another and say, "Let us go at once to entreat the LORD and seek the LORD Almighty. I myself am going." And many peoples and powerful nations will come to Jerusalem to seek the LORD Almighty and to entreat him.'

"This is what the LORD Almighty says: 'In those days ten men from all languages and nations will take firm hold of one Jew by the hem of his robe and say, "Let us go with you, because we have heard that God is with you." ' "24

I'm using the gospel here in its root sense: good news. The announcement of a decisive victory over a terrible enemy. News that awakens hope and courage in all who long for freedom. News that simultaneously brings terror and panic to all who are enemies of that freedom.

And this good news, this gospel, is for all nations. It's for all people. It embraces and welcomes all languages. Urdu speakers and Inuit and Norwegians and remote tribes tucked in the folds of Burmese mountain jungles. It's the homeless under the bridges of LA, the untouchables in the streets of Calcutta, the drug-addicted in sweaty apartments not far from where you live. It's rich people who live atop hills, and poor people who live in ditches. It's the old man in his lonely room, the teenage girl struggling with how she looks, the single mom wondering where the next meal's coming from, the salesman wondering if he can do this job another day, the celebrity wondering why being lavishly adored is not the same as being deeply loved. It's the discouraged dentist, the confused millworker, the weary postman. It's everyone, everywhere: "Let us go at once to entreat the LORD and seek the LORD Almighty. I myself am going."

This is evangelism, Bible-style. This is an evangelism that is cross-cultural, transpolitical, multiethnic, class defying, and wildly bountiful.

And it takes a village. It takes a church utterly God-smitten, who are in over their heads with the Holy of Holies. It takes a whole company of those who neither miss grace nor withhold it. For such a people, evangelism is almost effortless, the mere by-product of their God-smittenness. Otherwise, no one works at this. No one strategizes this. No one takes classes on this. It's just that a people who live with God at the center evoke, simply and powerfully, far and wide, curiosity about God. A community like that makes others envious in the best sense: they want what we have.[25] When God's way becomes our way, we become catnip to the world. The fragrance of Jesus is all over us.

This morning, my wife and I had breakfast with Rob and Andrea. Rob is one of the pastors at our church. I've been away all week on a writing break, and so I asked him what was going on at the church this week. He told me of several people — a dozen, in fact — all who had come to or called the church because they had heard "we help people." Rob told me about one of the people, a middle-aged single mom who had lost her husband, lost her job, and was losing her mind. She'd not been near a church since she was a young girl. Rob told her about the God who loved her and welcomed her, and she sat weeping to hear it. Then she looked up at him. "I had no idea," she said, "that a place like this existed on earth."

"In those days," it does.

CHAPTER EIGHT

EAT WHATEVER

WHEN GOD FIRST THUNDERSTRUCK ME about his heart for outsiders — for the many people he had in our city whom I'd yet to meet but for whose sake I was meant to stay[1] — I immediately got stuck. Where to begin? Does one just waltz into country clubs, biker houses, gay bars, crack dens, yoga studios and start handing out Bible tracts?

Well, it's been tried. The results are typically fruitless. Or worse: self-defeating. Tactics like that most often backfire. Regardless of how clean and humble our motives are, behavior like that smacks to the outsider as pretentious, smug, intrusive, mechanical. And weird. No one wants to be what we are. No one wants to be bitten by whatever bit us, smitten by whatever smote us, captivated by whatever's taken us captive.

I'll admit there are exceptions to this. Two come quickly to mind: Helen and Elizabeth. Both are women in their eighties, with bluish hair and failing sight and skin frail as crepe paper, but both are feisty and sassy and joyful and curious. Everyone wants to be like them. They hand out Bible tracts everywhere they go — in restaurants, in hair salons, in supermarkets, on street corners — and most people take them, and most, I think, read them, just because it was Helen or Elizabeth who gave it to them. If the secret to being like one of these two women lies hidden in the lines and pages of some little pamphlet, most people will scour it for clues.

But let's be honest. Few of us are like Helen or Elizabeth. I'm a bumbling fool with Bible tracts, napkin sketches of chasms and cross-shaped bridges. Lines like, "If you died tonight, do you know where you'd spend eternity?" come off flat and fatuous on my lips. I knew an elderly pastor, Leroy, who had a whole repertoire of evangelistic one-liners. Jump-starting a stranger's car battery in a mall parking lot (he carried cables in his trunk just to seize upon such opportunities), he'd stand at the open window of the driver whose car he'd just conjured back to life and say, "You know, forty-five years ago Someone came along and did that very thing to my heart. Would you like to know about that?" Or, riding in an elevator to the twelfth floor of some office tower, he'd turn to the person next to him and say, "The twelfth floor. Whoa! That's a long way up. But you know, I've met Someone who's promised one day to take me all the way up to heaven, free! Are you interested in meeting him?"

I watched him do this several times. He was very good at it, natural and affable. About half the people, maybe just out of politeness but I think a few out of genuine curiosity, agreed to hear him out.

I tried his methods out a few times. I don't know how many ways you can turn something simple into a disaster, but I managed it every time. I had a way of getting people's hackles up, and if they didn't walk away, I'd usually start to argue with them. After a few of these, I banned myself from attempting more. I even stopped trying to have "redemptive" conversations with Jehovah's Witnesses or Mormons who came to my door, for simple fear I was more deeply entrenching them in their views than coaxing them out of them.

In short, no one wanted to listen.

So when God thunderstruck me, I made a calculation: that there are few Helens and Elizabeths and Leroys in our church, or any church (I suspected that a hardier age produced whole pews full of them, but their stock's dwindled grievously), and that we would have to find a way of engaging our community more conducive to timid, prickly, awkward people like me.

And so we began.

And what we stumbled onto, formless and void at first, was a recovery of biblical hospitality. Two stories, one Old Testament and one New, have inspired and shaped that recovery. The first is the story of Abraham, in Genesis.

.   .   .

Abraham, father of the faith, was called out of Ur of Chaldees into a land God would show him. He was called to be a sign and symbol of God in the midst of those who did not yet know God. He didn't always live wisely—twice, in fear-driven acts of duplicity and self-preservation, he passed off his wife, Sarah, as his sister—but sometimes he lived brilliantly. He lived hospitably. Genesis 18, for example:

> The LORD appeared to Abraham near the great trees of Mamre while he was sitting at the entrance to his tent in the heat of the day. Abraham looked up and saw three men standing nearby. When he saw them, he hurried from the entrance of his tent to meet them and bowed low to the ground.
>
> He said, "If I have found favor in your eyes, my lord, do not pass your servant by. Let a little water be brought, and then you may all wash your feet and rest under this tree. Let me get you something to eat, so you can be refreshed and then go on your way—now that you have come to your servant."
>
> "Very well," they answered, "do as you say."
>
> So Abraham hurried into the tent to Sarah. "Quick," he said, "get three seahs of fine flour and knead it and bake some bread."
>
> Then he ran to the herd and selected a choice, tender calf and gave it to a servant, who hurried to prepare it. He then brought some curds and milk and the calf that had been prepared, and set these before them. While they ate, he stood near them under a tree.[2]

The thing to know is that Abraham, at first, doesn't know he's entertaining angels—or, more, the Lord of heaven and earth. He discovers that later. It's on the other side of his act of hospitality—a hospitality in keeping with the protocol of his Bedouin culture—that it becomes plain that these men are divine visitors. The opening line, "The LORD appeared to Abraham near the great trees of Mamre," is really the conclusion of the story, not its introduction. When the scene opens, all Abraham sees are "three men." Even though he calls the men "my lord," it's a different word from the one the story's narrator uses to identify the visitors as God himself. The narrator, every time, identifies these three men, collectively, as *Yahweh*, the sacred and exclusive name for God.[3] Abraham doesn't use that word. He refers to the men as *Adon*—a term sometimes used for God, to be sure, but just as equally a term of respect for a man of stature or power. *Adon* was a form of address a slave or servant would use for his master. But the word was commonly used as a polite salutation. It's like our English word *sir*.

I don't think, initially, Abraham knows he's welcoming any more than mere men—important men, lords, sirs, but still just men.

But he *sees* them. He sees these men clearly, from a distance. He sees them because he's sitting "at the entrance of his tent in the heat of the day." In a story like this, every word is handpicked. Every sentence is pared down hard and stark as bone. Every detail counts.

At the entrance of his tent. That detail counts. Abraham is neither inside nor outside. He's both in and out. Abraham inhabits, simultaneously, two worlds. This is a good posture for the father of our faith: at home, but facing the world.

This scene from Genesis 18 comes on the heels of three chapters that explore the divine and human meaning of God's covenant with Abraham. Genesis 15 narrates God's forming covenant with Abraham. Genesis 16 recounts Abraham and Sarah's ill-fated efforts to create an heir through the line of their Egyptian slave, Hagar, an anxiety-driven attempt to fulfill on their own one of God's covenantal promises. Genesis 17 tells the story of God's command to Abraham to seal and mark his covenant through the rite of circumcision.

So Genesis 18 is embedded in the context of covenant making.

God's overarching intent in his covenant with Abraham is twofold. God states most clearly that intent when he first calls Abraham:

> I will make you into a great nation
>   and I will bless you;
> I will make your name great,
>   and you will be a blessing.
> I will bless those who bless you,
>   and whoever curses you I will curse;
> and all peoples on earth
>   will be blessed through you.[4]

The covenant is about blessing. God's intent is to bless Abraham and all his descendants (a theme that emerges as the story unfolds) and it's to make Abraham and all his descendants a blessing. All peoples on the earth are to be blessed through Abraham—through him personally, and through his offspring.

To bless the man. To make the man a blessing.

Genesis 18 tells us, for the first time in this story, that Abraham just might take the second part of the covenant seriously. Up until now, besides passages that deal with the demands and promises of covenant, we've been regaled with stories of Abraham's trying to secure God's covenantal blessing for himself and his family. There's the account of Abraham's dividing land with his nephew Lot; there's the account of Abraham's arguing with God to rescue Lot and his family from God's wrath falling on Sodom. There's the account, as I've already mentioned, of Abraham and Sarah's masterminding a plot to secure an heir through Sarah's handmaiden, Hagar. In other words, Abraham is very busy trying to ensure that God makes good on the first half of the covenant — to bless him and all his descendants. This, it seems to me, is a human penchant, and certainly a North American one, and certainly a Western evangelical one: to resort to all manner of ploys and dodges to secure for ourselves God's blessing. I suppose we come by it honestly, since it appears to be the default of the father of our faith.

Abraham loves the first half of the covenant. He wants God to bless him.

What we haven't seen yet is that Abraham cares at all — or has even noticed — the other half of the covenant. God also wants to make him a blessing to all nations, to all peoples. To everyone he meets. To neighbors. To coworkers. To strangers. But Abraham's too busy chasing blessings for himself to concern himself with imparting any.

Abraham's lopsided interest in the covenant is curious not from a human standpoint — that, I'd argue, is natural — but from a theological one. It's the first half of the covenant — God's promise to bless Abraham and his descendants — which Abraham could safely ignore. After all, he can do nothing *on his own* to secure it. Blessings for Abraham and his ilk? That's all God's business, all God's problem. Abraham's role is simply to trust and obey, not to stage-manage, jerry-rig, bribe, browbeat, connive, or commandeer blessing. It's just to receive it. But that doesn't stop him from trying anyhow, in ways both comical and catastrophic. Abraham's great-grandson Jacob will prove a veritable genius at this kind of behavior, his whole life an odyssey of plot manipulations to try to wrestle blessing from God.

To be blessed: that can be safely left in God's hands. For Abraham. For Jacob. For you.

It's the other half of the covenant—*to be a blessing*—that should prompt Abraham to find strategic ways to "join God in what's he's doing." If any part of covenant calls for creative human-divine collaboration, this is it.

Yet Abraham seems indifferent to this part of covenantal relationship, perhaps even ignorant of it.

Until we reach Genesis 18. Then, suddenly, Abraham wakes up. Then, without warning, Abraham is ready. Perhaps he's been poised for this all along. Perhaps he's been sitting at the entrance of his tent for a while now. When the moment of opportunity arrives, he's there. He's ready. He sees. He acts.

Either way—whether he just showed up and woke up, or he's been here a while—to be a blessing means we sit between two worlds.

In the heat of the day. That detail counts too. This is the Middle East. Heat there is a devouring beast. Stones become coals. Air turns molten. All living things—tree, grass, gazelle, man—wilt beneath the ruthless gaze of it. Our culture is perhaps least hospitable in late evening; then, the world seems askew, we hold it at bay, and our bodies long to fold in on themselves and be still. But in Abraham's culture, the heat of the day was when earth bent off-kilter, when the world grew strange and menacing, and bodies drooped. "My strength was sapped as in the heat of summer."[5] It is the time of the day when hospitality to strangers is the farthest thing from anyone's mind—witness, many centuries later, maybe all of fifty miles from where Abraham sits, a Samaritan woman who's shocked at Jesus' request for hospitality in the heat of the day.[6]

In this culture, though famous for its hospitality, no one is looking to play host when the sun is out plundering.

Except Abraham.

As I've said already, I have a sense that Abraham's been sitting in the entranceway for quite a while, waiting for such a time as this. Paying attention. Hoping someone, anyone, would happen along whom he could rise up and bless. I think he's been ready for some time, now that God has shown repeatedly that he fully means to fulfill his promises to Abraham in the first half of the covenant—yes, Abraham's been ready for some time now to join God in fulfilling the second half of the covenant. The hospitality of the desert nomad, for sure, is an ingrained cultural trait with Abraham, bred in his bones. But the story aims higher than that. God takes Abraham's cultural posture, as he often takes ours, and redefines it. God co-opts and subverts a typical gesture of hospitality and turns it into a kingdom initiative.

Abraham has been blessed.

Now, he's ready to be a blessing.

And, of course, Abraham is not disappointed: the "three men" on whom he showers blessing, the three strangers he shows extravagant hospitality toward, turn out to be the Lord himself.

Rare, that this happens. Or is it? If what Jesus says in Matthew 25 is true — that the extent to which we've blessed others, shown hospitality to the least of these, is the extent to which we have "done it unto him" — then this story is common occurrence, or could be.

It could happen daily.

But it requires a spirit of hospitality: "Let me," Abraham says to the three men. *Let me* bring you water, provide you food, give you rest. Let me be your servant. Let me be a blessing.

There are spiritual disciplines for this, ancient ways that help cultivate this attitude of servanthood and hospitality. In a heart as self-regarding, indolent, and petty as mine, it takes long practice to grow this attitude. But I think I've grown in it. I think I'm growing.

. . .

But let's look at another biblical story, this one in the New Testament. It provides a surprising and important twist on the theme of what hospitality looks like. The story's from Luke 10:

> After this the Lord appointed seventy-two others and sent them two by two ahead of him to every town and place where he was about to go. He told them, "The harvest is plentiful, but the workers are few. Ask the Lord of the harvest, therefore, to send out workers into his harvest field. Go! I am sending you out like lambs among wolves. Do not take a purse or bag or sandals; and do not greet anyone on the road.
>
> "When you enter a house, first say, 'Peace to this house.' If a man of peace is there, your peace will rest on him; if not, it will return to you. Stay in that house, eating and drinking whatever they give you, for the worker deserves his wages. Do not move around from house to house.

"When you enter a town and are welcomed, eat what is set before you. Heal the sick who are there and tell them, 'The kingdom of God is near you.'"[7]

Abraham won the hearts of strangers by offering hospitality *to* them. Jesus tells us to win the hearts of strangers by accepting hospitality *from* them. This is the hospitality Jesus practiced with the Samaritan woman at the well: "Will you give me," he asks her, "something to drink?" Abraham's hospitality is a *Let me* kind: let me help you, let me serve you, let me give you water. Jesus' hospitality is a *Will you* kind: will you help me, will you serve me, will you give me water? This second form of hospitality, Jesus' kind, is the deeper of the two.

Why?

Because the first hospitality actually puts us in charge. We jump up and take action. We're the benefactor. We're the philanthropist. We're the merciful one. We have bread to spare.

We're the rich man.

But the second kind of hospitality puts us in need. We sit there and receive. We're the beneficiary. We're the supplicant and mendicant. We're at the mercy of others. We hunger and thirst.

We're the beggar.

The second form of hospitality is the deeper of the two, and the harder. There is no heroism in it, no largesse. No one sees the beggar and feels a rush of admiration. Pity, maybe. A tinge of scorn, perhaps. But not admiration. No one aspires to beggarliness. No one is inspired by it. Me, I'd rather, a thousand times over, a million, be the one who gives bread, gives water, than be the one who asks for it. Especially—*especially*—from a Samaritan woman who doesn't know how to stay married. Everything in me wants to maintain a distinct edge of moral superiority with someone like that. What has she got that I could possibly want or need? Am I not compromising my "witness" if I make myself vulnerable with her?

It's hard enough to practice a *Let me* form of hospitality even with heavenly visitors. To practice a *Will you* form of hospitality with trailer trash—well, that takes the humility of God.

And so God leads the way. And then he gives the command: "Eat and drink whatever they give you. Eat what is set before you."

For years I read this and never blinked. Now, it sends me reeling.

Jesus' first disciples observed kosher law, or *kashrut*. They observed the strictures of Levitical dietary rules: no pork, no dog, no snake, no crab, no horse, no blood. No cooking one thing in the pot of another thing. No this, and no that. No soft-pawed thing, no belly crawler, no bottom feeder, no carrion eater, no milk from the udder of an unclean beast. You could eat an animal that chewed the cud and had cloven hoofs, but not an animal that chewed the cud and didn't have cloven hoofs, or an animal that had cloven hoofs and didn't chew the cud.

There was a lot of food excluded by *kashrut*.

And then Jesus sends his followers out into highways and byways, into in-between places, and flatly says, "Eat ... whatever they give you. Eat what is set before you."

No strictures. No limits. No proviso. No saying no to this and no to that.

As I said, for years I read this and never blinked. I blink a lot now. Sometimes I almost hyperventilate. It strikes me that Paul must have had this story in mind when he gave the Corinthians mixed and confusing counsel about what to do with food sacrificed to idols: Eat it, and don't worry. Eat it, but don't cause someone else to stumble. Don't eat it. Idols are nothing. Idols are demons. Decide for yourself and don't let any man judge you. Make concessions to the weakest Christian in your midst.[8]

Well, it *is* confusing. I don't observe *kashrut*; in fact, this is the first time I've written about it, and I had to pause to go research it to get my facts straight. But I have my own private kosher laws, my idiosyncratic list of dietary restrictions. I don't drink hard liquor. I don't eat raw fish. I don't, I found out one day in Nairobi, eat goat intestines. I don't, I found out another time, eat pig brains. I don't, I found out with my First Nations friends, eat fishhead soup, which involves not just the head but every last little bit of the fish — scales and fins and entrails and eyeballs — all soaked together in brine. I like my steak medium-well and will send it back if it gushes blood as though hemorrhaging. I'm sure, if offered, I'd draw the line at cow eyes, uncooked liver, or moose testicles (affectionately called "prairie oysters" in the midlands of Canada).

But what if I'm in an in-between place? What if this is the hospitality of people to whom I'm announcing the kingdom of God? Would I have a glass of Scotch for the sake of the kingdom? If it was a Masai tribe and not a group of pastors offering me goat intestines, would I at least have a nibble? If a man or woman from the First Nations tribe in my area offered me raw fish, would I accept and partake?

"Eat ... whatever they give you. Eat what is set before you."

Jesus is giving his disciples more than a strategy for securing provisions. This is not about scrimping on the missions budget. He's telling us how to live in in-between places. Yes, we inhabit such places as Abraham did, ready to jump to our feet and declare, "Let me!" But even more, we inhabit such places as Jesus did, ready to just sit where we are and ask, "Will you?"

If I've learned anything about inhabiting in-between places, it's that Jesus' kind of hospitality is better *received* there than Abraham's form — or, more accurately, Abraham's form is suspect until we've practiced, repeatedly and genuinely, Jesus' form. Until we have humbled ourselves enough to receive wisdom, strength, truth, bread, water, from someone who's yet to enter the kingdom, we lack credibility with them. We seem arrogant to them. We come off as superior or sanctimonious or crusading.

Before Jesus offered the woman at the well living water — before he said, "Let me" — he asked her for water, because he was thirsty and he had nothing to draw with. "Will you give me something to drink?" he said.

And the kingdom broke in.

. . .

But most of us don't live in tents. Most of us don't draw water from wells, at least not communal ones. So what does biblical hospitality look like now?

The next chapter tackles that.

CHAPTER NINE

IN-BETWEEN PLACES

ONCE IN A WHILE, a word, a phrase, or an image is more than just a word or a phrase or an image: it's a Rosetta Stone, a voice from heaven, a final clue that solves a vast mystery. It's a password that opens a secret door into a hidden realm.

A friend of mine gave me a phrase like that. It wasn't original to him; he'd picked it up from some sociologist. But never mind that. It was a magic phrase, potent as incantation. It mapped and named the world afresh for me. It fitted me with special lenses that stretched my color spectrum into the ultraviolet. I could see deeper down, farther out.

The phrase: *in-between places*.

You must be crushingly disappointed. You must have thought I had the next *supercalifragilisticexpialidocious*. Or *flibbertigibbet*. Or, at least, the equivalent of *bibbitybobbityboo*.

But no, I just have *in-between places*.

Let me explain. In-between places are neither our own world nor another's. They're in-between: the space that runs, wide or narrow, between two worlds. They're not biker houses or gay bars or country clubs. But they're not sanctuaries or fellowship groups or Bible studies either. They're something in the middle, where everyone's both comfortable and uncomfortable, where everyone's forced to adapt by a few degrees, but only by a few. The ways we talk, the things we talk about, the food we eat, the interests we engage—everyone has to shift a little to fit into an in-between place.

And what we've discovered is that our community has many in-between places. And where they don't exist, they're easy to create. We actually started this awhile back, stumbling toward it. It was much later my friend used the phrase, and then everything lit up, like those big lights that turn a stadium field from blackness to radiance in one flick. But what we had found, and then began to create, and only later named, were in-between places.

An example would help.

In 2008, a massive in-between place was created by our community in our community. That summer, in August, our town and region hosted the North American Indigenous Games, which everyone here called NAIG. NAIG is the Summer Olympics for Indigenous people. It gathers young aboriginal athletes from almost every region across our continent (and a few from farther away) in an eight-day competition in sports ranging from soccer to canoe races to archery to boxing to short- and long-distance running, and many other things. During the games, cultural and entertainment events happened all over the town, from hoop dancing (a Plains Indian dance form) to drum-making seminars to an eclectic lineup of musical concerts, and much else besides.

It was a perfect in-between place: neither in nor out, not my world or yours, not ours or theirs, not us or them, but a place where worlds collide, intermingle, juxtapose, cross-pollinate. Everyone had to step out of what was known and comfortable, relinquish the need to have things on their terms and under their control, and enter a place where the familiar and the unfamiliar interwove. The watchwords became *Let me* and *Will you.*

About one hundred people from our church volunteered in one capacity or another.

It was brilliant. Eight days of this changed us. It changed the way we think about one another, relate to each other. It changed our ideas, many deeply entrenched, about who we think "the other" is. In so doing, it changed our ideas about ourselves.

I met Jenny during that time. Jenny is an elder of the Cowichans. She looks Indian: you'd never mistake her for, say, Italian or Spanish or Tibetan. She's pure Cowichan, and proud of it. She often dresses in black and crimson red, the signature colors of her tribe. She has three tattoos, two on her legs, one on her arm. "When I got this one, I didn't feel it at all," she says, pointing to the "Jenny" on her right arm, and referring to the stupor, the chronic state of numbness, she used to be in from her heavy drinking. "This one," she says, pointing to the eagle in flight on the outer shank of her right leg, "I felt a little. And this one," she says, pointing to the circle with the bear claw design on the outer shank of her left leg, "I felt a whole lot," meaning she'd sobered up when she got it and had nothing in her to naturally anesthetize the pain, "and so I decided that was enough tattoos for a while."

My wife first met Jenny in an in-between place. Actually, it was a place farther outside my wife's world than Jenny's: it was in a makeshift office set up in the inner hall of the Cowichan Cultural Centre, a series of buildings at the edge of town that are designed to resemble a traditional Native village. The office was in the stylized replica of a Coast Salish big house (or long house), a ceremonial gathering place where everything from weddings to funerals to potlatches to naming rites was held. For most white people, this is as close to being in a big house as any will ever get, or would want to get. Indeed, among most evangelical Christians, at least white ones, the big house is a locus of evil, a breeding ground for the demonic. Among Christian Native people, there are strong feelings on both sides about what the big house represents. Some believe it is evil. Some believe it is mostly cultural, and that most of its ceremonies can be redeemed.

It was here, in this replica of a big house, that Cheryl met Jenny. Cheryl was the unpaid coordinator for NAIG volunteers. She was working this particular day on entering names into a database. But things were a bit disorganized, so work was slow. Jenny walked in, sat down, asked Cheryl her name, and then told Cheryl her life story.

That day the two became friends. It turned out Jenny's son, Jason, already attended our church. Jenny, because of her drinking, had given Jason up for adoption when he was a tot, and their relationship was distant and strained. They hardly knew each other.

Jason had met a girl, Nadine, who once attended our church. They fell in love and wanted to be married. "I know a pastor who might do that," Nadine said, and called me.

That encounter, in time, led to Nadine's reclaiming her faith and Jason's coming to faith. At their wedding, I met Jenny — this is a few years before Cheryl and Jenny met—but she was cold and aloof and disdainful. She could barely look at me or speak to me. Later, after we became friends, she told me she didn't trust me when we first met because I was a Christian minister.

Jenny's suspicions had a deep root. She had been forced to attend Residential School as a girl. Residential Schools were a collaboration, for roughly one hundred years, between the Canadian government and various religious denominations to deliver education to First Nations people on the British model. It was boarding school, with militaristic discipline and a strong religious curriculum. Many of these schools were run by priests and nuns. In many, the priests and nuns abused the children—physically, verbally, emotionally, sexually. The stories are legion. And the enduring pain is colossal. A man in his seventies can recall his years in Rez and still collapse in anguish. The fallout from these places remains one of the most intractable problems for First Nations people in Canada.

So Jenny had a built-in reaction of distrust toward me. When we met, in my mind I made a calculation about Jenny: here is one who will never become a follower of Christ.

I had forgotten about Jenny when Cheryl came home one day and told me she had met Jason's mother.

"Who?" I said.

"Jason's mother," she said. "Jason Fraser. The lady I met today is Jason's birth mother. Jenny. Her name's Jenny."

Then I remembered. I didn't think much would come of Cheryl and Jenny's meeting.

Today as I write, not even two years since that first meeting between Jenny and Cheryl, Jenny is what I call the Queen of New Life. She sits in the front row and worships with her entire body. Sometimes she lets up a war whoop that sends holy shivers up your spine. The day she was baptized—the opening day of NAIG—she sang a song to the church in her own tongue about how God healed her broken heart.

I'm supposed to meet Jenny today at one of the big houses. There's a luncheon being held there in honor of actor Adam Beach, who's just moved to our area. When Jenny invited me this past Sunday, she looked at me and said, "I love you."

"I know," I said. "I love you too."

I call her Mom; though she's barely older than me, she seems much wiser. She calls me *whun'ni'tum muna'* (one-eye-*tum*-mun-ah*),* which in her language, *Hul qu'mi num* (*hulk*-a-me-numb), means something like "my white boy son."

In a couple of weeks, Jenny and I will spend a better part of a day visiting other Cowichan elders in their homes. We will be a two-person delegation, kingdom emissaries, going to invite these elders to a special event we plan to host at our church. The event, though, will be an in-between place: we will involve some protocols — welcoming and witnessing ceremonies, a blanketing ceremony — traditional to Coast Salish people. And we'll also pray to Jesus (which most Cowichans do anyhow, with their strong Catholic influence) and, as I said, meet in a church. Jenny's the perfect ambassador for all this. And me? I'm the student. As she says, "In this, I am your teacher."

This part of the story was to say simply that things like this don't happen when we stay safe in our own world. They happen in in-between places.

. . .

Here's the irony: many of us spend much of our time in in-between places. That's where we live and work and play. We don't live in Christian neighborhoods or eat at Christian restaurants or shop at Christian grocery stores. Few of us play in Christian sports leagues. None of us golf on Christian courses, or ski on Christian slopes. Not many of us work in Christian workplaces.

Most of our lives we live in in-between places. And yet the church, as a corporate entity, rarely goes there. We all gather from our in-between places, huddle together for an hour or two in our own little world, and then disperse again to inhabit once again the in-between places. But we rarely connect what we do in church with how we live everywhere else. In fact, part of the strangeness of evangelical Christianity is that the very idea of connecting the two tends to make us anxious rather than excited. We fear we'll compromise ourselves if we inhabit in-between places *as part of the church.* So we inhabit them without any clear and rooted identity.

It's no wonder the church is having little impact.

One practical thing we do as a church to connect our life together with our lives apart is collaborate widely, with almost anyone. We work with schools, with day cares, with women's shelters, with local government, with local businesses. We work with just about anyone. We collaborate promiscuously, in fact.

Why? Because this is how everyone actually lives. No Christian would, say, work at Burger King and refuse to labor alongside fellow employees because they didn't share your beliefs or values. If you did refuse on those grounds, you'd get fired, and rightly so. All of us work alongside atheists, Buddhists, lesbians, Hindus, and more, and think nothing of it.

Until we put our church hats on, and suddenly we get all skittish.

We decided to stop being skittish. I'm not saying we work *in* the church together with all and sundry. The church is *our* world, where we do things on *our* terms, without apology or compromise. And I'm not saying we create *partnerships* with all and sundry. I am saying we work *as* a church together with all and sundry. I'm saying we, *as* a church, inhabit in-between places. I'm saying we collaborate — literally, work together to accomplish a shared goal — widely. Our church takes part in the Walk of the Nations, an annual walk to celebrate cultural diversity and strengthen cross-ethnic friendships. Last year, I ended up walking behind the Pride people. I'm sure they felt as awkward about my proximity as I felt about theirs. But we weren't on a March for Jesus or a Gay Pride Parade. We were on a Walk of the Nations, and that turned out to be shared ground. An in-between place.

When we collaborate as a church, we don't make a condition of our collaboration that we share all goals and motives and values with whomever we're working alongside. A single shared goal is enough. You want racial reconciliation? I want that? Let's collaborate.

But when we inhabit those in-between places, friendships happen that probably wouldn't happen otherwise.

. . .

There is a monument that stands in the middle of east Africa's vast grasslands. The monument is sun bleached and weather worn, not much to look at. Its shape is a tapered oblong, about ten feet high, with a plinth that girds the base and serves as a bench for sitting. The monument stands in the middle of nowhere: a wide expanse of dusty earth pocked with tussocks of parched grass and ringed by a few scrubby acacia trees. It takes a long time to get there. No buildings or towns or villages are anywhere close. The setting commands little view: no forest, no lake, no river, no mountain. There are no animals around, which otherwise is the principal attraction in this part of Africa. Yet here, hundreds of people congregate throughout the day, people from every country — China, Ethiopia, Brazil, Canada, Germany, New Zealand, Kuwait, America, everywhere. The atmosphere is jovial. People try to overcome language barriers with gestures and loudness. Complete strangers take photos for each other. I'm sure that, several times in any given day, people exchange food, water, gas, whatever else you might need to continue your journey.

Why here?

The monument marks the boundary between two countries, Kenya and Tanzania. It stands at the point of intersection between two vast wildernesses, Kenya's Masai Mara Range, and Tanzania's Serengeti. On the monument, a line is inscribed down the middle of the plinth, dividing it evenly into two halves. That line marks the exact border between two worlds. You can stand on the plinth of the monument, straddle the line, and have one foot in one country, the other foot in the other. It's an in-between place.

The world converges on places like that.

CHAPTER TEN

A TALE OF TWO COMMUNITIES

I DO AN EXERCISE SOMETIMES when I'm asked to talk with church leaders. I draw a flat line on a chalkboard or flip chart. On the left side of the line I put a letter *A*. On the right side, I put a letter *H*. I call this, inventively, the "A to H Scale."

Then I assign Scripture verses to several people in the room. The verses are taken from the book of Acts, chapters 2 and 4, and from various chapters in the book of Hebrews. I have the people read these verses in a prescribed and alternating sequence: first a verse or two from Acts, then a verse or two from Hebrews, and then Acts again, and then Hebrews, back and forth until we're done.[1]

What I've paired up in the alternating readings are opposed realities. The world we see in Acts is miles and miles away from the world we glimpse in Hebrews. They comprise a series of before-and-after photos, except moving in the wrong direction: the *before* shots are splendid, captivating, inspiring; the *after* shots are shabby, embittering, depressing.

Like this:

> *Acts:* "They devoted themselves to the apostles' teaching and to the fellowship, to the breaking of bread and to prayer" (2:42).
> *Hebrews:* "Do not be carried away by all kinds of strange teachings.... Obey your leaders and submit to their authority. They

keep watch over you as men who must give an account. Obey them so that their work will be a joy, not a burden, for that would be of no advantage to you" (13:9, 17).

Acts: "All the believers were together and had everything in common. Selling their possessions and goods, they gave to anyone as he had need" (2:44–45).

Hebrews: "Keep your lives free from the love of money and be content with what you have" (13:5).

Acts: "Every day they continued to meet together in the temple courts. They broke bread in their homes and ate together with glad and sincere hearts, praising God and enjoying the favor of all the people. And the Lord added to their number daily those who were being saved" (2:46–47).

Hebrews: "Let us not give up meeting together, as some are in the habit of doing, but let us encourage one another" (10:25).

The journey from the community depicted in Acts to the community addressed in Hebrews follows an arc of shocking decline. The distance between the two, in only one generation, at most two, is stunningly wide. The comparison tracks a fall from a great height. It measures, like an astronomer's redshift, the fading of a brilliant light. It gauges, like a stockbroker's accounts on a Black Monday, the sudden gutting of mass wealth. The found are nearly lost again. The children of light live in shadows. The rich have become poor, with nothing to show for it.

After we've read all the Scriptures, I ask each person to draw the A to H Scale on their notepaper beside each set of Scriptures, and then to rate on that scale where they think their church falls in that area. (The midway ranking is around D or E on the scale.) And then I have them rate their church overall on the same scale. The scale looks like this:

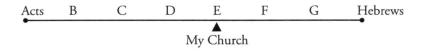

Acts   B   C   D   E   F   G   Hebrews
▲
My Church

And then we talk about it.

I have never had anyone rate their church in any area higher than a C, and never had anyone rate their church overall higher than a D. Every church, at best, is fair to middling, at least in the eyes of her leaders. A number of times I've done this, some leaders have ranked their church in certain areas, and sometimes overall, as G or H. They've bottomed out.

I usually at this point in our conversation make a little speech that goes something like this: "Now understand, Acts 2 and 4 depict the early church in its pristine form. The believers were living in the very light of Christ's resurrection: they had seen, touched, talked with, been instructed by the risen Christ. They were buoyed by an irrepressible joy and bolstered by irresistible courage. They lived in the overflow of this wild exhilaration. Everything was possible. Everything was new. And on top of all this, they had a sense that Jesus would return any minute, swooping down from heaven to make the kingdoms of this earth the kingdom of our God, to set all things to right and usher in the New Jerusalem on the ruins of Rome. What did a Mercedes Benz mean in light of all that? What value did money or status or stuff — or even health — have in comparison with that? So this moment was not to last. It couldn't. There had to be a coming back down to earth, a digging in for the long haul. All the same, we want to get as close to the world depicted in Acts as possible."

That's what I say. But I'm starting to regret my little speech. I'm starting to think it's a sidestep and a cop-out.

It's funny, but the older I get and the longer I'm in ministry, the more naive and idealistic I become, at least in some areas. For sure, in other areas I'm more cynical and pessimistic now than ever: I find, for instance, most people's reasons for leaving a church inanely self-serving, all the worse because the reasons typically come dressed in elaborate theological vestments. I have little patience left for debates about music. I have no patience anymore for people who tell me they're "sold out" for God or "radical for the kingdom," and who then bail out over a minor setback. I have a rapidly diminishing tolerance for the word *passion*, as in "I have a passion for [fill in the blank]": worshiping God, connecting ancient truth with beating hearts, restoring the arts to a place of honor in church, or some such. All these are noble pursuits. But having a passion literally means you'll die for the thing. I haven't seen a whole lot of that lately, but maybe I don't get out of town enough.

So I'm jaded.

But in some things, the trajectory is going the other direction. Here's one of them: I more and more believe that the church can look and sound and believe and act like the church did two thousand years ago, when the Spirit first fell like fire and came like a hurricane, and everyone liked everyone else, and shared as anyone had need, and bystanders rushed to become participants. I not only believe that this is possible; I believe it's normative. It's the way it's supposed to be.

Why else would the writer of Hebrews plead with and scold believers to return to what they once knew, if there was no way back?

.   .   .

In chapter 7, we walked through Zechariah 8. We looked at Zechariah's vision as a portrait of what a community looks like when God returns to and dwells at its center. I ended that chapter with the question, Could this be your church?

Yes.

And Acts 2 and 4 provide the beginning of an answer. Let's tease out a few things that would help us find the way back.

Here are the two passages spliced together:

> They devoted themselves to the apostles' teaching and to fellowship, to the breaking of bread and to prayer. Everyone was filled with awe at the many wonders and signs performed by the apostles. All the believers were together and had everything in common. They sold property and possessions to give to anyone who had need. Every day they continued to meet together in the temple courts. They broke bread in their homes and ate together with glad and sincere hearts, praising God and enjoying the favor of all the people. And the Lord added to their number daily those who were being saved.... All the believers were one in heart and mind. No one claimed that any of their possessions was their own, but they shared everything they had. With great power the apostles continued to testify to the resurrection of the Lord Jesus. And God's grace was so powerfully at work in them all that there were no needy persons among them. For from time to time those who owned land or houses sold them, brought the money from the sales and put it at the apostles' feet, and it was distributed to anyone who had need.[2]

A number of things leap out here, more than we'll take the time to examine. The first most obvious thing is how it opens: "They *devoted* themselves." That devotion describes a mindful, soulful, unwavering commitment to be something, to do something, to know something.

It is a deeply felt, fiercely resolved, strenuously disciplined, and highly focused commitment to a particular teaching, a distinct community, and a specific practice. Steadfastness in truth, family, and ritual. In sound doctrine, time with brothers and sisters, and simple but deep spiritual practices. These things, from the beginning, have been the heart of the church's life together. They will remain so until the end.

And there is worship too, unceasing, unrehearsed, flowing spontaneously out of hearts thunderstruck with thankfulness.

And there is awe. There is a continual sense of wonder at what God is doing in and through ordinary people. Yes, they witness unmistakable supernatural miracles: the lame walk, the blind see, the sick are made well. Even the shadow of an apostle is a balm of healing. But just as much — maybe more so, more unmistakably supernatural — they're in awe because generosity breaks forth every which way. The church erupts in an extravaganza of giving so sweeping it would be foolhardy if it weren't Spirit driven. People act like their stuff is everyone's: their house, their horse, their food, their money. A what's-mine-is-yours virus infects the whole lot. Listen again to the litany of wildcat, runaway acts of generosity: "All the believers ... had everything in common. They sold property and possessions to give to anyone who had need.... No one claimed that any of their possessions was their own, but they shared everything they had.... God's grace was so powerfully at work in them all that there were no needy persons among them. For from time to time those who owned land or houses sold them, brought the money from the sales and put it at the apostles' feet, and it was distributed to anyone who had need."

This just might be the greater miracle. This might be the critical factor in the church's "enjoying the favor of all the people" and the Lord's adding "to their number daily those who were being saved."

As I said, I'm cynical about a few things. One of them is the word *vision.* I know people who leave churches, or refuse to give to them, because there's not enough vision, or not one that captures their imagination and inflames their heart. Unless the leadership — though democratically — casts and casts and casts again a vision that is exciting, compelling, exotic, yet also manageable and affordable, able to be accomplished in less than two hours of personal commitment a week, people like this quickly get bored, sour up, cease contributing, and often leave.

It's worth noting that the leaders and the people depicted in Acts 2 and 4 aren't casting a vision: they're living a life. Their vision has already happened, has already been fulfilled: they have become children of God, invited into the kingdom of God. This is the unspeakable privilege. After that, it's enough—it's grace upon grace—to be together, to learn together, to grow together. It's enough to have good teaching and deep fellowship, and to share the sacraments. It's enough to worship alongside each other. It's enough to know that, should I need anything, someone here will help.

This is what every faithful church looks like, with or without some big hairy scary vision. When we do this right—when we devote ourselves to these things—vision is a natural consequence: we can't help but have impact on the community around us, and then dream ways to do even more.

The way ahead is the way back, and the way back is the way ahead.

.   .   .

I have a modest but subversive proposal. I suggest your church put a moratorium on vision-casting for the foreseeable future. Instead, I suggest you recover the vision that has already been fulfilled, that you are God's people, chosen and blessed and dearly loved. And then rally your church around simply being the church—*devote* yourselves to teaching, fellowship, sacraments, worship, and stewardship.

Do that, and I promise God will give you more vision than you can chase in a lifetime.

CHAPTER ELEVEN

WORDS MADE FLESH AND DWELLING AMONG US

"IN THE BEGINNING."

Two books of the Bible start that way. The first, obviously, is Genesis. In the beginning, God. God created. God spoke. God acted. In the beginning, there was God and nothing else. God and emptiness. God and chaos. And then God opened his mouth, and everything changed: light, life, you.

In the beginning.

The other book that opens this way is the gospel of John. In the beginning, the Word. The Word was with God, and the Word was God. The Word created, the Word spoke, the Word acted. And then, unimaginably, more: the Word became flesh. The Word dwelt among us. We touched the Word. We saw the Word. And all this came to be: light, life, you.

God is a creative creator. Genesis 1 makes that clear. God in creation turns words into realities. "Elephant": and there it is, grey and rumpled, lumbering, trumpeting, ears big as rugs. "Hippopotamus": and behold!

A giant wallowing cow looms up from muddy depths. "Rockies": and there they are, shearing up from flatlands, fierce and wild and blinding bright. What was not, now is. What no eye had seen nor ear heard is now a pageant of color and motion, a symphony of sound and song. And then God put mankind in the middle of it all, to rule it, to name it, to care for it. And to live in unbroken intimacy within it, with garden and wilderness, with grizzly and lizard, with each other, with God.

We threw it away. In a blink, with little provocation, the first man and woman reckoned they would be better served by heeding the enemy than God. What God made and gave and blessed, we spurned and broke, and then went looking elsewhere.

And the whole sad plight of humanity began. Our lostness. Our aloneness. Our not-at-homeness. Our frustration and anxiety and fear and anger. We live our lives now east of Eden, in sorrow, among thorns. In exile.

In the beginning, God created, and it was good. Then we came along, and it wasn't so good.

. . .

But there's another story being told. "In the beginning ... the Word." Not *a* word. *The Word.* The Word behind all the words, spoken and unspoken. The Word that was the creative genius behind elephants and hippopotamuses and Rockies, and the Word that is the sustaining power within all these things.[1] The Word that was with God and is God, was in the beginning.

And then an astonishing thing happened. At just the right moment, the Word became flesh and moved into the neighborhood.

If God is creative in creating, how much more is he creative in saving? If God displayed his power and goodness in giving us, for our existence, earth and sky and air and water, and all that lives within them, how much more does God display his power and goodness in giving us, for our salvation, Jesus Christ? God pulled out all the stops to create creation. How much more to create new creations?

To accomplish the first, God spoke.

To accomplish the second, God came.

. . .

"In the beginning." Scholars love the richness of this phrase in John's hands, in John's mouth. Listen, for example, to what renowned New Testament scholar Leon Morris, citing renowned scholar William Temple, writes about this: "'In the beginning' means that [Jesus] was before all else. But it probably means more. . . . 'beginning' can also denote 'origin' as in the sense of basic cause. Temple is probably right in thinking the phrase here combines two meanings, 'in the beginning of history' and 'at the root of the universe.'"[2] What Morris is saying, and he stands in a wide consensus on this, is that John is concerned with more than chronology. He's on about ultimate reality. The really real. It's not a "what or who came first" issue primarily for John, though that matters. He's equally if not more concerned with "what or who is at the center of everything."

The answer to both is Jesus. "In the beginning."

There is a phrase repeated three times in the New Testament that bears on what John is saying in John 1. The phrase is "before the creation of the world." Before anything was made, something was going on. Before one atom came into existence, a whole universe of divine love flourished.

Jesus is the first to use that phrase, in his high-priestly prayer: "Father, I want those you have given me to be with me where I am, and to see my glory, the glory you have given me because you loved me before *the creation of the world*."[3] Before the creation of the world, the divine love of Father and Son existed. And Jesus wants you and me to get in on that.

And then the apostle Peter says this: "For you know that it was not with perishable things such as silver or gold that you were redeemed from the empty way of life handed down to you from your forefathers, but with the precious blood of Christ, a lamb without blemish or defect. He was chosen *before the creation of the world*, but was revealed in these last times *for your sake*. Through him you believe in God, who raised him from the dead and glorified him, and so your faith and hope are in God."[4] Before the creation of the world, the Christ was chosen to redeem you.

And then the apostle Paul pulls it all together with this: "Praise be to the God and Father of our Lord Jesus Christ, who has blessed us in the heavenly realms with every spiritual blessing in Christ. For he chose us in him *before the creation of the world* to be holy and blameless in his sight. In love he predestined us to be adopted as his sons through Jesus Christ, in accordance with his pleasure and will."[5] Before the creation of the world, God in Christ also chose you to be his very own. He chose you before his creation to be his new creation.

Before God ever dreamed elephants or hippos or Rockies, he dreamed you. Before anything existed, his love existed, and that love sought and claimed you. He knew the mess he'd find you in. He knew the terrible cost to get you back. He decided anyhow, before he made a single thing, that it was worth it.

A lesser god would have decided before the creation of the world to leave well enough alone.

Our God decided before the creation of the world to get all in. Because before the beginning, before anything else existed, the Word was with God and was God, and the Word was not only making the world but, one day, coming into the world.

Before anything, God already had your salvation worked out. And, with it, your transformation. He set out not just to rescue you but to remake you. Not just to reconcile you to himself through his Son's cross but to conform you to the likeness of that Son through the Spirit's indwelling.

. . .

"The Word became flesh and appeared among us."

Jesus.

He looked just like us. He felt what we feel. He was tempted as we are. He ate and slept and laughed and wept and got frustrated with dunderheads and liked a good glass of wine. But what marked Jesus out as God of gods, King of Kings, Lord of Lords, was something we pay too little attention to, or so I reckon. It wasn't his miracles, though confused but otherwise smart men like Nicodemus thought it was, as did the crowds.[6] It wasn't his spellbinding eloquence or rapier wit or mesmerizing good looks. Many have this, and though we treat them at times like gods, we've proved the theory wrong. And maybe Jesus wasn't a standout in any of those things anyhow. As Isaiah says, there was nothing in him—no beauty, no majesty—to attract us to him.[7]

What made Jesus obviously the God-man were two things that combined in him as one thing: "he was full of grace and truth."

Full. The Greek means not one grain more of truth or one drop more of grace could be fit into him. He bursts at the seams with both.

Everything he is, everything he does, drips truth, exudes grace. There's never a moment when Jesus runs short on either. If Jesus were facing an enemy, or dealing with disappointment, or saw a beautiful woman, or was betrayed by a friend, or met a gay man, or was given a million dollars, or *whatever*, what he would say and what he would do would be the perfection of grace and truth.

This God-man chose you before the creation of the world. He became just as you are, and takes you just as you are, to make you just as he is: full of grace and truth.

. . .

When this becomes multiplied—three people full of grace and truth, thirty people, three hundred, three thousand—we call that church. A healthy church not only magnifies this effect; it mass-produces it. A healthy church is where I witness grace and truth in you, and you in me, but it's also the place where my own embodiment of grace and truth is catalyzed by your embodiment of it, and yours by mine. In healthy churches, something's in the air that makes each of us and all of us become more fully, more quickly, what God calls us to be.

Sick churches do the opposite. What's in the air calls out the worst in us, individually and collectively. They awaken, feed, indulge, reward our lowest impulses. If I'm a gossip or an angry man or full of resentment or a legalist or a grace abuser, a sick church makes me more so. It gives free rein to what's ugliest in me. It lets me justify my meanest basest self. And likewise for all: if we are altogether suspicious and unwelcoming, in a sick church we'll all only get worse.

But a healthy church brings out the best in us, individually and collectively. It awakens and strengthens and celebrates our noblest tendencies. If I'm a gossip, it will help me purify my thoughts and speech. If I'm an angry man, it will help me to seek and to impart the shalom of God. If I'm full of resentment, it will allow me to receive and to extend the grace of God. Or if I'm kind, generous, brave, a healthy church stokes that. It makes me more so. It enhances what's most beautiful in me. It helps me crucify my meanest self and spur on any sign of Christlikeness in me. And likewise for all: if we are altogether generous and hospitable, in a healthy church we'll all only get better.

All I'm saying is a version of what Paul and other biblical writers say in many places — Colossians, Ephesians, Philippians, Galatians, Hebrews, Peter's and John's letters. Our life together either eggs on a life according to flesh, or spurs on a life in step with the Spirit. It either keeps enslaving us to sin, or helps us live in the freedom for which Christ set us free. It either indulges our old ways of thinking and being, or helps us take every thought captive and make it obedient to Christ. It either keeps us as we were, or helps us reach maturity. Of course, most churches — all? — do both. But we're talking critical mass here. We're talking tipping points. Healthy church is where the likelihood of my being conformed to Christ increases exponentially.

I heard about an anthropology student who, many years ago, spent his summer living among the Navajo in New Mexico. He fell deeply in love with the people, and they with him. Especially, he was very close with an old Navajo woman. She was a grandmother to him. The day came when he left, and his hardest goodbye was with her. The Navajo are not known for long speeches, and she did not give one. All she said: "I like me best when I'm with you."

That's a good measure of the health of your church. Can you say of it, "I like me best when I'm with you"? Or better, "I like us best when we're together"?

If yes, my guess is that your church abounds with grace and truth, more and more and more.

. . .

"In the beginning."

God has been up to this for a very long time, and God has come a very long way to finish what he started. He has been dreaming and scheming, sending and moving, making and sacrificing, from before the world began until this very moment, to make for himself a new creation. How astonishing: that before God ever breathed a word of his first creation, he had already planned the Word's becoming flesh for the sake of his new creation. That new creation includes you, and your church, and all churches everywhere. The Word became flesh and came near for this very reason. The Word moved into your neighborhood, and mine, for this very reason.

In John's gospel, Jesus closes his earthly rabbinical ministry with a prayer, recorded in John 17. The Word in flesh saves his last words for the Father, but he speaks those words for the sake of his followers. It's really a prayer for the church to be full of grace and truth, which manifest as love and unity among us, and show up as purity and joy within us. Such a church, Jesus says, convinces an otherwise hateful world that he in fact has come from the Father.

And John already told us how he came: full of grace and truth.

Make this your resolve: that you and your church will know Jesus, the Word become flesh, so fully and so deeply that you and your church will also abound in grace and truth. May you and your church so resemble Jesus — the *neighbor* who moved into your neighborhood — that all the other neighbors, seeing you, also catch a glimpse of him.

CHAPTER TWELVE

WHEN CLEAN AND UNCLEAN TOUCH

RECENTLY, A YOUNG COUPLE started coming to our church. Both are funny, smart, attractive. They're very likable. They married a few years ago somewhere on the other side of the country, then migrated west until they arrived in our town, then moved around churches until they ended up in our church. Both are Christians who take their faith seriously. Both are seeking a place where they can worship, serve, grow. They want a loving and Christ-centered environment in which to raise their daughters in the "nurture and admonition" of the Lord.

Both are women. Linda and Rita are lesbians.

My first question to them: "Why us?"

There are two or three churches nearby that have no theological issue at all with same-sex marriages: they perform them, celebrate them, welcome those in them. Our church is not one of these churches. We're firmly embedded in our evangelical heritage: a strong emphasis on the Bible, on personal holiness, on evangelism and activism.

And strong feelings about homosexuality. Very strong feelings.

Linda and Rita actually grew up in this kind of a church, and that was part of their answer to "Why us?" The other part of their answer was more intriguing: they see life and joy in our church, and they want in on it.

We didn't know what to do with them. I lost more sleep over this than almost anything else in my twenty years of pastoral ministry. My heritage told me to give them the heave-ho. My theology told me they were living in defiance of God. But a stirring inside me which I can only describe as the Spirit of God told me something else: that God himself had drawn these women here. He had done that not so that we would overturn our heritage or revise our theology but because he was doing something deep in Linda and Rita, and he was entrusting our church to join him in his work.

. . .

But let me back up.

Our church embraces two values with equal vigor, and in the case of Linda and Rita, and many other people beside, those two values are in almost constant tension.

The first value is the truth and trustworthiness of the Bible. As good Baptists, we teach, believe, and try to live out that the Bible is "our one true guide for life and godliness." We believe we are *under* the Word of God, that though our understanding of it is often patchwork and our obedience to it halting, we have no right to impose on the Bible our own meanings or agendas. If we have done our best interpretive work with the Good Book and have concluded that it teaches a particular truth, then we are beholden to that truth no matter how costly or awkward or unpopular it might be.

That's one value.

The other value is that Jesus welcomed sinners and ate with them. He did this, and then asked you and me to keep up, on his behalf, his questionable work.

Jesus — we all know this — shocked, angered, and offended the religious community in his day by his easy rapport with disreputable people. He really liked being around people whom religious types aren't supposed to have anything to do with. He not only liked them; he sought them, welcomed them, invited himself to their houses, initiated conversations with them, enjoyed meals with them, let them off the hook, with scarcely a reprimand, for big-ticket sin items like adultery and thievery and shacking up.

The best I can make out here is that Jesus was working on the same stirring I had with Linda and Rita: God is doing something deep here, in Zacchaeus and Mary Magdalene, in the woman at the well and the woman caught in adultery and the woman who washes his feet with her tears; in all these sundry "sinners and tax collectors," God is revealing, convicting, wooing. And he invites Jesus to join him in his work. "The Son ... can do only what he sees his Father doing," Jesus said, "because *whatever the Father does* the Son also does."[1]

So Jesus watched his Father welcome sinners and eat with them. Jesus watched his Father stride over to Zacchaeus's house and scatter blessing on it. Jesus watched his Father welcome those whom Pharisees shunned. And Jesus jumped right in and joined his Father.

So we jumped right in (so to speak) with Linda and Rita and joined whatever the Father was up to.

As of this writing, we're still in the thick of it. It's been an interesting, often awkward, mostly grace-filled, always amazing journey. One of our pastors, Shane, was counseling Linda about some communication struggles she was having with Rita. Linda was trying to explain her frustration. Finally, she looked up at Shane and said, "Well, you're married to a woman. You know what they're like."

As Shane said later, "They never taught me at Bible college how to handle that sort of thing."

. . .

But our journey with Linda and Rita clarifies some of the convictions we've developed at our church. These convictions have been good companions as we wade through this situation and many others like it. These convictions help us keep our bearings. I've already shared two of those convictions—the Bible is our only true guide for life and holiness, and Jesus welcomed sinners, just as his Father did, and asks us to welcome them too—but let me walk you through a few of our other convictions. I think this will help if you find that your church is too safe—too prone to avoid "sinners and tax collectors"—and you would like your church to be more dangerous, more subversive, more out in the highways and the byways: in short, more ready to join God in the deep work he's doing in the lives of people all around you.

Conviction 1: God is here. One of our pastors was leading a staff time and wanted each of us to identify one or two "core convictions."

I was edified and fascinated to listen to the people I work with every day, some over many years, tell about what forms and transforms them.

I shared last and had only one I'd come up with: God is here. I could tell I underwhelmed the others with this, so I explained a little.

"There are few atheists in the world. But there are a lot of practical atheists — people for whom God's 'thereness' registers not at all. I sometimes call them apatheists — joining the word *theist* and the word *apathy*. Apatheists believe God exists but don't care.

"I'm trying not to be one. And so I nurture the conviction that God is right here, right now. In this place. Closer than a brother. And to believe that if my heart is fully devoted to him, he's come near to strongly encourage me. The main spiritual discipline for fostering this sense of God's nearness is curiosity. I try to stay more interested, regardless the situation, in what God is doing than in what man is plotting or in what the devil's up to. I don't want to be unaware of the devil's schemes. But I want to obsess over the Father's presence and the Father's work. I want to reserve all my strength for pursuing the kingdom of God and his righteousness.

"So my deep conviction is that God is here."

A few weeks later, the pastors and elders gathered to think through biblically and practically our response to our gay friends. I began the conversation with this question: "If gays and lesbians want to come to our church, do you see in that mostly God at work, or mostly the devil?"

To a person, everyone answered, "God."

God is here.

Which leads to our next conviction.

Conviction 2: When someone comes into the light, it's always God at work. God is the Father of light (Satan, the Prince of Darkness). Jesus said that he is the light that has come into the world, and he's come not to condemn the world but to shine his light. Those who come into the light step into a place where they can receive truth and grace (see conviction 4). Those who don't come into the light condemn themselves.

Anytime a man or woman brings their true self into the light — letting themselves be seen for who they really are — God's at work. Think of the two men in Luke 18 who go up to the temple to pray. One is a Pharisee, one a tax collector. The Pharisee is a moral exemplar. He is a paragon of virtue. He's a ready candidate for chairman of the board, president of the Rotary, spokesman for the Neighborhood Watch.

And he knows it. His prayer is lengthy, polished, eloquent, and the entire thing an extended brag on himself. I'm this; I'm that. I'm not this; I'm not that.

The tax man is a scoundrel. He's a bad egg. He's the sort of person whom "good" people point to — the Pharisee, in fact, does this — and say, "Thank God I'm not him." You give men like him a wide berth and never turn your back.

And he knows it. His prayer is short, stark, desperate. It is a confession and a plea. He's a sinner. He needs God's mercy.

Jesus is pointed in his verdict: the tax man walks away justified before God, the Pharisee doesn't.[2]

Why? Jesus says, "Everyone who exalts himself will be humbled, and he who humbles himself will be exalted."[3] But that exaltation and humbling has much to do with light and darkness. The Pharisee brings into the light only those parts of himself he wants God and others to see — his virtue, his fidelity, his generosity. But most of who he is remains in the dark. But the tax collector hauls his whole sorry, sordid self into the burning light. He hides nothing. He brings before God all his miserable fallenness, his deplorable folly, his pathetic brokenness, his real evil. He stands without excuse. He dares to ask for the only thing that can help: God's mercy.

And God gives him mercy in spades.

Jesus doesn't demand that first we sort ourselves out and clean ourselves up before we dare step into the light; he invites us to step into the light *in order* to get sorted out and cleaned up. It's impossible to clean a mess in the dark. We usually only make more mess.

Unless a man or woman of God will come into that mess, those in it are probably going to remain in it.

And that leads to the next conviction.

Conviction 3: When someone brings their mess into the light, their mess usually doesn't get cleaned up unless one of us wades into the mess with them. "Brothers and sisters," Paul writes to the Galatians, "if someone is caught in a sin, you who live by the Spirit should restore that person gently. But watch yourselves, or you also may be tempted. Carry each other's burdens, and in this way you will fulfill the law of Christ. If any of you think you are something when you are nothing, you deceive yourselves. Each of you should test your own actions. Then you can take pride in yourself, without comparing yourself to somebody else, for each of you should carry your own load."[4]

This is a remarkable passage. The role of the mature—those "who live by the Spirit"—is to wade into another's mess, not to judge them or join them or feel superior to them or codependently take responsibility for them ("carry each other's burdens," Paul says, and then right after says "each of you should carry your own load"). The role of the mature is to wade into another's mess in order to "restore that person gently."

The word *gently* is two words in the Greek: *pneumati praotçtos*, literally in "a spirit of meekness." Meekness is strength under control. It means that disciplinary encounters are not standoffs or court-martials. They're not a show of power. Discipline in the church is actually a ministry of the Spirit, the *Paraklete*, the one who comes alongside, gently, to counsel, comfort, plead, guide.

And the work of those who live by the Spirit is to restore. Again, the Greek here is worth noting: *katartizete*, literally "be ye attuning." The picture is of an instrument capable of producing beautiful, resonant, evocative music, but badly out of tune. Roughing up the instrument will only worsen and make permanent the problem. Discarding the instrument is stupid; it's a Stradivarius, a possession of great worth, inestimable value. It's just badly mistuned, and what should sing and woo instead squawks and yowls. It needs a gentle, masterful touch, a tightening here, a loosening there, a lowering of the strings or a straightening of the neck, a slow, painstaking removal of grime and a lavish, penetrating kneading-in of oil, to restore it to its true potential.

That's the work of those who live by the Spirit.

Often, those who step in to help clean the mess will look to others like they're endorsing the mess. I think of a pastor from another church who called me up a while back and told me he was concerned about our church. He had heard rumors. I asked what rumors. He listed three: a couple living together, a couple having sex outside marriage, and a gay man attending. All three were "messes" that we knew about and had stepped into in an effort to "gently restore." When I told him that, it made matters worse. "What are you doing helping these people?" he asked. "I would have kicked them out a long time ago. I don't understand how you can tolerate sin in the camp."

I don't know how I can avoid it. Several years ago, our church made it our prayerful ambition "to win the heart of the Cowichan Valley." We've been doing that, but the heart of the Cowichan Valley is coming to us broken, afflicted, dark, confused. It is, for the most part, a deeply hurt and unhealthy heart.

But we asked God for that heart. And so we're trusting God that, as we live by the Spirit, he'll give us what we need to tune that heart to sing his praises.

Which leads to the next conviction.

Conviction 4: *What we bring to the work of tuning hearts is grace and truth*. According to John's gospel, Jesus Christ, as a reflection of the Father, came full of grace and truth. We talked about this in the last chapter. Here, again, are some key verses: "The Word became flesh and made his dwelling among us. We have seen his glory, the glory of the one and only Son, who came from the Father, full of grace and truth.... Out of his fullness we have all received grace in place of grace already given. For the law was given through Moses; grace and truth came through Jesus Christ. No one has ever seen God, but the one and only Son, who is himself God and is in closest relationship with the Father, has made him known."[5]

John wants to make clear the nature of Jesus' relationship with the Father, primarily by telling us how Jesus reveals the Father. It's through grace and truth. John contrasts this way of revealing the Father with Moses' way of revealing God—through law. The Mosaic law is an unambiguous manifesto of the standards of a holy God. Nothing in the law is up for discussion or debate. Law largely deals in commands and prohibitions—do this, don't do that. It's cut and dried. It's black and white. It's short on interpretation, long on pronouncement.

Then Jesus comes and changes the rules (see conviction 5). It's not that God no longer cares about his own standards of holiness.[6] But Jesus brings a fresh revelation. Where Moses revealed, in stone, the unbending standards of a holy God, Jesus reveals, in flesh, the beating heart of a Father God. It's a heart full of grace and truth.

Full. God is full of grace and truth, and so Jesus is full of grace and truth. Jesus never had to wonder or ponder how to act or to speak in any situation. His holy instinct, wired in by the Father, was always and everywhere to act and to speak with complete grace and complete truth. He didn't choose between the two. He didn't dial one down to play one up. He didn't alternate from one to the other according to the situation at hand. Every time Jesus spoke, everywhere Jesus acted, he revealed God in the fullness of truth and grace.

That day the pastors and elders met to talk about how to respond to our gay friends, we spent most of the time looking at John 1. "What does it mean," I asked, "that whatever we say or do be full of truth?" That generated a lot of discussion that, frankly, was well-trod territory for Baptists: sin is sin.

But then I asked, "What does it mean that whatever we say or do be full of grace?" It means, we concluded, that at every point Linda and Rita—or anyone else we "who live by the Spirit" come near to—should know in their bones that we love them and that our deepest desire is for them to win.

We ended that day by coming up with a little proverb of sorts. It's this: when we speak truth, it should be so grace-soaked it's hard to reject; when we show grace, it should be so truth-soaked it's hard to accept.

All this leads to what may be our most startling, and most subversive, conviction.

Conviction 5: *Jesus reverses the flow of influence between clean and unclean, and empowers us to do the same*. The teachers of the law accused Jesus of breaking the law of Moses. What Jesus actually did was more radical: he reversed it. The law was established to keep us safe from moral and spiritual taint. But Jesus, full of grace and truth, came to make us dangerous. He came to turn us into agents of moral and spiritual cleansing and wholeness. He meant for any ordinary Christian to be able to show up at the gates of hell with no more than the Holy Spirit brimming inside them, and for the gates of hell to collapse beneath the weight of our presence.

That's how Jesus did it. Jesus didn't run from sin; he put sin on the run. He didn't fret about corpses or invalids, blood or open sores, whores or lepers, demoniacs or Gentiles. He didn't flinch from brushing his robe or hand against sin and sinners, and worry that he'd thereby stained his unblemished whiteness. He got very close to all and sundry, reaching out to touch, to embrace, because his holiness exerted an irresistible power over the unholy. Unholy things had no power to corrupt him. Unclean things had no power to taint him. They either submitted to his influence or fled.

This is not the way Moses envisioned it. Moses wrote law upon law to uphold this fundamental spiritual truth: to "keep the Israelites separate from things that make them unclean."[7] And for good reason: if ever something clean touches something unclean, the clean thing always—*always*—becomes unclean. It never works the other way around, not in the law of Moses. So the law—primarily the three books of Leviticus, Numbers, and Deuteronomy—has warning upon warning to steer clear of unclean things, and rule upon rule about what rigmarole is required of you—penalties, quarantines, sacrifices—if you don't.

And then Jesus comes and changes the rules. He reverses the way spiritual things work. He reverses the flow of clean and unclean. Now, astonishingly, when clean and unclean touch, the unclean becomes clean. This, in a word, is a revolution. It is a revolution of staggering proportions. It is a revolution that the church has mostly ignored or opposed. Jesus, after all, called his followers the salt of the earth and the light of world (an appellation he also uses of himself). Light assumes darkness, and salt assumes both blandness and rot. But both salt and light need to get up close to do their work.

Jesus sends his followers into a dark and bland and rotting world, to get up close to do our work. He looses this revolution upon the earth. He makes several comments announcing this revolution. "Do not think that I have come to abolish the Law or the Prophets," he said. "I have not come to abolish them but to fulfill them." But even more, Jesus commits several acts that stage the revolution. We'll take a close look at two.

The first is in Luke 8, the account of the woman who has had a flow of blood for twelve years. The story is embedded in another: Jesus is on his way to the house of Jairus, whose twelve-year-old daughter is dying. Both stories are embedded in yet another: Jesus' demonstration of power over both the natural order—he calms a storm with just a word—and the supernatural order—he calms a demon-stormed man with just a word. The Jairus story and the story of the woman with the flow of blood form a pair, linked by a chronology of events but also by the number twelve: in the case of the woman, twelve years is too long to suffer on this earth; in the case of the girl, twelve years is too soon to leave this earth. Together, with the twelve-years-afflicted woman, with the twelve-year-old dead girl, Jesus demonstrates his power over sickness, no matter how chronic, and his power over death, no matter how sudden.

The ground themes of all four stories—storm-tossed sea, demon-tossed man, sickness-tossed woman, death-tossed family—are twofold:

human fear in the face of such tossings, such turnings, and Christ's power in the face of the same. Jesus emerges as Lord over all these realms. He's Lord over the natural, the supernatural, the physical. He's Lord over death.

And one more thing besides. There's one more area over which Jesus is Lord that this sequence of stories shows: the religious world. Jesus is Lord over the Law. As Christ meets with Moses and Elijah (representing the Law and the Prophets) in Mark 9, God says about him, "This is my Son, whom I have chosen; *listen to him*."[8] "Listen to him." The Son has the trump card. The Son possesses overruling authority. The Son has the last word. In fact, Jesus' lordship over the religious world may be the loudest statement of all in Luke 8, but it takes a little teasing out for most of us to see.

The portrait of Jesus' lordship over religion is evident in the Legion story and the Jairus story, but especially in the story of the woman with the flow of blood.

First, that:

> As Jesus was on his way, the crowds almost crushed him. And a woman was there who had been subject to bleeding for twelve years, but no one could heal her. She came up behind him and touched the edge of his cloak, and immediately her bleeding stopped.
>
> "Who touched me?" Jesus asked.
>
> When they all denied it, Peter said, "Master, the people are crowding and pressing against you."
>
> But Jesus said, "Someone touched me; I know that power has gone out from me."
>
> Then the woman, seeing that she could not go unnoticed, came trembling and fell at his feet. In the presence of all the people, she told why she had touched him and how she had been instantly healed. Then he said to her, "Daughter, your faith has healed you. Go in peace."[9]

This woman is the poster girl for Leviticus 15:25–27: "When a woman has a discharge of blood for many days at a time other than her monthly period or has a discharge that continues beyond her period, she will be unclean as long as she has the discharge, just as in the days of her period. Any bed she lies on while her discharge continues will be unclean, as is her bed during her monthly period, and anything she sits on will be unclean, as during her period. Whoever touches them will be unclean; he must wash his clothes and bathe with water, and he will be unclean till evening."

This is that woman. For twelve years, this has been that woman. She is a breeding ground of ritual uncleanness. She is an infestation. Her chairs, her bed, her sofa, her car seat—she's tainted it all. And not just inanimate things, not just furniture and tableware and haberdashery. Leviticus 15:25–27 three times compares a woman's chronic bleeding to her monthly period, and simply says, As with that, so with this. So we're required to include this detail from Leviticus 15:19, concerning regulations around a woman's monthly period: "When a woman has her regular flow of blood, the impurity of her monthly period will last seven days, and anyone who touches her will be unclean till evening."

Anyone who touches her becomes unclean. And anyone she touches. Her husband, if she has one, if he's stayed around these twelve years, is in a perpetual state of uncleanness because of her. Her friends—well, they must have all left by now, or simply wave to her from a distance.

It's why she's so afraid. When Jesus demands, "Who touched me?" she must hear in his voice anger, annoyance, accusation. "Power's gone out from me," he says. Literally, "Virtue's gone out of me."

Jesus keeps insisting that whoever touched him show themselves. "Then the woman, seeing that she could not go unnoticed, came trembling and fell at his feet." This isn't shyness on her part. She's terrified. She knows she's in for a good scolding. She's made him unclean. He's on a mission to save a little girl from death, and now he'll have to quarantine till evening. How inconvenient. How selfish and foolish of her.

So she comes trembling, falls at his feet, and explains herself "in the presence of all the people." That detail is important, as we'll see. She was sick. The touch healed her. All the people hear this. And then Jesus does the unexpected, the shocking: "Then he said to her, 'Daughter, your faith has healed you. Go in peace.'"

Why is this so unexpected, so shocking? Because everybody knows two things should happen now. One, she shouldn't be able just to walk away. Leviticus is explicit: "When she is cleansed from her discharge, she must count off seven days, and after that she will be ceremonially clean. On the eighth day she must take two doves or two young pigeons and bring them to the priest at the entrance to the Tent of Meeting. The priest is to sacrifice one for a sin offering and the other for a burnt offering. In this way he will make atonement for her before the LORD for the uncleanness of her discharge."[10] But Jesus simply says, "Go in peace."

The second thing is even more shocking: Jesus turns Leviticus on its head. Page after page after page of that book is dedicated to the theme of clean and unclean. One conclusion from all that verbiage is inescapable: when clean and unclean touch, the unclean always, *always*, taints the clean thing. It never works the other way. A clean thing never, not once, sanctifies, purifies, restores to wholeness an unclean thing.

Until now.

Now, in Jesus of Nazareth, the direction of influence is completely reversed.

One more story, from Matthew's gospel:

> When Jesus came down from the mountainside, large crowds followed him. A man with leprosy came and knelt before him and said, "Lord, if you are willing, you can make me clean."
>
> Jesus reached out his hand and touched the man. "I am willing," he said. "Be clean!" Immediately he was cleansed of his leprosy. Then Jesus said to him, "See that you don't tell anyone. But go, show yourself to the priest and offer the gift Moses commanded, as a testimony to them."[11]

"Jesus reached out his hand and touched the man." This is an out-and-out breach of Levitical law. A person with leprosy had a clear mandate: "Anyone with such a defiling disease must wear torn clothes, let their hair be unkempt, cover the lower part of their face and cry out, 'Unclean! Unclean!' As long as they have the disease they remain unclean. They must live alone; they must live outside the camp."[12]

But this man with leprosy understands that a new power is loosed on earth, a power that emboldens him to move among "large crowds" without uttering the mandatory warning, that emboldens him to run right up to Jesus and fall at his feet: "Lord, if you are willing, you can make me clean." How did he know? Anyone else would have recoiled in horror at the man and been shocked by his effrontery and delusion. But this man knew, knew as certain as he knew fire's hot and water's cold, that in Jesus the world has been turned upside-down. Now when clean and unclean touch, it's the unclean that must surrender its claim. No wonder Jesus sent the man to tell no one but the priest, "as a testimony to them." The priests, of all people, would get this. The priests, of all people, would understand the revolutionary force of this.

I don't think I'm claiming too much to use that word, *revolution*. This reversal of influence — the clean can make the unclean clean — represents one of the biggest insurrections that's ever occurred within any religion anywhere, where its own rules get rewritten in a single stroke. But it's one revolution the church has many times in many places lagged behind on. We sometimes just don't get it. We oftentimes just don't practice it. I suspect we sometimes just don't believe it.

Our church is starting to believe it. Our church is starting to get it, and put it into practice. Our church is trying to catch up with the revolution Jesus started two millennia ago. We've a long journey still ahead of us. We're making as many mistakes as discoveries as we go. But more and more, as we walk in the fullness of Christ's grace and truth, we find him right alongside, ready to tune even the most out-of-tune heart to sing his praise. And we find that as we walk in the power that was in Christ, we can touch unclean things and not only are we not tainted by them, we make unclean things clean.

But any church that does this will encounter opposition. As we're about to see.

CHAPTER THIRTEEN

JESUS AND THE THREE SPIRITS

THINGS COME IN THREES.

That's the folklore, anyhow. Good things, bad things: all follow a trifold pattern. You lose your car keys, then break the coffee urn, then your water tank ruptures. One, two, three. Or, pleasantly, you win dinner for two at the new Italian restaurant, then get an unexpected check in the mail, then the boss gives you a raise and a week's getaway for your hard work and great attitude. One, two, three.

Well, maybe it works that way.

Just as often, though, things come in ones or twos or a dozen. I think, more likely, our minds have a certain Trinitarian structure and rhythm to them, so threefold patterns tend to light up our grey matter, set our synapses humming.

All the same, I have noticed a threefold repetition in the ministry of Jesus, and by extension, in churches who join Jesus' mission in the power of his Spirit.

Almost every time Jesus said anything or did anything, three spirits attended. Almost, you could say, three spirits woke up. They stood to attention, at high alert. They engaged. They stopped whatever else they were doing and came running.

The first, most obvious, is the Holy Spirit. It's unhelpful, I know, to talk about the Holy Spirit's "waking up." But we do know that we can quench the Holy Spirit. We can refuse or sabotage his fire and passion and vigor so frequently that, for all intents and purposes, he dies within us.[1] And we know that we can grieve the Holy Spirit. We can spurn or trample so often his love and compassion and wisdom that the Spirit within us is wrenched with sorrow.[2] I think, also — this is only a hunch, with thin biblical warrant but ample empirical evidence — that we can bore the Holy Spirit. We can love comfort and evade the kingdom so habitually, the Spirit eventually loses interest.

Whenever and wherever Jesus showed up, the Holy Spirit began leaping. You see it as early as the day Mary, ripe with child, showed up in the home of her relative Elizabeth, who was even riper with child. John the Baptist, just hearing the voice of the Christ-bearer, leaps in the womb. It's deep unto deep. It's the Spirit testifying with his spirit that the Son of God is in the house. And we see the Holy Spirit roused to full alert whenever, wherever Jesus appears. Jesus comes to town, and crowds come running, demons start shrieking, the desperate become hopeful, the powerful grow afraid.

All in all, the Holy Spirit's afoot and afire. This is arguably the most obvious thing about Jesus and the early church: wherever, whenever they appeared, the Holy Spirit showed up, howling down the rafters, shaking lintel posts, loosing tongues, giving valor, healing sickness, raising the dead.

But other spirits showed up too. Evil spirits. Vicious, malicious, predatory, unclean things awakened and mobbed together, wreaking havoc however they might. I'm not sure, I've already said, whether Christians sometimes bore the Holy Spirit. But I am close to a hundred percent certain that Christians sometimes, maybe ofttimes, bore evil spirits. Too seldom do we pose any threat. Too seldom we live in such a way as to arouse even faint alarm in the heart of Beelzebub. Too often we get so preoccupied with Screwtape's[3] old shopworn tricks — jealousy, suspicion, divisiveness, discouragement, a spirit of complaint, and so on — we give him no cause to come up with anything fresh. He can toss into our midst a little bone of rumor and get us fighting over and gnawing that, and meanwhile he can just keep doing whatever he does in his spare time, never mind us.

Not so when Jesus arrives. Then, all hell breaks loose, since it's the only tactic the devil has when all heaven breaks in. He typically puts on quite a display — bellowing, writhing, gnashing, mouth frothing. It's Linda Blair on speed.[4] All his antics pose not the slightest twinge of worry in Jesus. He deals with it, fast, hard, decisively. And so too his disciples, once they get their training wheels off. One thing is clear, though: that when Jesus is on the move, the demons get no rest, find no shelter, lose all cool, drop all guises. They resort to open, unconcealed aggression of the nastiest sort. Jesus deals with it, lickety-split, and plants the kingdom ensign on the rubble. The church doing Christ's mission with Christ's heart in Christ's power should expect no less — full demonic assault met with decisive kingdom conquest.

Those are two of the three spirits awakened by Jesus and his bride.

The third spirit is often more noxious than the second. Indeed, it is often simply the second spirit — evil spirits — masquerading as something good.[5]

I speak of the religious spirit. Wherever Jesus arrived, the religious spirit was soon aroused, to withering disdain, to cold fury and malice aforethought. This is a spirit the evil spirits enjoy taking captive.[6] It's a dangerous spirit because it's evasive and camouflaged. It shape-shifts. It's seditious, insidious, always posing as its opposite: keeper of virtue, upholder of purity, protector of doctrine, defender of truth. It's rigidity masked by piety. It's control pretending to be watchfulness. It's judgment posing as discernment.

The Holy Spirit is only ever what it is: the pure presence of Christ.

So too an evil spirit. It is only ever what it is: the pure presence of the Antichrist.

But a religious spirit is never what it seems. It's corruption masquerading as goodness.

And it's very hard to cast out. Almost impossible. Jesus could dispense with evil spirits with a single word. One command, and they were flung headlong into fiery torment, shrieking their protest in vain.

But Jesus could not cast out a religious spirit with a thousand words. Indeed, the more he spoke to it, the more it cloaked itself with God talk and strutted its impeccable credentials. You know the general list: sat on this board since before the dawn of time, taught these studies for years beyond numbering, read the Bible end to end every year for decades, tithed and then some since childhood. And so on.

Jesus met those people all the time, and made nary little headway with any. Consider, for example, the trajectory of John's gospel, from chapter 7 through chapter 12. The religious leaders mount an increasingly belligerent attack on Jesus personally and on his work. They begin with semipolite requests for his *bona fides*, move to increasingly shrill accusations against him—he's got questionable parentage, he's had no schooling, he's a Samaritan, he's demon possessed, he's an enemy of Rome—to, finally, hatching a plot to kill him. All the while, Jesus explains to them who he is and what he's doing. But with every word he speaks, their ears grow duller, their opinions louder, their vision cloudier.[7]

It's hard to get past all that, or through to that.

An example. This portrait is fictitious, but assembled from many real encounters.

Let's call her Deirdre. Deirdre grew up in a good Christian home. In fact, her religious pedigree goes back centuries and includes prominent and founding members of churches stretching all the way back to the Scottish Highlands on her dad's side, the English Midlands on her mom's. Her grandmother and grandfather met at a holiness conference in Keswick, England. Her own mom and dad attended Sunday school together at First Church in a small farm community in Saskatchewan, and both can tell funny stories of their third-grade teacher, the formidable but lovable Ms. Doolittle, who drilled them with Scripture and made them learn it by heart. Deirdre's father was First Church's youngest lay preacher—people compared him to C. H. Spurgeon. He went on to become a full-time pastor, then a missionary in Indonesia, and then an officer in their denomination. He died of a stroke at age sixty-three, speaking at a Revival Conference.

Deirdre was married at seventeen to a boy she had met in Sunday school, just like her parents. What was never talked about was that she *had* to get married because there was a problem—she was pregnant. Deirdre was sent to Calgary for her last year of school, and the baby was promptly given up for adoption, but she was made to marry the boy anyhow. They've made the marriage work, largely by staying busy and staying out of each other's way.

Deirdre and her husband came west for reasons they've never talked about. Within weeks, she was involved in three or four things: teaching Sunday school, organizing the women's ministry, delivering hot meals to shut-ins, and volunteering to answer phones at the church when the secretary needed to get the bulletin ready for Sunday. Within six months, she was superintendent of the Sunday school and helping with the youth group. She's also mentored three young moms and visited the shut-ins she delivered meals to.

The pastor couldn't believe his good fortune. He didn't know how the church had ever managed without her. When a position on the deacons council came available, he heartily suggested her name. She happily accepted it.

And then the trouble began.

There are a number of things Deirdre has observed at the church, and she feels she must, now that she has been given the sacred responsibility of being a deacon, speak them out. To wit:

- The toys in the nursery are not properly sanitized, and a number of them are unsafe for small children.
- The sign at the church entrance does not say that we're part of the Convention of Bible-Believing Kingdom-Come Teetotaling Baptists. People should know this before they come through the doors.
- Nowhere in our constitution have we taken a position on the events surrounding the second coming of Christ. This is potentially confusing for people. And where *do* we stand on those matters?
- Likewise in the constitution, nowhere have we spelled out our position on creationism, biblical inerrancy, birth control, drinking and smoking, or what we'd do if we found a gay person in our midst.
- She saw one of our youth leaders talking with a married man downtown. She'd like the pastor to deal with this.
- Is there a policy about how short the skirts can be for people on the worship team? If not, can we make one?
- Is she the only one who sometimes finds the pastor's sermons a little — she doesn't want to say liberal, but doctrinally fuzzy? She's kept a record of instances of this, and she'd be happy to share that with any of the other council members.
- She appreciates our church's helping street people and the like, but should we put our energy (and money) into *those people* when our own church members rarely if ever get a visit from our own pastor?

And that's just the first round.

The pastor now wonders how to get rid of her. Every time he tries to talk with her about any of this, either it goes nowhere or it gets worse. And it turns out that Deirdre talks with a lot of people. She freely shares her growing concern about all the things with which she's growingly concerned, and she tells the pastor "a lot of people" feel this way. When he asks her to name anyone, she replies that sharing names would be a breach of confidence, and she's surprised the pastor would even ask her to do such a thing.

Most of us who've spent any time in the inner workings of a church will find this portrait, fictional though it is, eerily familiar. And most of us are nonplussed by it. No prayers, no confrontations, no frank discussions, no backroom deals make it go away. One day, mercifully, Deirdre and her ilk usually leave of their own accord. They leave embittered, accusatory, and often try to sabotage the church from a distance. The pastor is relieved almost to giddiness. The only thing that spoils his happiness is the thought that seven Deirdres, each worse than the last, might be on their way.

Deirdre is the embodiment of the religious spirit.

.   .   .

Now the point of saying all of this is to say that all three spirits — the Holy Spirit, evil spirits, and religious spirits — rouse whenever Jesus is in the house.

They can't help it.

The Holy Spirit is necessary, since apart from him we can do nothing.

The evil spirits are inevitable, but easy to identify and clobber.

But the religious spirits are inescapable, and nearly impossible to deal with.

So what shall we do?

I'm learning the art of holy indifference. One of John Wesley's biographers described the man's "regal disdain for trifles." That's brilliant: a kingly contempt for trivialities. Most of what the religious spirit cooks up is too petty to waste a moment on, too paltry to dignify with a response. And too toxic. This spirit's offerings are not just flighty things pretending to be weighty things, but rancid things posing as sacred things. It's bile passed off as holy water. Poison hidden in a chalice.

What I'm learning is that we don't have to drink it. This is one cup you can let pass. In my early days of pastoring, I didn't heed that. I drank from the cup every time it was offered to me. I drank, and it rankled, twisted, and inflamed me. I allowed it to eat me alive. And always I would find that the more I fought against the religious spirit, the more I became it. I fought bile with bile, pettiness with pettiness. I rarely did this openly. But that's part of the way it works: rarely is anything done openly. Instead, it's done secretly, furtively, in a sideways manner.

Wisdom refuses to stoop to this.

Which isn't to say I just ignore it. We still need to confront the religious spirit. Jesus did this repeatedly. He called it out of the shadows, named it for what it was, and made it clear that the kingdom of God will not be beggared by this spirit. It will not be held ransom. It will continue its work of healing and liberating and proclaiming.

If the religious spirit is at all as I've been describing it, then of course its preferred haunt would be synagogue on Sabbath or church on Sunday. Its stage is not the public square. It shows up on hallowed ground, amid consecrated halls. It inhabits the place set apart for worship and prayer and the public reading of the Word. This is the place the religious spirit gravitates to, because it's camouflaged for just such an environment. It can perfectly mimic the gestures, postures, tone, and language of this place. It can go for years undetected in these quarters.

Until provoked. Until Jesus shows up.

So Jesus often encountered this spirit at church, as you do.

There was, for instance, the man with the shriveled hand. I think I met this guy once, so to speak: one hand perfectly fine, wide and leathery and strong as a hydraulic pump from having to do double duty, and the other a wilted and bony rag of a thing, curled in on itself like a small animal dying. His bunged hand trundled up under his arm, carried there like a loose package awkwardly jutting, threatening to drop.

Anyhow, if that was him, Jesus ended up meeting him in church. And the watchdogs were watching. The religious spirits were hovering. They figured Jesus might be stirred with one of his odd emotions — love, compassion, tenderheartedness, that sort of thing — and that he might make a move. And he doesn't disappoint. Best I give the story in full:

On another Sabbath he went into the synagogue and was teaching, and a man was there whose right hand was shriveled. The Pharisees and the teachers of the law were looking for a reason to accuse Jesus, so they watched him closely to see if he would heal on the Sabbath. But Jesus knew what they were thinking and said to the man with the shriveled hand, "Get up and stand in front of everyone." So he got up and stood there.

Then Jesus said to them, "I ask you, which is lawful on the Sabbath: to do good or to do evil, to save life or to destroy it?"

He looked around at them all, and then said to the man, "Stretch out your hand." He did so, and his hand was completely restored. But they were furious and began to discuss with one another what they might do to Jesus.[8]

These stories can be multiplied. Maybe most glaring is the account that follows Jesus' most spectacular miracle, raising Lazarus from the dead. The Pharisees are so alarmed by this, they call an emergency meeting of the Jewish high council, the Sanhedrin, and after urgent debate they come to fierce resolve: "from that day on they plotted to take his life."[9] They don't in any way deny the miracle; they defy it. They pull out all the stops to destroy the author of such wonders because "if we let him go on like this, everyone will believe in him, and then the Romans will come and take away both our temple and our nation."[10]

The last thing the religious spirit wants is Jesus "going on like this." It's dangerous, subversive, a threat to order. It imperils temple and nation, the touchstones of religious pride and identity.

Stories like this must have fed the imagination of Russian novelist Fyodor Dostoyevsky as he wrote his famous "Grand Inquisitor" chapter in his masterpiece, *The Brothers Karamazov*. In that riveting piece, Ivan Karamazov, ever bent on destroying the sweet faith of his brother Alyosha, tells him about Jesus walking into Seville, Spain, "during the grimmest days of the Inquisition. When throughout the country fires were burning endlessly to the greater glory of God and ... wicked heretics were burned."[11] Ivan goes on to explain, "Of course, this was not the coming in which He had promised to appear in all His heavenly glory at the end of time ... No, He wanted to come only for a moment to visit His children ... He came unobserved and moved about almost silently but, strangely enough, those who saw Him recognized Him at once ... drawn to Him by an irresistible force." But the crowds surging around him draw the attention of the Grand Inquisitor, a man ancient, austere, terrifying. He seizes and imprisons Jesus, and intends to execute him, but only after he spends the night lecturing him on why he is a threat to the church and to public order. He explains to Jesus that only three forces can "overcome and capture once and for all the conscience of these feeble, undisciplined creatures, so as to give them happiness. These forces are miracle, mystery, and authority." He claims that Jesus "rejected the first, the second, and the third of these forces and set up his rejection as an example to men" when he spurned the devil's three temptations. What Jesus offers people, the Grand Inquisitor accuses him of, is freedom.[12] And that is an intolerable gift. People don't know what to do with freedom.

Ivan ends his story this way:

> The Grand Inquisitor falls silent and waits for some time for the prisoner to answer. The prisoner's silence has weighed on him. He has watched him; He listened to him intently, looking gently into his eyes, and apparently unwilling to speak. The old man longs for him to say something, however painful and terrifying. But instead, He suddenly goes over to the old man and kisses him gently on his old, bloodless lips. And that is His only answer. The old man is startled and shudders. The corners of his lips seem to quiver slightly. He walks to the door, opens it, and says to Him, "Go now, and do not come back ... ever. You must never, never come again!" And he lets the prisoner out into the dark streets of the city. The prisoner leaves.
>
> Alyosha asks Ivan, "And what about the old man?"
>
> "The kiss," he says, "glows in his heart ... But the old man sticks to his old idea."[13]

"The old man sticks to his old idea": the epitaph of those who love the religious spirit.

This is not a counsel of despair. It's a counsel of reality. It's facing squarely a biblical fact: wherever the kingdom of God forcefully advances, opposition mounts fast and hard, and much of that opposition comes from within the camp. I have stopped counting the churches I know where a great vision embodied in a godly pastor has died a brutal death at the hands of those with a religious spirit. I wonder how many of those pastors would have carried on in the face of that spirit if they had known, for one, that these spirits always show up when Jesus is on the ground and, for another, that the best way to deal with them is to defy them.

The next chapter shows why that matters.

CHAPTER FOURTEEN

WRECK THE ROOF

Your church is too safe.

One sign that it might be so is a roof in good repair. I mean this as a metaphor.

Sort of.

A roof in good repair is a sign that no one wants so desperately to get within your walls that they'll resort to extreme measures. No one is ready to vandalize the place for the sake of finding Jesus inside. No rumor is afoot that would drive people to acts of forcible entry.

They were ready to do that in Jesus' day, according to a well-known story of an event that occurred in Capernaum, Jesus' neighborhood, his home turf. The scene and the event:

> So many gathered that there was no room left, not even outside the door, and he preached the word to them. Some men came, bringing to him a paralytic, carried by four of them. Since they could not get him to Jesus because of the crowd, they made an opening in the roof above Jesus and, after digging through it, lowered the mat the paralyzed man was lying on. When Jesus saw their faith, he said to the paralytic, "Son, your sins are forgiven."
>
> Now some teachers of the law were sitting there, thinking to themselves, "Why does this fellow talk like that? He's blaspheming! Who can forgive sins but God alone?"
>
> Immediately Jesus knew in his spirit that this was what they were thinking in their hearts, and he said to them, "Why are you

thinking these things? Which is easier: to say to the paralytic, 'Your sins are forgiven,' or to say, 'Get up, take your mat and walk'? But that you may know that the Son of Man has authority on earth to forgive sins ..." He said to the paralytic, "I tell you, get up, take your mat and go home." He got up, took his mat and walked out in full view of them all. This amazed everyone and they praised God, saying, "We have never seen anything like this!"[1]

"He preached the word to them," is how Mark puts it. Even Jesus, the Word, uses the word. Jesus preaches the Bible.

So this is a story about the power of the preached word.

But it is also a story about the limits of its power. It's a story about the need for the word to be preached, but also for the Word to be made flesh and dwell among us. The word preached with power and fidelity draws the world, that's clear enough. But it's the Word loosed, the Word incarnate, the Word speaking our truest names and naming our deepest wounds and ministering God's deepest remedy, that transforms the world. The word preached draws a crowd. But the Word made flesh makes a church.

But first the roof must be broken.

The irony in this story is an irony present even in some of our best churches: that the preaching of Jesus doesn't always make us more like Jesus. The proclamation of the word does not always translate into our doing of the word. Here, Jesus is both preaching and being preached. He is both herald and fulfillment of the good news.

People flock to hear it. People fail to heed it.

Because at the heart of the word and of the Word is welcoming the stranger. It's loving the least of these. It's becoming those who bring shalom to those who lack it.

This church couldn't give a rip. It's about getting the best seat, damn all the rest of you. So a man on a stretcher, a woman in a wheelchair, a woman of the night, a man with a monkey on his back, a kid with ADHD — I'm not going to give up my privileged position for their sake. If they didn't have the good sense to get here on time, that is not my problem. I'm here to hear a good sermon, and if that single mother can't keep her kid quiet — that's what medication's for, honey — the ushers should escort them out.

A young lady in our church moved to another city to attend university. I knew of a good church in that city — the word was preached there—and I recommended she try it. Her first Sunday, she arrived early and took a seat near the front. A few minutes later, a couple walked in and stood over her. She looked up and asked if she was in their seat.

"Yes."

She got up and moved three rows back. The next person just told her straight up, "You're sitting in my seat." She moved again, this time to the other side of the sanctuary and farther back. Shortly, another couple came, sat in the pew directly in front of her, and turned and glowered at her.

"Am I in your seat?"

"Yes, you are. That has been our seat for forty years."

She got up, sat in the balcony, and thereafter never returned.

The good news: I know the pastor of that church and contacted him about what happened. The following Sunday, he put on his prophet hat and called the church to do better. And I told the story in our church, names disguised, and said to the people, "If ever someone is sitting in 'your' seat, consider it divine appointment: God's given you a lunch date." Afterward, several people told me how that one challenge opened up new friendships.

But I wonder about that couple who have sat for forty years in the same pew. This is a church renowned for its pulpit ministry. As far as I know, they've never had a mediocre preacher. All the pastors I've known who held that pulpit—I've known four—were or are masterful homileticians. They've handled the word of God correctly, and declared the word of God with vigor and passion.

Forty years of that. Forty years of the word preached. Forty years of gospel proclaimed. Forty years, Sunday upon Sunday, of sermons that must have declared God's scandalous welcome to the stranger among us. Had they not, many times, heard John 4 (Jesus meets a woman at the well) or Luke 7 (a woman anoints his feet with her tears) or Matthew 25 (Jesus divides us, as sheep from goats, based on whether we welcomed the stranger)?

Forty years, and still they'd not heard.

. . .

A church will cease to be a church if the word of Jesus is not preached. But a church will fail to become a church if the Word made flesh does not appear among us, and we touch him, and see him, and he us. And sometimes, that happens only when someone has the gall, the audacity, the desperation to break the roof open.

So some friends come with a paralyzed man. Some friends, indeed. But they can't find a seat. They can't get past the people who have sat in that pew for forty years. They can't even get through the door. People must see them. People must have an inkling why they're here, what they're hoping. They must be able to intuit that these men have shown up for something other than a good sermon. Perhaps that's the problem: they do intuit exactly that. They reckon that, should these men get through the crowd, the sermon will abruptly end, and other matters will leap to center stage. They're preempting interruption, watching for drunks and squalling babies and men in wheelchairs, and other sundry distractions.

Which leaves it to some friends to choose from two courses of action. One is to leave. They tried. They get points for trying, surely. It's Miller time.

The other is to commit an act of holy vandalism. If legal means fail, find illegal ones. If politeness and decorum fall short, resort to rudeness and disruption. If the kingdom comes near and there's no neat tidy way to get in, come up with a messy havoc-wreaking way.

And that's what they do.

They break the roof. They clamber up and, bare fisted, tear tile and thatch, strut and truss. They make a gaping hole, large enough to wangle down a man in his gurney. Daylight cascades through the opening, blazing up the room like a theophany, and dust and rubble tumble down the light shaft. All eyes turn upward. From below, the broken roof, raggedy edged, drinks the sky. A huge angular shadow appears in that opening, eclipsing the sun. It's a silhouette of sorrow and longing. Faces stare down from the edges. Down it comes, this shadow, this silhouette, until everyone sees what it is: a gaunt and motionless man, wild eyed with hope.

Jesus has stopped preaching. The silence in the room swells to fill the farthest corners. You can hear the drumming of your own blood. The seesawing of your own breath. Jesus looks at the man and says, "Son, your sins are forgiven."

Which is an interesting way to begin. Does Jesus not get it? This man has just fallen from the sky. He's a parachutist entangled in his ropes. He's a puppet on a string. He's a moth in a spider's web. He's desperate to be set free from this snare. He wants to walk again. He wants to will his arms to move, and for his arms to obey. He wants to hold his wife, and toss his daughter in the air and catch her, and drink coffee with friends without their having to hold the cup to his lips. Sin? When did you think I had time and opportunity for that, Jesus?

Clearly, something else is going on here. Some other threat, worse than physical brokenness, stalks this man's life. Jesus deals with that greater threat first.

Which lights a firestorm in the room. "Now some teachers of the law were sitting there, thinking to themselves, 'Why does this fellow talk like that? He's blaspheming! Who can forgive sins but God alone?'"[2] A wider drama is taking place here. This is not just about preaching or healing or being kind to vandals. This is about authority. With what authority does Jesus speak and act? Preaching is one thing, forgiving quite another. That's God's bailiwick. That's God's exclusive territory, and to enter it is to cross a line. Jesus claims more power than a mere mortal is permitted to wield. Human forgiveness is always and only personal. I hurt you, let's say — took your money, insulted your children, broke your roof, some awful evil thing — and you, with or without my saying I'm sorry, forgive me. Only you can decide that. Not even God can decide that for you.

But Jesus here is not offering personal forgiveness ("You bumped my head on your fall from the sky, but I forgive you"). No, Jesus is issuing a decree. He's ruling on cosmic matters. He declares that, start to finish, every twisted thought and nasty deed and poisoned word that ever came out of this man is, here and now, washed away. Scrubbed clean. Dead and buried. It is finished. These things no longer defile him, define him, or bind him. The whole weight of a whole lifetime of getting it wrong is lifted from him. He can walk free.

And that shocks and angers people who know better.

So then Jesus heals the man simply to vouch for his authority to forgive the man. "Immediately Jesus knew in his spirit that this was what they were thinking in their hearts, and he said to them, 'Why are you thinking these things? Which is easier: to say to this paralyzed man, "Your sins are forgiven," or to say, "Get up, take your mat and walk"? But I want you to know that the Son of Man has authority on earth to forgive sins.' So he said to the man, 'I tell you, get up, take your mat and go home.' He got up, took his mat and walked out in full view of them all."[3] Clearly, it's easier to say to the paralyzed man, to anyone, in fact, "Your sins are forgiven." Words like that are cheap, unless they're not. A pronouncement like that, when made generally and not personally, to cover all sin and not just *this* sin, is impossible to verify. Who will know? How can anyone check? You can't hack into God's computer to find out whether there's still a "Sin" file with the guy's name on it, or whether that's been erased from the hard drive.

It's easier to speak forgiveness, but harder to enact it. Forgiveness is harder to authorize. Healing is the other way around. With healing, the proof is in the walking, the authority in the results, which can be verified empirically and immediately. It can be tested in the shop. To command a paralyzed man to "get up" demands instant validation. A demonstration must ride the heels of the pronouncement, or else we're dealing with a charlatan.

Jesus heals the man to prove he has the authority to forgive the man. He does that which is harder to say and easier to do — heal him completely, head to toe — to establish that he has also done that which is easier to say and harder to do — forgive him completely, head to toe.

·   ·   ·

But I want to go back to that broken roof.

A broken roof is maybe the only door the desperate have to get into your church. It's what they resort to when all polite efforts fail, when they're not welcomed through the front entrance, and not at the side door either. But if Jesus is actually in the building, some desperado and his buddies will figure that out and finagle a way in.

I want you to see what happens when that happens. Prior to the sick man's getting himself to Jesus, that church had good preaching. The best: Jesus himself. Imagine such a thing: the Word made flesh declaring, interpreting, applying the word. That must have been a feast for mind and heart.

But after one sick man gets into the center of things, the word becomes flesh. The gospel is not just preached — always a good thing — but unleashed, set in motion. Through that unleashing, five radical acts are committed: radical welcome, radical forgiving, radical healing, radical confrontation, and radical worship. I'm using the word *radical* in its root sense, literally: *radix*, "roots, foundations, the stuff underneath." That which holds up and gives life to everything else.

It begins with radical welcome. The first word out of Jesus' mouth is "Son." This is spoken in the same breath forgiveness is pronounced, but it is prior to that pronouncement, almost the coil spring of it. We know, if we're careful theologians, that the right to become children of God follows, rather than precedes, "receiving Christ."[4] In other words, first we receive Jesus, believe in him, are forgiven by him, and then we become sons and daughters. But isn't that what this man is doing, receiving Jesus, receiving him in his wildly inelegant fashion, bumbling, tumbling, roof-wrecking his way to Jesus? Isn't that what his crashing the party is all about? Isn't he like so many others whom Jesus radically welcomes and accepts, who find out they're forgiven only *after* they step full into the embrace of Christ's acceptance? That Christ has first forgiven them (did any of them ask?) may very well be the basis on which Jesus now accepts them, but in real time his acceptance seems to release his forgiveness. At the very least, it announces it. I'm thinking of the woman at the well, or the woman caught in adultery, or the woman who anoints Jesus' feet with her tears, or Zacchaeus: all people who first received Jesus' radical welcome, and then only after discovered that, *ipso facto*, they'd also received his radical forgiveness. It was a package deal. "He welcomes me as his own and he forgives me." He forgives my marital disasters. He forgives my adultery. He forgives my years of turning tricks and burning bridges. He forgives my dastardly unscrupulousness, my stealing bread from children's mouths.

I'm accepted. I'm forgiven. That's all they know, and not one of them seems theologically vexed about which came first.

. . .

So there's radical welcome. And radical forgiveness. When the roof opens, when the word becomes flesh, radical forgiveness rushes down in the waterfall of acceptance. "Son, your sins are forgiven." Never mind that the paralyzed man didn't ask for this. Never mind that he has other matters on his mind. He's likely not theologically vexed about which came first, acceptance or forgiveness, but I'm guessing he's vexed that forgiveness is on offer at all. What about this picture, Jesus, are you not getting? I'm P-A-R-A-L-Y-Z-E-D!

But, of course, paralysis is not this man's most pressing problem. He only thinks it is. Which puts him in good company, or at least in common company, with the rest of us. Most of us think our most pressing problem is something other than sin. It's financial or relational or vocational. It's that I have a poor self-image, or others are routinely mean to me, or I never got the same breaks my younger brother got. Jesus, fix that. Heal that. Take that away. Give me something else instead.

Say what? My sins are forgiven? What about the drunk driver who put me in this place? What about the negligent medical team who, had they handled me with greater skill and care, it might have meant only a short stint in a neck brace, not this infernal, eternal sentence of memorizing every last inch of every last ceiling I've ever lain beneath? Huh? What about my wife, who couldn't take having a cripple for a husband and hightailed out of here with her office manager three months after the accident? You want a list of people needing forgiveness, I'll write you one.

Well, I'm making this up. But something akin to that very well could be swirling around inside his head.

I think in general we don't take sin seriously. We cheapen it, and so cheapen forgiveness. In fact, clear evidence that we don't take either seriously — sin or forgiveness — is the massive amount of unforgiveness among otherwise Bible-believing Christians. Unforgiveness is itself a terrible sin. It is a prison, dark and cold, we put ourselves and others in. That so many hold on to it so tenaciously is a sign they don't even see it as sin. It's a *right*. Bitterness is the collateral they're owed until they get their pound of flesh.

But when the roof gets broken, radical forgiveness breaks out. It has to: the kind of people who come in the roof hole, tumbling down from the sky, are not, generally, garden-variety sinners. They're spectacular sinners. They're hothouse varieties. They come in exotic strains. Their sexual escapades, their history of violence, their carnivorous tendencies, their appetite for illegal substances, their skill at working every angle, means that patness and vagueness won't cut it. Mere forbearance won't touch what really aches in them. They need something bone deep and heartwrenching. They need to know that this forgiveness — Christ's forgiveness enacted by Christ's community — goes all the way down, even to *that*.

Not long ago, I visited a church in my town to hear a good friend preach. He was speaking on how the truth of God makes us feel unworthy and so makes us want to run from him, but the grace of God lets us know we're accepted and so we want to run to him. A lady in front of me began weeping almost at the start, and by the end was sobbing loudly, almost wailing. When my friend invited people to come up to the front for prayer, she flew up there. She crumpled on the steps, heaving with her sobbing, thanking Jesus. I have no idea who she is. But I'm guessing she's no garden-variety sinner. I'm guessing she has a past that they don't make medication strong enough or therapy deep enough to banish. I'm guessing she's done things so indelibly staining, no self-help manual can even lighten them a tone. Only the blood of Christ can make them white as snow. I'm guessing she loves much because she's been forgiven much.

I was so moved by how her church embraced her, I started wondering if somewhere there was a hole in the roof.

· · ·

And then this story takes a dark turn, sounds a bleak note. The Pharisees don't like this talk of forgiveness. They resent it. The religious spirit we talked about in the last chapter wakes up howling, except silently, only on the inside. These men are too cowardly to say what they're thinking. They'll save that for the church parking lot, after the service. But it's already too late: they're outed by their inner dialogue. With Jesus in the room, to think a thing is the same as speaking it. "Immediately Jesus knew in his spirit that this was what they were thinking in their hearts."

What happens next is one of the most important parts of this story: Jesus confronts them. He stands them down.

Now listen. If you should choose to make your church more dangerous—choose to let your roof be broken, sometimes even aid the breaking of it—you will arouse the religious spirit. That's a promise. It will, as we talked about earlier, be sly at first, hard to catch, all murmurs and rumors, taking cover beneath pious questions. It will keep to the shadows until it's gained enough momentum to mount a frontal attack.

And as I have said, this spirit is harder to expel than Beelzebub himself, which is why it's his favorite tactic, why he loves to take churchgoers "captive to do his will."[5] But regardless of that, this spirit must be confronted. Left to breed in the shadows, it does more damage than hauled into the light. Unchallenged, it multiplies. Exposed, it rarely backs down, but it does lose much of its credibility or power to intimidate. Resisted, it will flee.

. . .

And then radical healing takes place. This healing is one of the ways Jesus confronts the religious spirit. This isn't the first or the last time Jesus will heal someone in open defiance of religious rules, in the face of fierce but veiled opposition. He will also heal a man with a withered hand and a woman with a hunchback. But what's to be noted is that Jesus' confrontation is not just mere words: it's active. The story I opened the book with—from Mark 9, in which Jesus' disciples get in an argument with the teachers of the law over a boy afflicted by an evil spirit—reminds us of the uselessness of confrontation without action. When we do not act on our deepest convictions, only speaking them, we are no better than those we confront. Indeed, according to that story, it was his disciples' failure to act that frustrated Jesus the most: "O unbelieving generation. How long will I put up with you?" Anytime we dare to confront the religious spirit, we should be prepared to back our words with a demonstration of the Spirit's power. We can't accuse religious people of not loving the poor, for example, if we're not living sacrificially for the sake of the poor, or denounce them for not caring for the creation if our own carbon footprint is only a half size smaller than anyone else's.

Confrontation is worse than useless if it's just accusing words.

We also see that though physical healing and spiritual healing don't always come conjoined like they do in this story, "getting up and walking" is always a sign that we've been forgiven. Forgiven people "prove" they're forgiven by walking in newness of life. They walk in the light, walk by faith, walk by the Spirit. Forgiveness sets us in motion. It acts upon us to make us act. It gets us up and gets us going. It does not indulge one more minute of lying around waiting for things to happen, waiting for others to do something, blaming others for the way I am. "Get up, take your mat, and go home." This getting up, taking our mat—once the symbol of our inability to move at all—and going home in full view of everyone is what every forgiven man and woman is supposed to do every day.

When we're new creations, we act like it.

We need more of this — this active response to the good news of what God has done for us — in most of our churches. Holes in the roof help by adding a sense of urgency to the matter. When there are no holes in the roof of our church, no one desperate for the touch of Jesus, our church becomes nothing more than a country club where we while away a few hours each week, swapping gossip and sizing each other up. But when someone comes among us who desperately needs to know that Jesus forgives and heals, that life can start afresh, the urgency of walking out our faith in full view is instantly heightened. There is a fresh urgency for elders and pastors and Sunday school teachers and worship team members to get up, every day, pick up their mats, and walk, always in the direction of home. That's church.

. . .

One last thing breaks out once the roof breaks open: radical worship. "This amazed everyone and they praised God." Everyone. Even, we're led to believe, the grumblers. That itself is amazing: that faultfinders become praise givers.

Again, a hole in the roof heightens the urgency of this. Anyone who has ever been restored even a little bit to the fullness of their humanity has been so because they learned to truly worship. It's why Jesus takes as much time as he does with the woman at the well to explain true worship to her. It's why Gideon's first act after tearing down his father's idols is to "build a proper kind of altar to the LORD your God on the top" of the ruins.[6] It's why Paul tells us, "in view of God's mercy," to offer ourselves "as living sacrifices," because the promise is that when we do, we will be transformed by the renewing of our minds.[7] No one continues to walk in newness of life without a life of radical worship.

All these are the blessings of having a hole in your roof. It almost makes you want to make a few holes yourself.

. . .

A number of years ago I was attending a conference in another part of the country, and was invited to speak at a nearby church for Sunday worship. I arrived at the place half an hour before the service began, only to find the place locked up. So I drove down the main drag. It was a small community right beside a lake. The street was thick with people. It was a party. The town was hosting a marathon, and hundreds of runners and their well-wishers were out in force. Everyone was in a festive mood. Dancing tempos pulsed from speakers lining the street, and tempting aromas wafted from food vendors' kiosks. There must have been, all told, three thousand people.

I got back to the church ten minutes before the service began, and a deacon had just arrived, alone, to open the door. He seemed surprised to see me. When I explained that someone in the church had booked me to speak there that morning, he said, "Well, it wasn't me, and nobody told me."

Two other deacons showed up, and we went into the photocopier room to pray. Only, no one prayed. All three deacons groused bitterly. The Friday before, the church parking lot had been freshly paved, the final touch on a major building renovation. Sometime between Friday night and Saturday, someone had driven an RV onto the lot — the men speculated it was "one of this riffraff come to run in the marathon" — and had left a thick crease in the soft asphalt. We all walked out to look at it. It seemed to me nothing that a handyman with a blowtorch and a piece of plywood couldn't repair in a blink. But they were infuriated. We walked back into the building and the service was starting, so we skipped the prayer.

At exactly the hour, about thirty-five unsmiling people shuffled into the sanctuary and sat near the back. We endured fifteen minutes of listless singing. There were some announcements. And then I was up. I had twenty minutes.

I there and then decided to change my text. I can't recall what I had planned to speak on, but on the spot I changed my mind and read the story of the paralyzed man. I talked to the congregation about all the people in their town today who didn't seem at all interested in coming through the door of their church, let alone breaking through the roof. I complimented them on their recent building renovations, but then asked, "Are you willing to see this building beat up a little — stains on the carpet, scuffs on the wall, gouges in the asphalt — in order to see a few of the people on the street here with you?"

It didn't go over well. No one talked to me afterward — well, one person did, but they just wanted to know if I knew so-and-so from the community next to the one I lived in. The rest emptied out in less than five minutes, as unsmiling as they came, maybe more so. The deacon who opened the door was standing at the door, ready to lock it, when I exited. No one thanked me. I was, it probably goes without saying, never invited back.

That was a long time ago. One can only hope that, somewhere along the line, someone broke the roof.

CHAPTER FIFTEEN

UNITY FOR THE SAKE OF THE WORLD

"HOW GOOD AND PLEASANT IT IS when brothers live together in unity!"[1]

Thus effused David.

He would have known. He'd tasted the rapture of brotherly unity: his deep-unto-deep bond with Jonathan comes instantly to mind. And, more often, he'd suffered the rupture of brotherly unity: his own brothers scorning him, his father-in-law hunting him to kill him, his henchmen wearing him out with their relentless bloody-mindedness. The absence of brothers dwelling together in unity was David's portion for most of his existence. It made him relish the few scraps of it he got. It made him hunger for more.

In Psalm 133, David compares brotherly unity to anointing oil poured over Aaron's head in his priestly consecration. And he compares it to the dew on Mount Hermon, and imagines that falling on Mount Zion. Much can be said about both images, much more than I'll take the space for here. The anointing of a priest—especially Israel's first priest, Aaron—was a thing of great and solemn wonder. And the dew on Mount Hermon was a feat of nature—a nightly ritual of air and earth that restored to pristine lushness a landscape blighted daily by pounding, withering heat. What David is in essence saying is that brotherly unity compares with the best the religious world can offer, and the best the natural world can produce.

And then he goes one step farther: "For there the LORD bestows his blessing, even life forevermore" (v. 2).

Unity is like heaven. It is the fullness of God's shalom. It is, to use David's imagery, Mount Zion here and now, the everlasting borne among the everyday. Unity is a prelude to eternity, which, as we'll see in a moment, is something very close to what Jesus says.

The Bible is little interested in equality. It aims much higher than that. From Genesis to Revelation, it calls us to this deeper, greater, tougher, sweeter thing: oneness. Oneness in our relationship with God. Oneness in our relationship with our spouse. Oneness with our relationships with other Christ-followers. Oneness in the church.

Oneness beats equality every time, because equality demands sameness. To be equal to you, I have to be as smart and strong and kind and generous as you. But oneness presumes difference. To be one with you, I have to accept your gift of otherness. I can be weak where you're strong, and vice versa. Oneness requires my life to complement yours. It calls us to complete one another. In marriage, for example, who wants equality? "We're even" is hardly a motto for lifelong affection. Whereas oneness is intrinsically cooperative, equality is inherently competitive, a recipe for endless one-upmanship. Or worse: a recipe for disaster. Equality was the false dream of Marx and Lenin, an ideology so unworkable in real life that its architects created one of the deadliest and darkest social nightmares in history. On a more personal level, equality is what people strive for in a divorce: half the assets, half the money, half the time with the kids. The scales must be exactly even then. But in a thriving marriage, the husband can be good at cooking and the wife at house repairs, each serving the other, and the resulting oneness means they both eat well in a house well kept.

Oneness, dwelling together in unity, is a good and pleasant thing in itself, much better than equality, and much, much better than animosity.

So God calls the church to oneness. He does that so that we can enjoy the goodness and pleasantness of it. God is a giver, and "every good and perfect gift" is from above.[2] But he has another reason for calling us to unity: nothing rehearses the kingdom of God better than our oneness. A church unified is an ensign and a showcase of the kingdom. It's a pageantry of the kingdom played out before a broken world to convince those who are far away to come near.

That's actually the argument Paul makes in that famous passage in Ephesians 4. On the surface, Paul seems only to advance a case for church unity for the sake of the church, for us to enjoy its goodness and pleasantness, and as a staple ingredient in the church's maturity. To be sure, these are desirable and needed things. But Paul, more subtly but just as forcefully, also advances a case for church unity for the sake of the world, for the world to glimpse the kingdom and to long for the wholeness and purity and maturity within it.

First, the key passage:

> As a prisoner for the Lord, then, I urge you to live a life worthy of the calling you have received. Be completely humble and gentle; be patient, bearing with one another in love. Make every effort to keep the unity of the Spirit through the bond of peace. There is one body and one Spirit, just as you were called to one hope when you were called; one Lord, one faith, one baptism; one God and Father of all, who is over all and through all and in all.
>
> But to each one of us grace has been given as Christ apportioned it.
>
> So Christ himself gave the apostles, the prophets, the evangelists, the pastors and teachers, to equip his people for works of service, so that the body of Christ may be built up until we all reach unity in the faith and in the knowledge of the Son of God and become mature, attaining to the whole measure of the fullness of Christ.
>
> Then we will no longer be infants, tossed back and forth by the waves, and blown here and there by every wind of teaching and by the cunning and craftiness of people in their deceitful scheming. Instead, speaking the truth in love, we will in all things grow up into him who is the head, that is, Christ. From him the whole body, joined and held together by every supporting ligament, grows and builds itself up in love, as each part does its work.[3]

Church unity, Paul says, is a gift of the Spirit held together by the presence of Christ ("the bond of peace") rooted in the character of God ("there is one God"). Yet even with all this—the gift, the glue, the root—unity still requires our every effort to keep, something that any-one who's been part of a church community for more than, say, three weeks knows is true. We join a church not because it's already whole, pure, and mature but to help it become so.

That is a compelling enough reason for unity. But that says nothing about the claim I am making, that we're to make every effort to keep unity not just for our own sakes but for the sake of the world. To see that, we need to go back to what Paul says earlier in Ephesians:

> But now in Christ Jesus you who once were far away have been brought near by the blood of Christ.
>
> For he himself is our peace, who has made the two one and has destroyed the barrier, the dividing wall of hostility, by setting aside in his flesh the law with its commands and regulations. His purpose was to create in himself one new humanity out of the two, thus making peace, and in one body to reconcile both of them to God through the cross, by which he put to death their hostility. He came and preached peace to you who were far away and peace to those who were near. For through him we both have access to the Father by one Spirit.[4]

This is a complex bit of Scripture, and I don't intend to comment on all of it. For one, Paul builds his argument on an analogy with the temple in Jerusalem and uses that to picture those outside of Christ as those stuck in the court of the Gentiles—"excluded from citizenship in Israel and foreigners to the covenants of the promise, without hope and with-out God in the world."[5] And he depicts Christ's death as breaking the wall—"the dividing wall of hostility"—between the outer court and the inner courts, allowing the outsider free access to the inside, a thing that before would have been punished by death.

But here's the passage that I want to focus on:

> His purpose was to create in himself one new humanity out of the two, thus making peace, and in one body to reconcile both of them to God through the cross, by which he put to death their hostility. He came and preached peace to you who were far away and peace to those who were near. For through him we both have access to the Father by one Spirit.

This, simply, is remarkable. It's revolutionary. What Paul says is that unity with others comes prior to reconciliation with God. In order for someone far from God to be reconciled with God, they first must be brought into unity with someone near to God. Let me put it plainly: no outsider will believe in Jesus until an insider treats him as a brother.

We actually already know that. Anyone who has led anyone to Christ knows it began not with judgment but with acceptance. You treated your Buddhist or atheist or lesbian neighbor as, well, a neighbor. You trusted her to look after your kids while you ran to the grocery store, and picked up milk for her while there. You invited the man next door, though his mouth is like a gutter and he openly mocks Christians, over for burgers and told him how much you admire his carpentry skills.

You lived as though there was no dividing wall of hostility between you.

This is the life Paul commends to the Corinthians. In 2 Corinthians, Paul says that God makes his appeal to others to "be reconciled to God" through us. That message comes through our mouths and our lives. Why us? God first reconciles us to himself, then gives us the ministry of reconciliation and commits to us the message of reconciliation, and so we become his ambassadors of reconciliation.[6] To be that, Paul says, requires two things: we open our new "grace-healed eyes"[7] to see others, and we open our new grace-filled hearts to receive them. Paul says it this way: "from now on we regard no one from a worldly point of view," precisely because God doesn't, and from now on we do not count "people's sins against them," precisely because God doesn't.[8] Grace-healed eyes. Grace-filled hearts. We treat people like they already belong to God in order to invite them to belong to God. We treat them as brothers and sisters so that they might become brothers and sisters. Our appeal for anyone to be reconciled to God is rooted in a demonstration of reconciliation: we accept them first. This acceptance is a prelude, a foretaste, a heralding of God's acceptance of them. We, like Jesus, do not condemn the world: we are a light within it.

. . .

What does all this have to do with unity within the church? Well, simply, if we can't live reconciled lives with one another, how will God make his appeal through us? We will be sweet water and salt water coming from the same spigot. We will be walking, talking contradictions. If we lack oneness with those already in the church, how will we possibly convince anyone outside it that this is God's main business, reconciling the world to himself in Christ?[9] They'll see right through our little facade.

Unity within the church is the heart of our appeal. Living reconciled lives with other believers validates our message to a fragmented, isolated, divided world. Unity among us vouchsafes our ambassadorial authority. It is our diplomatic calling card. Without it, the emperor—or ambassador—has no clothes.

Jesus said all this to his disciples just before his death: "My prayer is not for them alone [the disciples in the room with Jesus]. I pray also for those who will believe in me through their message [you and me], that all of them may be one, Father, just as you are in me and I am in you. May they also be in us *so that the world may believe that you have sent me.* I have given them the glory that you gave me, that they may be one as we are one—I in them and you in me—so that they may be brought to complete unity. *Then the world will know that you sent me* and have loved them even as you have loved me."[10] Earlier in his prayer, Jesus acknowledges that the world does not know God and hates his followers.[11] This is an unpromising platform to begin from. Any church that has attempted to reach its community, though, knows of what John speaks: scant knowledge of God, often contempt toward his people. In a world like that, all the church has to convince the world is the clear evidence that the cross works: once we were far away, divided by a wall of hostility, and now we're one with God and, as a sign of that, with each other.

John says in another place that anyone who claims to love God but hates his brother is a liar. "For if we do not love a fellow believer, whom we have seen, we cannot love God, whom we have not seen."[12] That's the whole point. The world cannot possibly begin to believe in the reality of an unseen God, extravagant in mercy, lavish in goodness, bent on redeeming and reconciling and restoring the creation, until our churches are living object lessons of this very thing.

Unity among us is inherently good and pleasant. For that alone, it's worth pursuing. But such unity is also the only litmus test the world has to test our claims and see if they be true.

For that, make every effort.

. . .

In twenty-two years of pastoral ministry, I have seen much to both encourage and discourage me on this score. I have seen great feats of peacemaking: a marriage that was beyond all hope restored through forgiveness and repentance and heroic hard work; a friendship that was destroyed through gossip rebuilt through heartfelt apology; an entire church that was riven by Luciferlike hubris healed by Christlike humility. I have witnessed, though not as often as the cross of Christ merits, fathers running to embrace prodigals, Hoseas seeking out unfaithful Gomers, Esaus welcoming home thieving Jacobs. Each is utterly breathtaking, a pageant of Christ's wild-faring redemption, his willingness to turn the house inside out to recover one lost coin, to pick his way over craggy heights to rescue one lost lamb, to wait in prayerful heartbreak to welcome home one lost son.

Too often, though, I've seen the other side. I've watched people fall out with one another over the tiniest infractions—a slight, an oversight, a mild rebuke. I've seen whole wars erupt from minor provocations. Rather than make every effort to keep unity, there are those who spare no expense at sowing discord. I sometimes call this the Euodia and Syntyche syndrome. That's a reference to the two women Paul addresses near the end of his letter to the Philippians, sisters turned rivals, colaborers cum combatants. Once they stood side by side in the good fight. Now they're just ripping fur in a catfight. Paul pleads with them to "agree with each other in the Lord," and enlists those around them to help.[13]

"In the Lord." That's the key. Agreement with one another, period, is hard to find, harder to maintain, and of little value anyhow. I disagree with my closest friends on a whole range of things: books, movies, music, places to vacation, ways to discipline children, and on and on. On many matters, we have no equality, nor want it, nor seek it. But on deep matters, we have oneness. Differences of opinion serve only to enliven rather than undermine our friendship. They make for fun banter. They spice and vary our conversations, keeping our relationship from staleness and blandness.

We don't need sameness. We don't need to agree with each other on everything. How tedious that would be.

We need only to agree with one another in the Lord. The things that matter most—the list of "ones" Paul rattles off in Ephesians—"one body and one Spirit ... one hope ... one Lord, one faith, one baptism; one God and Father of all, who is over all and through all and in all"[14]—these are the truths we're to hold to unswervingly. Paul's exhortation to "make every effort to keep the unity of the Spirit through the bond of peace" is best done by fostering convictions about these "ones."

My experience is that any group of Christ-followers committed to that will, as a fruit of that, have oneness with one another. And, as a bonus, they will be a ringing endorsement for the kingdom of God among those yet far from it.

.   .   .

Paul prays early in Ephesians that "the eyes of your heart may be enlightened in order that you may know the hope to which he has called you, the riches of his glorious inheritance in his people."[15]

"The riches of his glorious inheritance in his people." The dullest saint is a treasure trove of heaven's bounty. The most malformed believer is a cache of divine wealth. You and I sit weekly in the company of staggering riches, much of it hidden in plain sight. So, of course, the eyes of our hearts must be opened to see it, and that through fervent prayer.

My recommendation: if you don't see it yet, start praying hard, and keep praying until you do.

And this: whether you see it clearly already or simply must take it on faith, make every effort to keep the unity with these holy people. It will be pleasant in its own right. But it will also be a token to a broken, scattered world of a God who brings far things near and makes old things new.

CHAPTER SIXTEEN

HEALING IN
OUR WINGS

ANCIENT MARKETS WERE DIRTY PLACES. You stood cheek by
jowl with a ragtag bunch of sneezing, sputtering, coughing humanity.
Mobs with filthy hands, open sores, nasty contagions, jostled shoulder to shoulder. All handled the same merchandise. Ten people groped
nectarines, dried figs, pistachio nuts, and the eleventh person bought
and ate them. Twenty people, some whose bodies had not seen water
in a fortnight, tried on sandals before one man finally purchased and
wore them. Tablefuls of crockery and basketry and jewelery, of fresh
vegetables and dried peppers and ham hocks and bread loaves, of leather
aprons and cotton jerkins, all were caressed by a hundred fingers that
also grubbed gardens and swabbed counters and dabbled in places
unmentionable. At the market, small pieces of the debris of each and all
were swapped about freely. Humanity's earthiness was bartered along
with its wares. Everyone steeped in the broth of everyone else's breathing and sweating. Everyone took home a little souvenir from everyone else's personal collection, a memento or three from the man who
slopped pigs, the woman who cleaned latrines, the boy who caught rats.

You have to walk a marketplace in some part of the developing
world to get a real feel for this. I've walked in a few such places, in
Africa and India and Southeast Asia. Most recently, I did it in La Paz,

Bolivia. I meandered for miles through a narrow maze of stalls and storefronts cluttering and climbing a steep web of streets. Many peddlers just heaped their wares on the road or sidewalk, maybe on truck pallets, and constructed over top makeshift canopies from sticks and tarps. There's a certain order in the chaos: tubers are over here, dried peppers there, fruits around the corner, fish down the lane. The butchery was my favorite. It had the shock of carnage to it, and a pungency that a lifetime of perfumes could not mask. Until I first visited one of these, back in my twenties, I thought meat was brilliant red or luminous white, wrapped in small portions artistically arranged on styrofoam trays under clear cellophane pulled to a creaseless tautness. I thought meat departments were germless places, shiny and pretty and, above all, odorless. But such sanitary luxury is a new thing on the earth. La Paz's meat market is more like the old days: mounds of black-red flesh, crusting in the heat, jutting with bone, bristling with hide, swarming with flies, laid out on bloodstained wood counters. It's cooled, if at all, by a bored fat man standing behind it, idly flicking a fan, but mostly just to chase the flies off. Prospective buyers rummage through the meat folds like they're fingering towels in a white sale. But that's not it: they handle the meat with a gruff impatience and matter-of-factness like they're trying to rouse an incorrigible uncle from a drunken stupor, grabbing it hard, poking it, shaking it, heaving it back on the counter with feigned disgust. And nothing of the animal is not for sale. Its head and hooves. Its brains and tail. The lining of its stomach. Its plumbing.

It's no wonder careful, well-bred people find the market distasteful, even revolting. They're rank, dirty, dangerous places, and that's to say nothing of pickpockets, mountebanks, snake-oil salesmen who mingle in the throng. Just the raw, unfiltered ebb and flow of sheer earthiness makes marketplaces dangerous places. They're deep swamps of virus. They're breeding grounds of plague.

The Pharisees were careful, well-bred people. They took many necessary and wise precautions whenever any one of them was reduced to a visit to the market. Picking up some bug — the sniffles, a lingering cough — was the least of their worries; indeed, in a prebiotic age, it wasn't their worry at all. Though their codebook for cleanliness, Leviticus primarily, was in part a primer for good hygiene, they didn't know that at the time. For them, Leviticus dealt with a different kind of uncleanness: moral, religious, spiritual. An open sore wasn't just infectious; it was a token of sin and a threat to intimacy with both God and others. Certain kinds of food were not just writhing with parasites or teeming with cholesterol, putting those who ate them at risk for gastrointestinal complications or heart disease; they were despised things that put those who ate them at risk of sullying themselves and alienating God.

So it's no surprise that Mark records this in his gospel:

> The Pharisees and some of the teachers of the law who had come from Jerusalem gathered around Jesus and saw some of his disciples eating food with hands that were defiled, that is, unwashed. (The Pharisees and all the Jews do not eat unless they give their hands a ceremonial washing, holding to the tradition of the elders. When they come from the marketplace they do not eat unless they wash. And they observe many other traditions, such as the washing of cups, pitchers and kettles.)
>
> So the Pharisees and teachers of the law asked Jesus, "Why don't your disciples live according to the tradition of the elders instead of eating their food with defiled hands?"[1]

The Pharisees and lawyers are not offended, to repeat, because of the disciples' glaring lack of hygienic discipline; they're offended because of their conspicuous lack—indeed, their out-and-out defiance—of well-established and widely agreed-upon moral standards. Jesus' disciples are scofflaws. They flout tradition with recklessness. They trespass clearly marked boundaries and vandalize the no-trespassing signs on their way across. They are men without scruples. They are men devoid of good sense, good breeding, good manners. They are men who, if their rabbi can't restrain them, then sterner measures should be employed.

All's to say, this scene that Mark records should in no way surprise us. To give his non-Jewish readers a little orientation, though, Mark inserts parenthetically a comment about Jewish protocol for visits to the market. This is not just for Pharisees; it's for "all the Jews." These scruples—flagrantly thrown off by Bartholomew and the two Jameses and Peter and Judas, that whole sorry mob—are to be the badge of the law-abiding. Mark's little tableau of Jews in the marketplace would not register even the slightest qualm for a good Jew. Nothing would seem amiss. They'd all be on the side of the Pharisees against Jesus and his unruly disciples. That would raise the alarm. Even more, what would alarm them—or, more likely, send them into paroxysms of moral shock—is the scene Mark records just prior to this: "When they had crossed over, they landed at Gennesaret and anchored there. As soon as they got out of the boat, people recognized Jesus. They ran throughout that whole region and carried the sick on mats to wherever they heard he was. And wherever he went—into villages, towns or countryside—*they placed the sick in the marketplaces*. They begged him to let them touch even the edge of his cloak, and all who touched him were healed."[2] Look what gets hauled into the marketplace, and look who goes touching it. This portrait of people openly, deliberately placing the sick in the marketplaces reinforces every scruple a good Jew has about such places: avoid them, and when you can't, take a good, hot, long shower as soon as you get home. For someone to openly, deliberately bring sick people into such places, and for anyone to openly, deliberately touch them (and then, the pairing of these two texts hints, not even to wash up afterward) is, well, scandalous.

Mark no doubt juxtaposes these two scenes from the marketplace to set up a stark and sharp contrast, and to underline how radically Jesus changes the rules. In Jesus, as we saw in an earlier chapter, holiness is no longer a hothouse flower that wilts on contact. It is a cedar of Lebanon, the balm of Gilead, and even the edge of his cloak spills with healing. His holiness is not a delicacy to be primly guarded; it is an invading force that overwhelms resistance. It is a force to be reckoned with, not some keepsake to be safely stowed away.

What I want to emphasize here is that this is a template for the church. The market is a classic in-between place, where cultures and classes come together. Markets intersect the rich and poor, the old and young, the good and bad, the beautiful and sordid. It's everyone's world in general, and no one's in particular.

The way the traditionally religious inhabit such places is that they don't; they make forays into them, guarded, priggish, stealthy, squeamish, fleeting. In and out. They rush in, holding their noses, closing their eyes. They get what they need. They rush out, and try to scour any residue of the place from skin and heart and mind.

The way Jesus inhabits such places is subversively, massively, invasively. He comes with healing in his wings.[3] He moves toward those who move toward him, the kingdom of God on a collision course with a world half pleading, half defying. His arms are spread wide, to make more of himself, to gather more into himself, to pour more out of himself. He is large with compassion. He is unstoppable with redemption. He is a holy terror. When the kingdom within him collides with the world as it is, the kingdom will break that broken world, break and break it until it makes it anew. The lame will walk, the blind will see, the mute will speak, the deaf will hear. The foolish will become wise, the cowardly brave, the stingy generous. Angry people will first taste peace, in their bones, and then start making peace, from their hearts. Bitter people will forgive. The joyless will become joyful.

This is, I said, a good template for the church.

I'm thinking of Father John Sergieff. John was a priest in Kronstadt, Russia, in the mid- to late-nineteenth century. That was a time and place of dirty marketplaces. Imperial Russia was decadent, rotting beneath its own weight, and the streets were dangerous, rife with poverty and depravity. Crime ran amok. Alcoholism was rampant. Prostitutes crowded the corners, thieves the alleys. There was no safe place, so most people who weren't part of that world didn't venture out into it. Most of the clergy, used to a life of privilege and status, used what waning powers they had to insulate themselves from the widespread peril and hardship.

Not so Father John. His daily practice was to don his robe and descend into the meanest part of the city. He'd walk among the addicts and the predators, the whores and the thieves, the orphans and the widows, and he did it with healing in his wings. He would find the most broken and dissolute man or woman he could track down, lying in a gutter or standing on a street corner. He would cup their chin in his large hand and lift their face so they were looking directly in his eyes. "This," he would say, meaning this way of life, this means of survival, this condition I found you in, "this is beneath your dignity. You were created to house the glory of the living God."

Father John, in his lifetime, was called the Pastor of All Russia. And everywhere he went, revival came with him.[4]

.   .   .

In chapter 3, I began to share how God gave me his heart for the First Nations people. In these parts, the people, mostly, are part of six traditional Indian bands collectively known as the Cowichans. (Perhaps you've heard of Cowichan sweaters, a knitted jacket of thick wool with distinctive Coast Salish designs, in black or brown or grey, woven into the arms and body; those originated with *my* tribe.) When it became clear to me that God was asking our church to be part of a force for healing and reconciliation with and to the Cowichans, I began, with a small team of people who felt similarly called, to dream how this should look. Our first step was to design a workshop to help educate the churches in our region on the history, culture, and current issues of the Cowichan people, and to address what role the church may play now.[5] Nearly one thousand people from eight or nine churches went through this five-hour workshop over the course of fourteen months.

There were many other initiatives our church undertook during and after that time, including our participation in the North American Indigenous Games (NAIG), which I mention briefly in chapter 6. I also sat on many community forums and councils and boards, trying to learn as much as I could about our community, trying to do as much as I could.

It was all good, but it lacked one thing: we weren't actually doing anything. We lacked redemptive, incarnational presence and action. We weren't going into the market with healing in our wings. We weren't going there at all. So in the spring of 2010, we launched a children's ministry on the playground on Boys Road. That's the heart of Cowichan territory. It's the epicenter of the tribe's reservation, the Rez. It is nothing like the playground in your neighborhood, unless you live in a war zone, an inner city, a slum. The playground has been vandalized repeatedly, so none of it works: the slide is smashed, the swings are broken, the seesaw is twisted on its hinge. Every piece of equipment is spray bombed with expletives, skulls, Nazi symbols, the florescent outline of anatomical parts. The chain-link fence around the playground is torn away from whatever posts are still standing, and the playground itself is strewn with glass, garbage (here and there, mounds of it; evidently some people use the area as a garbage pit), dog feces, hypodermic needles, beer cans, discarded furniture, sometimes dead animals.

This is our staging area. We roll in here with a large van and an eighteen-foot trailer that converts into a stage, and put on a high-energy program aimed at children but which also, at least from a distance, attracts teens and adults. The program takes about half an hour. But it's just the beginning. It's just to get everyone's attention and convey, through song and story and puppetry, the gospel. But after, we try to make the Word flesh. We share a hot meal with the people. We talk with them neighbor to neighbor. We play basketball or tag. We discuss how to join with them in renewing their community, which everyone who speaks with us longs for but has lost hope in its ever happening.

It's still not much, what we're doing, but it's more than it was. And it is stimulating creative thinking about what steps to take next. Just yesterday I sat in a two-hour meeting with highly engaged and gifted people, discerning where to go from here. We all have a clear idea of where this will go eventually: a Zechariah 8–type community (see chap. 5), which we call Sanctuary. That vision is what compels us and keeps us going when we lose nerve or steam, or both. What we get confused about sometimes is not where we're going but where we're going next.

One thing's for certain: we must carry healing in our wings. The Cowichan people hurt deeply and all over. Their history over the last hundred and fifty years or more, from first contact with the British (before that, sporadically, the Spanish) until now, has some high points, but those are thickly mixed with, almost eclipsed by, a welter of low points. As my friend Dr. Daniel Marshall, the foremost historian of the Cowichan people, says, "Imagine tomorrow a foreign invader, under the guise of friendship, took your culture, your language, your land, forcibly removed your children from your home to educate and board them, and often sexually, physically, and emotionally abused them, created a massive federal law to maintain the status quo around this, and then after several generations of it blamed you for drinking too much or not working enough, and told you just to get over it. Imagine this was your story. How would you feel?" Daniel, of course, is describing in broad outline the last hundred and fifty years of colonialism and its impact on the First Nations people in Canada. (The "massive federal law" is called the Indian Act, an entrenched piece of legislature that treats First Nations people as wards of the state. It almost singlehandedly has created the welfare mentality widespread among the First Nations, and is so bound up with the conditions that prevail in First Nations communities that eliminating it would cause greater heartache and destruction than maintaining it. The closest analogy I can think of is the *perestroika* era in Russia, which seemed brilliant to the Western world but created daily conditions for most Russians that were many times worse than what it replaced.)

Solving any of this is miles outside my bailiwick. All I know is that many of the Cowichan people, like the inhabitants of Jerusalem in the time of Nehemiah, are in "great trouble and disgrace."[6] And the deeper we go, the more we need flowing through us the healing that Christ had flowing through him, running down him even to the hem of his robe.

I came to this task — of being a pastor, a writer, an advocate for First Nations people — poorly equipped. Of all the roles I play (and there are more: husband, father, friend, home repairman, dog owner — you get the picture), the one I'm most trained for is writer. The downside of this is that I talk (and write) better than I live. I "write pretty," to quote a friend. But I live messy. Most things I start I half finish, and cobble together that half. But in virtually every other task I'm required to do, by law or God or duty or conscience, I'm beginning to see that my most glaring deficiency is an inadequate — nay, almost bankrupt — theology of healing. What follows, then, is part confession, part repentance, and part — and very modest — proposal.

· · ·

Jesus said that we would do even greater things than he did.[7] Likely, the "greater" refers not to quality but to quantity: it's hard to top feeding five thousand with a few loaves and fishes, walking on water, turning water into wine, healing the sick, raising the dead. But what can't be improved on can be expanded. We can nourish even more, transform even more, overcome even more, restore even more. From a strictly statistical point of view, we have done greater things. Jesus fed a large crowd in the wilderness once (maybe twice). We have, in Sudan and Pakistan and Angola and Sri Lanka, and many other places, done it almost routinely. Jesus changed water into wine. We have changed a multitude of things into something else — corn into fuel, binary electronic impulses into computers, microwaves into cell phones that, lickety-split, you could use this moment to connect with someone clear across the globe.

But Jesus wasn't referring to humanity's growing brilliance with technology when he said we would do greater things. He was talking about the Holy Spirit. Christ's death and resurrection and ascension — his "going to the Father" — released the "descent of the dove," the wind from above, the fire from heaven. The return of Christ to the Father inaugurated the Father's sending his Spirit to all his children. That

Spirit did not just come for a visit—that was common enough in times past—but took up permanent residence in every son and daughter. Thus, Christ's real presence and power lives in every Christ-follower, and that real presence and power is multiplied by however many of us as there happens to be on the earth at any given moment. The triune God flows in and through us—in us to make us as he is, through us to empower us to do as he did.

How can we not do greater things than Jesus did? Jesus was a one-man show in a one-act drama in a one-horse town. The body of Christ is, at current count, two billion strong engaged in a drama that straddles the globe, embraces every culture, unites both genders, encompasses all generations, and has been playing in a theater near you now for nearly two thousand years, day after day, night after night. How can we not do greater things?

Yet something is lacking. All this real power and presence, magnified billionsfold, seriously underwhelms. Fathers keep pleading with the disciples to do something with their demon-afflicted sons, and the disciples keep arguing among themselves, or simply shrugging their shoulders, admitting defeat, and leaving the scene.

I am increasingly distraught about this. Increasingly convicted. Increasingly shamed and angered by it. Increasingly driven to repentance. Increasingly awakened to holy desire. I want more of the "he who is in me" to be obviously, demonstrably greater than he who is in the world.

I want to do greater things than Jesus did.

.   .   .

A theology and practice of healing begins with a theology of suffering, and with practicing the presence of those who suffer. We live in a broken world. Paul in Romans says that the whole creation is frustrated—subject to frustration, and that by God—and groans beneath it. He also says it waits in eager expectation for the children of God to be revealed—or, as Clarence Jordan vividly renders that in the *Cotton Patch Gospel*, "The fondest dream of the universe is to catch a glimpse of one real son or daughter of God."

There is a deeply affecting scene in the classic movie *Ben Hur*. Ben, the once-time nobleman now enslaved, is shackled together with other slaves and driven by belligerent Roman centurions through the searing Judean wilderness. Ben is dying of thirst. A child offers him water in a hollowed-out gourd, but a gruff soldier takes it from him before he gets a drop. Ben collapses. He begs God to help him. A shadow falls over him, and a man kneels down. He begins to wash Ben Hur's sweaty dirty face and hands. Then he lifts Ben's head and brings a cup to his lips.

Though we can't see his face, we know—from the calm authority with which he moves, the focused compassion in which he acts—who this Good Samaritan is: it's Jesus.

When the gruff soldier sees Jesus helping, he bellows at him and charges over, hand on sword hilt, to stop him. Jesus stands and faces the soldier, who stops in his tracks. All we see is Jesus' back. But the soldier's face says everything: this is not someone you mess with. This is someone you submit to. This is someone with authority much greater than your own, even if yours comes from Rome.

The power of that scene is, in part, that any one of us could play the role of Jesus: give a cup of water to the thirsty and resist the evil that demands we cease. Any one of us can be the answer to the groan of creation, be the reality that fulfills the universe's fondest dream. Part of the "greater things than these" is our willingness to mourn with those who mourn, to defend the defenseless, to bind the wounds of the brokenhearted.

There is a variant translation of John 9, the story of the man born blind, that captures this well. That story's opening scene is usually translated thus:

> As [Jesus] went along, he saw a man blind from birth. His disciples asked him, "Rabbi, who sinned, this man or his parents, that he was born blind?"
>
> "Neither this man nor his parents sinned," said Jesus, "but this happened so that the work of God might be displayed in his life. As long as it is day, we must do the work of him who sent me."[8]

The disciples are asking about *the cause* of this man's suffering. Jesus rules that question invalid. The real issue, he says, is *the purpose* of the man's suffering: that he might become a showcase for God's glory. This is an improvement, for sure, on the disciples' simplistic, reductionist theology of suffering ("bad things happen to bad people" is the sum of it), but not by much. Does Jesus mean this man has endured a lifetime of blindness—

stumbling and groping his way through the unlit maze of the world—so that, almost at random, God might one day show up and show off?

That's where the variant translation helps. Jesus' remarks can just as naturally be rendered this way:

> "Neither this man nor his parents sinned," said Jesus. "But *so that the work of God might be displayed in him, we must do the works of him* who sent me as long as it is day."[9]

"So that the work of God might be displayed ... we must do the works of him." The man's blindness is not occasion for theological speculation; it's an invitation to care, to act, however blundering and patchwork our acting might be. This willingness to act is the greater part of our greater works. Whether we deal in supernatural miracles—the dead raised, the blind seeing, the lame walking—or in everyday miracles—the naked clothed, the hungry fed, the imprisoned visited—doesn't matter: all are the works of him who sent Jesus. "The fondest dream of the universe is to catch a glimpse of one real son or daughter of God."

·   ·   ·

But first, we must see the blind man. The irony of the story in John 9 is how poorly everyone else sees—the disciples, the blind man's neighbors, especially the Pharisees and other religious rulers. Jesus alone is keen-eyed. Jesus alone looks without blinders at the blind man's blindness. That's our first task. And we must know that for every blind man or thirsty man or dying child or lonely woman—for every suffering person—for whom we do the works of him who sent us, there are myriad others we miss. This whole moaning, howling, writhing thing called creation is a train wreck, strewn and smoking in a million twisted pieces. The reality is that reality is skewed. Nothing is as it ought to be. Everything is amiss: misplaced, misfiring, mistaken. Our bodies wear out. Their silky smoothness turns leathery and wizened, their willowy suppleness gets creaky and brittle, their tautness puckers, their shapeliness whittles or bloats. Once flowing hair becomes scruffy and tufty. Once mellifluous voices turn croaky. And our minds, which spend half their lives accumulating, spend the next half jettisoning, and tend to retain the least valuable or helpful parts of the cargo: the trivia, the resentments, the grudges, the shame, the self-pity.

The whole creation groans, and we along with it.

Any theology of healing that doesn't start here, and stand here, and face this unflinchingly, is going to do more harm than good. I could cite you instances. I have sat too often with bewildered and deeply hurting men and women from churches that have no theology of suffering and so offer no comfort to those whose suffering proves intractable to their prayers and declarations of healing. I think particularly of a woman who came to see me after her husband died of cancer. They had served their church for more than twenty years in key leadership positions. All their children had been married in the church. They had faithfully tithed, and beyond, to the ministries of the church. They had stood by the leaders of the church through several crises and one very nasty scandal. But when the husband was diagnosed with cancer, and steadily declined, and then died, and then refused to sit up when, at the very last, the leadership commanded him to rise from the dead, they blamed the man and his wife for lacking faith, and shunned her.

She was devastated. She wondered when, under rules like this, anyone could legitimately die without it impugning their faith. Is every death short of those that come softly, swiftly, chariotlike, and snatch us from our sleep, old and full of years, a failure to believe? Is every sickness that doesn't retreat before our fiery, defiant prayers a sign of something deficient in those prayers?

I've had enough of these kinds of experiences to realize that an insufficient theology of suffering will produce, every time, a woefully inadequate theology of healing. All healing presumes two things: a broken creation, and a dream of wholeness. Something's gone awry, and somehow a rumor got started that it could be otherwise. Healing operates in the space between this awryness and this rumor, between grief and hope, between what is and what could be. A wound, a sorrow, a loss, a disruption — some such thing always serves as a precondition for healing. A promise, a possibility, a longing, a vision — some such thing always serves as a catalyst for it.

But there are no guarantees. Healing is always a gift, never a right. It's something we ask for humbly, look for hopefully, and, if given, receive gratefully. But it's not something we demand and then expect. The difference between those two postures — asking and demanding — is vast. The first is the attitude of the child or the servant, the second of the spoiled child or the despot. It seems to me that some sectors of the church, perhaps in a misplaced desire to protect God's reputation, have so backed away from a theology of healing that they can't even bring themselves to ask for it. And, as I've already said, some sectors of the church, perhaps in a misplaced desire to restore God's reputation, have so embraced a theology of healing that they can't bring themselves to ask for it either: they just demand it.

I'm arguing for a middle ground, which I think reflects mostly what we see in Scripture: the centurion pleading for his slave, the nobleman for his servant, the father for his son, Mary and Martha for their brother. They stood between pain and promise, between the thing gone awry and the rumor of wholeness. But they stood there as supplicants, not tyrants.

Faith is a part of this asking, this pleading. Jesus, not always but often, either performed a healing in response to someone's faith or credited a person's faith for their healing: "Your faith has made you well."[10] But faith works two ways here. It is clearly an ingredient in healing. It has to be, since faith is the only way we can approach God. But faith is also a refusal to demand healing. It's a refusal, if healing doesn't come, to blame anyone, God or the person who prayed. Faith is always the substance of things hoped for. It is always the certainty of things unseen. Once we turn hope into demand, it ceases to be hope. Once we insist that the unseen become seen, right here, right now, it stops being certainty and starts being a kind of hostage-taking.

If faith is to remain faith, there must always be both two clauses to it: "our God is able" and "but even if he does not." Those phrases, those clauses, come from the story of Shadrach, Meshach, and Abednego in Daniel 3, when an enraged King Nebuchadnezzar threatens to throw them in a fiery furnace unless they bow to his idol. They respond: " 'O Nebuchadnezzar, we do not need to defend ourselves before you in this matter. If we are thrown into the blazing furnace, the God we serve is able to save us from it, and he will rescue us from your hand, O king. But even if he does not, we want you to know, O king, that we will not serve your gods or worship the image of gold you have set up.' "[11]

"The God we serve is able to save us ... and he will rescue us ... but even if he does not." I can't think of a better summary of faith than that.

My modest proposal is that we pray for healing with faith like that. We approach every situation of awryness — lousy marriages, horrible jobs, sickness and disease, depression and boredom, war and oppression and poverty and famine, and everything else wrong with us and the world—with the boldness and humility of Shadrach, Meshach, and Abednego: our God is able, our God will (which, after all, is a guarantee—it's just that the timing for its fulfillment is beyond our knowing), but even if he does not.

This little I know: the more I pray this way, the more I see God do exceedingly abundantly more than I asked or imagined. I see sick people get well in ways that defy medical prognosis. I see marriages restored that everyone, especially those in them, thought beyond help. Recently, I watched as a man in our church, a quadriplegic bound seven years to a wheelchair from a spinal cord injury, get up and walk across the stage.

Our God is able.

Our God will.

But even if he does not, we will not stop serving him, or praying in his name, or caring for the sick, or serving even those who oppose our God and threaten us.

A church like that could bring pagan kings to their knees. A church like that would do greater things than Jesus.

CHAPTER SEVENTEEN

BREAK WALLS AND BUILD THEM

THERE ARE TWO WALLS IN THE BIBLE.

One is standing. It is high and thick and foreboding. It is impregnable. It must come down if the kingdom is to move forward.

The other has fallen. It is ruined, burnt, and unimpressive. It keeps nothing out. It must be rebuilt if the kingdom is to move forward.

Every church has to decide in their time and place which wall is which, and what they will do to remove the wall that opposes the kingdom, and what they will do to build the wall that advances it.

The first wall in the Bible is Jericho. Gateway to Canaan. It was a fortress town, a walled garrison designed as much to keep people in as out. As Israelites crossed the Jordan into Canaan, they knew that unless the walls of Jericho fell, the whole enterprise of inheriting and occupying the land would stall at the threshold.

But how? How does a poorly armed community breach and raze walls that big and fortified? Well, we know this story: not by might nor by power. Not with the weapons of this world. This kind comes out only by prayer. A stronghold this strong gets demolished only by divine power.

And so a strange counsel is given Israel's leader, Joshua. Actually, two strange counsels are given him. The first is to "make flint knives and circumcise the Israelites again," which, as the rest of the text explains, implicates all males born in the desert, including all those of "military age." The command itself is good. Circumcision is Israel's mark of covenant faithfulness. This is unfinished business, something forgotten or neglected during Israel's forty years in the desert. The old ways are revived in a single day, in one mass ceremony of blood and honor when the "whole nation" is circumcised.

The problem isn't the command. The problem is its timing. And the problem is location. A few weeks earlier, precrossing, and a few miles back, east of the river, would have been a much more appropriate time and place for a command like this. Now urgent matters are at hand. Now a whole city, a whole country, is poised to be conquered. In fact, here's what we're told at the opening of Joshua 5: "Now when all the Amorite kings west of the Jordan and all the Canaanite kings along the coast heard how the LORD had dried up the Jordan before the Israelites until we had crossed over, their hearts melted and they no longer had the courage to face the Israelites." Good military strategy dictates immediate action. The leadership of the enemy nation has collapsed. They are in puddles on the ground. They are reduced to quivering mounds of cowardice. They will offer frail resistance, if any. Strike now. Strike, before they muster courage and join ranks and sort out a plan of defense, or even attempt a preemptive strike.

This is the moment God gives his military strategy: "At that time the LORD said to Joshua, 'Make flint knives and circumcise the Israelites again.' So Joshua made flint knives and circumcised the Israelites at Gibeath Haaraloth."[1] Well, God is God and can advise as he wishes. But this does seem to me spectacularly bad timing and location. There were forty years or so to get around to this, and a vast desert to get it done in. God decides to do it here, to do it now.

Why?

Let's admit that if the command had been issued, say, six months prior and a hundred miles afield, it would have been relatively easy — a simple matter of tying up loose ends. Getting the house in order in preparation for the big outing. Going through a proper checklist of things to be done before you invade a foreign nation.

But because it comes here and now, on the eve of invasion, with all the kings quailing, it instead becomes a profound object lesson in radical trust.

Circumcision—and this in the day before anesthetic, antibiotics, Tylenol 3, sterilized surgical tools—makes a big man stoop. It makes children out of warriors, turns he-men into ninety-pound weaklings. The men of Israel must sit and nurse their wounds, immobilized, knowing a child with a stick could defeat them today, and tomorrow, and the next day too. Knowing it could well be a week or two before they're up for so much as a stroll let alone a fight.

Sitting there, hurting, one thought must dominate all the rest: do I trust God now?

Which is a good thing to wonder. Because what God tells Joshua and the people to do next defies belief.

There is, it turns out, no military strategy. All God wants is for Israel to go in circles. Just walk around the wall. Blow your horns. Repeat the next day. Multiply times seven.

You know how this goes. This otherwise bizarre tactic is exactly what it takes.

So that's how you break a wall. Or at least, that's how Joshua and the people leveled the walls of Jericho. As far as I know, this was a one-off. Is there any take-home for us? Is there any lesson here, even by way of allegory, that might help us?

I think so.

To get at that, let's think of the only person we know from Jericho, Rahab. Rahab was either an innkeeper or a prostitute. Likely both. She's the one the Israelite spies, dispatched at the command of Joshua, throw their lot in with, and she with them. That in itself is worth reflecting about.

Joshua sends two spies. He tells them, "Go, look over the land." Forty years earlier, he was recruited by Moses as part of a spy team. There were twelve back then, men whom Moses sent with almost the same mandate—"See what the land is like." But only two came back with a good report: Caleb and Joshua. The others turned the hearts of the people to wax. They stirred up fear about the perils, the risks, the costs. They obsessed over the daunting hugeness of the task, not the bigness of God and his promise. For their faithlessness, and Israel's faithless reaction, the nation was doomed to forty years of desert wandering.

Now the promise has come due again. And Joshua picks not ten men but two. My guess: he chose them not solely on the basis of their stealth and astuteness. They are more than crack operatives, cagey and skilled in the art of lipreading and lock-picking and homemade explosives. My guess is he handpicked two men because he recognized in them a kindred spirit. These were men who saw obstacles as opportunities. They were men who saw giants not as those too big to hit but as those too big to miss. They were men who believed God is always larger than whatever sets itself up in pretension against him.

And they knew a kingdom person when they met one, regardless of how unlikely a candidate that person seemed. Rahab would not have been on most people's radar for the person most likely to advance the kingdom of God. Even if she was just an innkeeper, a tavern owner, that's no work for the faint of heart. Jericho was a garrison town, a colony of scrappers, scofflaws, mercenaries, arms traders, black market dealers. A brawling, drinking town. Any innkeeper here would have to be tough talking, hard bitten, trusting no one, taking no guff from anyone, demanding cash up front. And Rahab was likely not an innkeeper, or not only. The Hebrew word to describe her, *zune*, is ambiguous, but the most sensible translation is harlot, a rendering with which the writers of both Hebrews and James unambiguously concur.[2] Indeed, that makes good sense of the story itself: the Hebrew spies are instructed to go about their business secretly. Checking in at the local hotel is hardly a way to remain inconspicuous. But procuring the services of a prostitute would be, especially since this is not the kind of behavior that a Canaanite would suspect from an Israelite. This is a shrewd ploy to fit in with the culture, blend in with the scenery.

But they must see a quality in Rahab that no one has noticed before. She's more than the golden-hearted whore. She's cut from the same cloth as Naomi's daughter-in-law, Ruth; as the Samaritan woman Jesus meets at the well; as the "sinful" woman who crashes Simon the Pharisee's house party to anoint Jesus' feet; as the Syrophoenician woman who will not take no for an answer, even from Jesus, especially from Jesus; as Mary Magdalene, from whom Jesus cast out seven demons and who now cannot say thank you enough. She's the woman who's been waiting her whole life to find out there's something more, something other, than all she's known all her life, and who'll now go to extravagant and dangerous lengths to get in on it. Since the days of John the Baptist until now, the kingdom of God has been violently advancing, and violent men lay hold of it. And since the days of Rahab the prostitute until now, the kingdom of God has been violently advancing, and violent women lay hold of it.

The spies spy that. In all this suspicious, vicious town, where dogs eat dogs, literally, and humans exploit other humans for their own gain, there's one lady who's had enough and will risk it all to leave it all. They see it, whatever it is they see: a look in her eyes, of hunger and wildness and sadness and hope; a laugh both cynical, mocking the world that is, and raucous, welcoming the world that's coming; a quickness of reflex, a sharpness of insight, a willingness to put to work all that the culture's taught her in order to take back all that the culture's stolen from her.

The spies spy that.

And she's no fool. She's spying things too. What she sees are two men who, though they look like everyone else, though they act like just two more customers out to slake their lust, are like no one else she's ever met. They have qualities about them that defy description — courage, perhaps, and something that only later Rahab will learn to call holiness — which no outward guise can fully conceal. Something beyond dress and facial features distinguishes these men from every man she's ever known.

It must be God. Years earlier, Moses stood on a mountaintop and pleaded with God to go with Israel wherever they went. "If you do not go with us," Moses argued, "what will distinguish us from all the people on the face of the earth?" That clinched it. God agreed. God bowed to Moses' request. God conceded to Moses' flawless logic that no human can produce from within themselves the mark of transcendence. The kingdom of God is among us only when the King himself is among us.

Rahab must smell God on them. Rahab must see God in them, in some subtle hand movement, some cadence of speech, some flicker of awareness. Something in their faces or their eyes that reveals something on their insides. She must know that whatever else these men are about, they embody some reality that she would risk her life to be part of. And if she can't be part of it, she'd rather die trying.

So she throws herself in with them and they with her. From here on, the fate of any one of them rests with the trustworthiness of the others. An act of betrayal on either side is death. Each now risks everything on the belief that the kingdom is coming.

And so it does. And so their faith proves of greater worth than gold.

. . .

This is where the story of Jericho's walls enters our own. It is, from top to bottom, on the grand scale and on the intimate, a story about betting the farm on the trustworthiness of God and the certainty of his kingdom. It is about one woman and two men who stake everything on the hope that their personal stories are part of the bigger story: that what God is doing for all people he's also doing for each of them.

It's about those who know that any wall built to keep God out is a wall whose only value is in being demolished. As the apostle Paul later says, "I beg you that when I come I may not have to be as bold as I expect to be toward some people who think that we live by the standards of this world. For though we live in the world, we do not wage war as the world does. The weapons we fight with are not the weapons of the world. On the contrary, they have divine power to demolish strongholds. We demolish arguments and every pretension that sets itself up against the knowledge of God, and we take captive every thought to make it obedient to Christ. And we will be ready to punish every act of disobedience, once your obedience is complete."[3]

God empowers Israel with divine weapons to demolish the stronghold of Jericho. And this is meant to be the ongoing ministry of the people of God: that whatever walls exist that keep God stranded outside and Rahab trapped within, captive to living "by the standards of this world," their only value is in coming down.

This book is about that. It's about your church, in your community, discerning and acting in the authority God has given you to reduce to rubble — not with weapons of this world but with God's quirky agenda and home-tooled methods, however those get revealed — all the walls that keep the kingdom out and Rahab captive.

Rahab the prostitute shows up three other places in our Bible. Two I've already alluded to, the letter to the Hebrews and the letter of James. In Hebrews, she appears alongside the patriarchs and right next to Moses, just before the judges. She's hailed, as are the rest, as an example of those who lived by faith. In James, she's compared with Abraham, father of the faith. There she is, a onetime prostitute, an outsider to the covenant until she got on the inside by hook and by crook, holding her own in the company of prophets and sages and kings. There she is, former harlot, held up for your mother and your grandmother and your wife and your daughters to emulate.

As if that weren't enough. But the other reference is breathtaking:

Rahab appears in Matthew's genealogy of Christ. She's the tenth name counting down from Abraham. (Or eleventh: she's named as the mother of Boaz, and so the wife of Salmon, in a list that, with five exceptions — Tamar, Rahab, Ruth, Bathsheba, and Mary — lists only the names of fathers; Matthew, with a penchant for the scandalous, feels compelled to include in an otherwise paternal list the names of a rape victim, a prostitute, a Moabite outsider, an adulteress, and a pregnant virgin.) That makes Rahab a great-great-great — great times twenty-nine, by my count — grandmother to the Messiah. Had there not been a Rahab, there would not have been a Boaz, and then not an Obed, and not a Jesse, and not a David, and so on, right down to Jesus — generations of those who never came to pass.

But there was a Rahab. She was faithful. She believed in the King. She believed in the kingdom come and in the kingdom yet to come. She staked her life, and the lives of her family, on this wild extravagant hope. She mortgaged her entire future, not one thing held in reserve, on her certainty of things unseen, her assurance of things hoped for.[4] She believed that God exists and rewards those who earnestly seek him.[5]

And she was right.

The kingdom of God broke through her walls. In the fullness of time, because of her faithfulness and the faithfulness of many others like her, the kingdom of God broke through your wall too.

And now you too get to walk free.

. . .

To break a wall requires more trust than work. That's what Israel discovers at Jericho. And every Christian and every church that have attempted to go and do likewise have discovered the same thing. These kind come out only by prayer. These walls come down only in God's way, with God's weapons, or else they either never fall or, if they do, whatever breaks in and breaks out after that is not the kingdom of God.

To break a wall requires more trust than work.

But to build a wall takes more work than trust.

Nehemiah could tell you as much.

Nehemiah is our other biblical story about a wall. This time, the kingdom of God is itself in rubble until the wall gets built. So there are walls that must come down if the kingdom is to move ahead, and there are walls that must go up if it's to be so.

Again, let's take a close look at the story.[6]

Nehemiah works for a powerful and capricious man, Artaxerxes. Artaxerxes, like his father, Xerxes, is equal parts statesman and madman. He's whimsically generous, dangerously volatile, wildly self-indulgent, unpredictable in his anger and his kindness. Implore him for a favor, he might give you exceedingly abundantly more than all you ask or imagine, or he might have you summarily executed. You never know one way or the other, one day to the next.

Nehemiah is Artaxerxes' slave. That meant he was completely at the beck and call of the man. He was a high-living slave — Artaxerxes lived lavishly and ensured that all who served him did as well — but there was no question about where the power resided: the king had it all; the slave had none. The king could wield his power however he thought best, to suit whatever whim took hold of him at the moment, to indulge whatever impulse flitted through him in that instant.

One day Nehemiah's brother Hanani comes for a visit. We have some historical evidence that Hanani was a local politician in Jerusalem — in fact, that he may have been governor on either side of Nehemiah's own term in that office. At any rate, he has information Nehemiah wants. So Nehemiah gets right down to business — no small talk, no cocktails and canapés, just a blunt question: what's happening with Jerusalem and her inhabitants?

That's the question burning in Nehemiah's mind. How the fire started, we don't know. He's been a slave for a long time, dutifully doing his duty. He must be good at it. You don't serve a king of Artaxerxes' rank without a high level of swank and polish. He needs a firm grasp of the big picture and, simultaneously, his fingers on every last little detail. He needs both panoramic and microscopic vision. He must be a master of decorum and a paragon of discretion. He must possess extraordinary eloquence, tact, and finesse, combined with ruthless efficiency. He must be the consummate courtier, poised, shrewd, intuitive, unfailingly professional, fawning with overlords, brusque with underlings.

He has all that. And now, messing with all that, he has a fire in the bones.

Hanani's answer only fuels the fire. "Those who survived the exile and are back in the province are in great trouble and disgrace. The wall of Jerusalem is broken down, and its gates have been burned with fire."

Nehemiah's response: "When I heard these things, I sat down and wept. For some days I mourned and fasted and prayed before the God of heaven."

The fire rages, and it won't go out. Nehemiah spends weeks and weeks stoking it.

And then one day, some three months after Hanani's visit, he can no longer bear it. He walks in to Artaxerxes' throne room on a wing and a prayer: "Give your servant success today by granting him favor in the presence of this man," he Hail Marys to God.

Nehemiah's three months of prayer has shaped in him a risky strategy: he walks into the king's presence downcast. His sadness is all over him. This is a ploy that might backfire tragically. Ancient Eastern kings were not overly disposed to pander to their servants. Servants served kings, not the other way around. It was an act of brazen audacity to display human frailty to Artaxerxes. He paid you, so to speak, to be above all that. Fake it if you must. Just don't drag your personal problems to work with you. With this king, it is definitely not about you.

Nehemiah understands that perfectly well: "I had not been sad in his presence before." Nehemiah doesn't mean he'd never *felt* sadness in the king's presence. The entire chapter preceding this comment is the diary of his broken heart. Nehemiah has been coming into Artaxerxes' presence for ninety days with sorrow ravaging his insides. It's just that Nehemiah had never let on. He'd managed his sorrow in closed quarters. He'd kept his grief to himself. When in the presence of the king, he'd mustered whatever forces of courage and connivery he needed to put on a happy face. He'd kept a stiff upper lip. He'd worn a plastic smile.

But today would be different. Nehemiah's three months of soaking his pillow with tears, of seeking the face of God, has distilled to a single, crazy, do-or-die ploy: don't mask your sadness anymore. Let the king see in your face what you feel in your heart. Who knows, maybe today his mood is generous, his disposition kind.

And it is. Artaxerxes' comment reveals a depth in the man easily missed. "Why does your face look so sad when you are not ill?" the king asks. "This can be nothing but sadness of heart." The king must himself be a man of sorrows, familiar with suffering. He's been here before.

All the pomp and lavishness of his kingdom, all his harem girls, all his conjurers and jongleurs have not kept the wild plundering thing called sorrow out of his heart. On this day, at least, Artaxerxes knows what heartbreak is. His sympathy is aroused. His compassion is awakened. On this day, he grieves with those who grieve.

"I was very much afraid," Nehemiah says next. Of course. The king's question, the king's remark, has probably been delivered poker-faced. Is the king seething? Is he genuinely curious and concerned? Is this a day he's feeling bountiful, or vengeful?

Nehemiah has no time to weigh that out, only to plunge in. Which he does with astonishing forthrightness: "Why should my face not look sad when the city where my fathers are buried lies in ruins, and its gates have been destroyed by fire?"

Artaxerxes' next question changes history: "What is it you want?"

. . .

What is it you want?

It's a question that unlocks our deep self. What is it I want? Why do I keep avoiding certain things, long after I've proven the worthlessness of that tactic? Why do I keep pursuing certain things, even after a lifetime of disappointments, either from missing it or, more often, from getting it? Psychiatrist Dr. Irvin D. Yalom uses that question to dismantle people's defenses and pull off their masks. He conducts a simple exercise in which he gathers a roomful of total strangers, randomly pairs them off, and has each partner ask the other, repeatedly, "What do you want?" He writes:

> Could anything be simpler? One innocent question and its answer. And yet, time after time, I have seen this group exercise evoke unexpectedly powerful feelings. Often, within minutes, the room rocks with emotion. Men and women—and these are by no means desperate or needy, but successful, well-functioning, well-dressed people who glitter as they walk—are stirred to their depths. They call out for those who are forever lost—dead or absent parents, spouses, children, friends. "I want to see you again." "I want your love." "I want to know you are proud of me." I want you to know I love you and how sorry I am I never told you." "I want you back—I am so lonely." "I want the childhood I never had." So much wanting. So much longing. And so much pain, so close to the surface, only minutes deep.[7]

What is it you want? Jesus asked that. Indeed, we have two stories, back to back, in which he asks it twice. The first time, he asks it of James and John. The second time, he asks it of a blind man, Bartimaeus.[8]

All three approach the King with a request. All three angle in on him, hoping to exploit his power and wealth for their benefit. None has the reserve of Nehemiah. None resorts to a subtle ploy to arouse, hopefully, the king's curiosity and sympathy. James and John simply blurt it out: "We want you to do for us whatever we ask." Blind Bartimaeus bellows it out, over the din of the crowd and the stern warnings of the disciples: "Jesus, Son of David, have mercy on me!" What each lacks in tactfulness they make up for in directness. Their brashness has the virtue of eliminating all guesswork.

The King, Jesus or Artaxerxes, asks, "What is it you want me to do for you?"

None has any problem answering. Each has thought this out. Each has distilled it into a very clear and very big ask. No time for sidelong hints and cryptic suggestions. No room for winks and nudges. Just get straight to the point.

What James and John want: "Let one of us sit at your right and the other at your left in your glory."

What Blind Bartimaeus wants: "Rabbi, I want to see."

Jesus refuses James and John's request. Or, at least, he tells them those seats are already taken, without saying by whom. Maybe Rahab. Maybe Bartimaeus.

Jesus grants Bartimaeus's request. Instantly. Without quibble or condition.

In one sense, both are selfish requests. James and John's, blatantly so. They are asking to co-rule with Jesus. They are asking for something that would benefit themselves and no one else.

But so is Bartimaeus. I realize that his request for sight is inherently less selfish than the brothers' request for power and status. But there's nothing selflessly grand about it either. And maybe there is, underneath the blatant selfishness, hidden in the fine print, something noble and altruistic in James and John's request: "Jesus, we simply and humbly request more power in order that we might serve the needs of widows and orphans—and, yes, that poor blind man over there. If you give us those seats, we will use our authority to uphold the cause of the oppressed and relieve the plight of the distressed. Trust us."

That's unlikely. But equally unlikely is any lofty motive at work in Bartimaeus's request. The brothers Boanarges were just being sneaky and acquisitive, is the most likely explanation: "Give me mine." But Blind Bart is just being candid and acquisitive: "Give me mine."

Jesus says no to the brothers.

Jesus says yes to Bart.

Is that fair?

But there's a clue in the second story, the blind man's story, about what each will do if given what they want.

In Mark's gospel, which mostly I'm relying on here, we're told what happens when Jesus grants Bartimaeus his request and restores his sight: "Immediately he received his sight and *followed Jesus along the road*."

A few verses earlier, Mark records the reaction of Jesus' entourage to Blind Bartimaeus's crying out to Jesus: "Many rebuked him and told him to be quiet." Luke in his gospel actually identifies "the many": "*Those who led the way* rebuked him and told him to be quiet."[9]

"Those who led the way." I assume James and John are among these. I assume they have positioned themselves prominently in this group, leading those who lead the way. They are, after all, the group's self-appointed leaders. They are born leaders, legendary leaders, leaders who lead. And they are doing what leaders do: telling others what to do. Barking orders. Commanding and commandeering. Lording it over the little people. Exercising authority over them.

All the things Jesus told them not to do.

"You know that those who are regarded as rulers of the Gentiles lord it over them, and their high officials exercise authority over them. Not so with you. Instead, whoever wants to become great among you must be your servant, and whoever wants to be first must be slave of all. For even the Son of Man did not come to be served, but to serve, and to give his life as a ransom for many." This was, in fact, the last speech Jesus gave to his disciples before they met Bartimaeus.[10]

Something must have got lost in translation.

When Jesus granted Bartimaeus's request — to see — immediately he followed Jesus. Luke adds that he also praised Jesus. Immediately, he used his sight to obey and to worship. He used his newfound power to seek and honor Christ.

Not so James and John. I'm guessing that, even after Jesus' clear instructions to them about the nature of kingdom leadership, those who led the way still felt it was their prerogative to lead the way. To give the orders. To tell the least of these to shut up, and now.

What would men like that do if you gave them more authority, if you let them sit at your left and at your right? What would they do with power of that magnitude, when they already use the little power they have to bully blind men?

Well, we don't know for certain. But here's the more pertinent thing: what is it you want him to do for you?

And what will you do should he grant your request?

. . .

What is it you want? The king asks Nehemiah that question. And Nehemiah has no problem answering. He's thought this out. He's distilled it into a very clear and very big ask. " 'If it pleases the king and if your servant has found favor in his sight, let him send me to the city in Judah where my fathers are buried so that I can rebuild it.... If it pleases the king, may I have letters to the governors of Trans-Euphrates, so that they will provide me safe-conduct until I arrive in Judah? And may I have a letter to Asaph, keeper of the king's forest, so he will give me timber to make beams for the gates of the citadel by the temple and for the city wall and for the residence I will occupy?' And because the gracious hand of my God was upon me, the king granted my requests."[11]

What is it you want him to do for you?

And what will you do should he grant your request?

. . .

Nehemiah had prayed, just as he went in to see Artaxerxes, this: "Give your servant success today by granting him favor in the presence of this man."

"Give your servant success." Nehemiah defines success, it turns out, not by upward mobility but by downward: from the luxury of the palace to the squalor of the slum. From wearing silk to wearing coveralls. From eating delicacies to eating bologna. For Nehemiah, success is losing his life for the sake of others' finding theirs. It's to give himself to a task and a purpose that require toil, hardship, and sacrifice, and no great reward for him other than knowing he's served God's purposes in his generation.

That's success.

And it takes work.

That's where the story also informs ours, where it gives us a template for what it is to be the church. The kingdom is about walls coming down. And it's equally about walls going up.

Walls coming down requires work, but mostly it requires trust. Every attempt to tear down walls of oppression and defiance, Jericho walls, that does not rely deeply, almost solely on God always fails.

Walls going up requires trust, but mostly it requires work. Every attempt to build walls of protection and blessing, Jerusalem walls, that does not demand our best efforts and call out our hardest toil always fails.

Nehemiah knew Jerusalem's walls were more than walls (just as Joshua knew Jericho's walls were more than walls). Jerusalem's walls were stone and mortar. But they were also symbols of protection and blessing. They were catalysts of restoration. They reawakened identity and calling. Through building them—not just *having* them, but *building* them, stone on stone, the scrape of trestle on rock like a throaty song, the slap of wet mortar on hard surface like the footfalls of a river dance—the people rebuilt themselves. They discovered what they had forgotten or forsaken: that they were God's very own possession, his peculiar people.

For good reason, then, Nehemiah ends with the entire community gathered in exuberant worship: this is where the sweat and toil and endurance have been heading all along. They once were not a people. Now they are the people of God. So they will proclaim the praises of him who brought them out of darkness and into his marvelous light.

Every church that seeks the kingdom must break walls and build walls. And the walls we build are not the walls that sometimes the church has built—walls to isolate us and insulate ourselves, walls to intimidate others, walls that forbid the least of these to enter. Walls that keep Rahab out. Walls that reinforce our Jonah contempt and our Simon the Pharisee disdain.

No, instead we build walls that remind us we're peculiar people.

Work. Worship. When the early church was looking for the right word to describe their life together, their seeking God and serving God, they found one word that meant both work and worship. *Latreuō.* *Latreuō* is an act of worship. And *latreuō* is a public work. It is building the wall, and then dancing on it. It is digging a well, and then drinking from it. It is constructing a bridge, and then crossing it.

It is building an altar, and then laying yourself down on it as a living sacrifice.

. . .

What are the walls you need to tear down? What are the walls you need to build? What are the bridges you need to create or remake? What liturgies does your church need to initiate and enact?

Let me stop speaking figuratively and talk plainly.

I'm thinking of Mike's church. It was once, in the 1980s and partway through the '90s, a flagship church in our denomination, thriving and innovative. Under the wise leadership of a committed team, they'd almost mastered that elusive rhythm of the "journey inward, journey outward":[12] people were growing more and more in love with God and neighbor, were conforming more and more to the likeness of Jesus, were doing more and more the work of Jesus in the power of the Spirit, within the church and without.

It was all good until it wasn't. The senior pastor, after twenty-three years at the helm, became disheartened over a minor squabble and resigned. Then began The Troubles. Years of them. Splits and exoduses. Expulsions and implosions. Long volatile meetings filled with accusation and recrimination, the kind that leaves everyone with a bitter aftertaste in their mouths. A rapid decline in attendance. A pervasive discontent among those who stayed. Good people leaving and wounded people staying. Disgruntled people leaving, but only in a kind of self-imposed exile, sabotaging from a distance.

It went on a very long time.

Mike was the associate pastor. Mike is maybe the most intuitive leader I know, but he has no formal theological education and, until this church, no pastoral experience (though he served for many years in a couple of parachurch ministries). His role through most of the debacle was to support and walk alongside the senior pastor, a good man who was becoming the scapegoat for most of what ailed the church. During this dark time, I offered—twice, if recollection serves—Mike a position at our church. I thought he'd crawl over cut glass to get away from his current situation. But he stunned me, both times, by turning me down.

Three things tied him to the helm. The first was his deep loyalty to the senior pastor. The pastor was a good man, a gifted preacher, a man of prayer. He was marked by deep and genuine humility. Mike signed up to be one of his "mighty men," and he was not about to abandon post just because the job got hard. The second thing was Mike's deep loyalty to the church, toxic as the church was. Mike was being tested and refined in one of the hardest and yet most important areas of spiritual formation of any Christian leader: to love people whom you have every reason to despise. And as is always the case, there was a remnant of prayerful, godly, long-suffering people, and Mike refused to leave them in the lurch. He had been a part of the community for a decade before being called to his pastoral role, and these people had helped him work through some difficult times. It was now his turn to stand in the gap for them.

The third reason Mike didn't bolt was his unyielding conviction that God had him in this place for such a time as this.

I admired his courage. I applauded his conviction. And I thought him crazy.

God proved me wrong.

But not immediately. The senior pastor left, defeated and dejected. The leadership, such as it was, asked Mike to step into the role of interim senior pastor. For another year and a half, Mike was hard pressed. He was faced, like Nehemiah, with the challenge of rebuilding a community in the midst of devastation. And those who were devastated didn't know what to do.

Complicating matters were the frequent but unpredictable health issues plaguing his adopted daughter, Monica. Mike and his wife, Sue, had spent many hours in hospital wards with Monica, anxious as they awaited doctors' diagnoses or proposed treatments, in agony as they watched their daughter's tiny arms bruise with needles. Mike and Sue skirted the edge of a long fall as they attended to the fragile health of their daughter and their church.

And then, when it couldn't get any worse, it didn't. Beyond all reckoning, a miracle happened: the church got well. Not only well. It has become an embodiment of the kingdom of God.

How?

Well, mostly, because God's grace abounds. It's never in short supply, never rationed to make it last or to stretch it to go around. As my friend Graham Cooke likes to say, "God has abundance; the enemy has a budget." Mike and Sue, and a small group of prayerful people, kept running into God's throne room to get all the mercy and grace they needed, and then walking out flush, with armloads.[13]

In grace, they loved. They confronted. They pleaded. They rebuked. They persevered. Grace prompted them. Grace sustained them. Grace poured out through them.

The church is now called The Forge. "A forge is a place of refining and strengthening," Mike says. "God turned up the heat, and it was forging us together into what he desired us to become. It was God's forge, and he was the blacksmith. Heat isn't a bad thing. It's active, not passive. It's not always comfortable or pleasant, but you get good stuff out of it."

Indeed.

The Forge has created an atmosphere in which anyone can belong. Their focus is on the community, and especially in giving dignity to those who are often marginalized in churches. They openly talk about being a church for the 95 percent, a phrase that represents the percentage of nonchurchgoers in their area. They include children as part of the service. They have made space for people with handicaps to share and participate in their gatherings. People who come with broken lives are embraced.

Here's an example. Cobbs Bread opened a local bakery in The Forge's community. These are bread stores that bake loaves and buns made from exotic flours ground on-site and that turn stale by next day because they have no chemical preservatives, loaves and buns chock-full of seeds and nuts and fruits and spices, each selling for five or six dollars apiece (the loaves) or per half dozen (the buns). It tastes like the bread angels must eat.

Every day, Cobbs stores have bread to spare, bread left over. Lots of it. In a year, hundreds of thousands of dollars of it, if it were sold at retail prices. But it didn't sell. Most bakeries (I am sad if I'm breaking news here) throw their surplus away, for reasons that make business sense, but not common sense.

Not Cobbs. They give all their surplus, every day, to organizations in their community. The Forge has set up a system two days a week to retrieve the surplus, sort it, and then give it all away. They have a team of people who take bread to single moms, seniors' homes, neighbors.

Few of these people go to The Forge, at least not when they first start getting the bread. There are no strings attached. No one has to come to a meeting or endure a visit from the elders. There are no Bible verses that The Forge twist-ties to the loaves or gospel tracts they insert in the bread bag.

It's just giving bread, really good bread.

And many of these people wake up one day and realize that in the Father's house, in Mike's church, at The Forge, there is food to spare. They wake up and realize that they don't live by bread alone. And so they make the journey to the place from where the bread came, and find there a God who runs to greet them, calls them sons and daughters, puts robes and sandals on their feet, rings on their fingers, and who has fatted calves awaiting the barbecue.

They've removed walls that isolate and separate.

They've built walls that bless and protect.

CHAPTER EIGHTEEN

EVEN THE SPARROWS

Your church is too safe.

I hope by now I've convinced you it is, and given you resolve, and maybe a few workable ideas, to go and do otherwise.

Hoping I have, let me now say this: your church is not safe enough.

I think this claim goes hand in hand with the other. We can take, on principle, that wherever our churches are too safe—havens of comfort for ourselves, breeding grounds for our prejudices, catering services for our preferences—they also will be not safe at all—not for us, not in the ways that matter most, and certainly not for anyone who breaks the roof or crashes the party. When our churches are mostly about insulating us from a broken world, they most tempt us to sit in judgment on that world, and applaud ourselves for doing so. A friend of mine described to me the church she grew up in this way: "Every Sunday, the sermon was about why what we believed was superior to what everyone else believed, and here are five ways to spot why they're wrong and we're right, and here are three steps to guard yourself from any compromise. And now, go out into the world and guard fiercely what you have." That's probably a caricature, but not by much. And for the record, I think there are right and wrong beliefs. But always the church needs to return to the fundamental covenant God made with Abraham: that we are blessed—materially, spiritually, in every way—in order to be a blessing. Or, as Paul puts it, "You will be made rich in every way so that you can be generous on every occasion."[1] God's riches—whatever form they take—are never for hoarding or squandering but always for sharing; they are given in order both to make us rich and to make us generous. They're never just for you, though by all means enjoy them. God "richly provides us with everything for our enjoyment."[2] Yes and amen. But that declaration is conjoined to—indeed, embedded within—an imperative: "Command those who are rich in this present world not to be arrogant nor to put their hope in wealth, which is so uncertain, but to put their hope in God, who richly provides us with everything for our enjoyment. Command them to do good, to be rich in good deeds, and to be generous and willing to share. In this way they will lay up treasure for themselves as a firm foundation for the coming age, so that they may take hold of the life that is truly life."[3] In the kingdom of God, there is no possibility of wealth apart from generosity. A stingy rich man, a cheapskate millionaire, a miserly moneybags—one cannot be such a thing and at the same time an authentic Christ-follower. Christ in me, if that's for real, will always depose mammon. The Holy Spirit has perfected the jujitsu move that touches my heart and, reflexively, loosens my grip on things.

Generosity encompasses both stuff and spirit. It touches things seen and unseen. It's about the cars and appliances and shoes and frozen meat and canned peaches and T-shirts I have. And it's about the hope and joy and peace and truth I have. Both comprise a vast inventory of wealth. All's to be enjoyed, none's to be hoarded. God gave the whole lot to make me rich and generous both.

This reality bears directly on our corporate life. Whatever God has richly provided, share. That's a command for you personally, but it's also one for us to hear and respond to collectively. Does your church meet in a beautiful building, or at least a sound one? Are there others in your community who might benefit from its facilities the six days it mostly sits empty? Are there people in your pews who, even when all the bulletins have been handed out and the Sunday school classes staffed and the coffee detail covered, still have no job to do? Might they volunteer to scrub graffiti off downtown walls, pick up garbage off city streets, visit the elderly in their cramped humid rooms, maintain community gardens? Whenever God gives more than we need, makes us "rich in every way," he does it to bless us but also to make us a blessing, so that we can be "generous on every occasion."

. . .

Part of biblical generosity is biblical hospitality, which is not quite what we've made hospitality into in North America, at least the part I'm from. Our version of hospitality is inviting friends or at least acquaintances two weeks from now to come for dinner at six, with the implied proviso that they'll be out the door by nine. The menu is fussed over. The house is scrubbed and tidied, at least its public areas, to spotlessness. If the guests show up more than a half hour early or a half hour late, or stay longer than a half hour past when they ought to go home, it's cause for fuming. We keep the conversation, for the most part, light. If someone ventures too far down a narrow back alley — politics or religion or feuds over sports teams — the hostess will cheerily, but with thinly veiled steeliness, call them back to less contentious matters.

And so on.

In short, our hospitality is inviting friends to visit and enjoy some superficial artificial conviviality for about three hours in which we all observe an unspoken rule to be on our best behavior. Biblical hospitality, on the other hand, is welcoming strangers to abide with us for who knows how long, in which we all observe an unspoken rule to help each other live well. These two things are almost polar opposites.

Some Bible scholars believe that the principal trait of God is hospitality: he goes to extravagant lengths — roaming highways and byways, scouring ditches and brothels, knocking at any random door — to invite not just strangers but enemies to his banquet. And he pays the ultimate price — his own Son killed outside the camp — to make a way for them to come in, and abide with him, and dwell in the house of the Lord forever. And he's not content merely to reform the errant sinner and feed the wandering vagrant: he's bent on nothing less than full adoption rights. He wants sons and daughters. And he wants them for all time.

That's hospitable.

Jesus makes biblical hospitality a touchstone of true discipleship. He runs a little test with Christians and churches, one which has enormous and far-reaching consequences. He comes among us disguised. And not just the disguise of the ordinary, the nondescript, the mild-mannered and well-mannered. That kind, though easy to miss, is easy to embrace. No, his disguise is outlandish. In very bad taste.

Dirty.

Homeless.

Poorly dressed.

Poorly nourished.

In trouble with the law.

That kind. He looks exactly like that smelly drifter who begs by the post office, with the mess of homemade tattoos down his arms and that mouthful of bad teeth. He bears uncanny resemblance to that over-the-hill whore who stands shivering on the street corner by the bikers' pub. He rolls around in a trash bin before knocking on your door. He comes to us dogged out, and arouses every instinct we have to turn away, to turn him away. "I was a stranger," he says. "And you invited me in."

Or not.

That's the test. It seems patently unfair. "If we knew it was you, we wouldn't have called the police." His point exactly.

There was a movie made in 1961 called *Whistle Down the Wind*. Some children stumble on a homeless drunk asleep in their family's barn. Startled, they ask who he is. Equally startled, he replies, "Jesus Christ." He utters it as profanity. The children hear it as revelation. They welcome him and honor him as Christ among them, and their hospitality transforms both the man and the family—in fact, the entire community.

A Sunday long ago, I was away and Shane, one of our pastors, spoke. Twice during his sermon, he had the congregation break into small groups to discuss a question. Both times Shane did this, he sat on the stairs leading up to the platform in our sanctuary while everyone else huddled in conversation. A First Nations lady, new to our church, and who may have had a little too much to drink that morning, came up both times, sat with him, put her arms around him, and leaned her head into his shoulder. He put his arm around her, and the two sat, without speaking, until Shane called the congregation back to attention. Then she got up, went to her seat, and listened with the rest.

It had an electrifying effect on our church. A few, I think, were appalled. But most were enthralled, thrilled, moved. They felt that this *was* the sermon (which was based on the last part of John 6, where Jesus challenges people to "eat my body, drink my blood"). Shane and this frail woman had, unrehearsed, enacted a parable of what it means to have Christ in the inmost places, bone of my bone, flesh of my flesh. What it means to welcome the stranger.

I wish I'd been there. It reminded me, just a little, of something that happened to Jesus.

I'm thinking of the story in Luke 7, where a woman barges in on a high-society dinner party and anoints Jesus' feet with her tears, dries them with her hair. She has a shady past. Well, maybe not shady enough: she's well known in town for her unsavory character, her deplorable conduct. She hasn't a name; she has a label: sinner. She wouldn't have ventured into the house at all—this was not an in-between place by any stretch—except Jesus is there, and for that she'll risk much: break the roof, poison the guard dog, hoodwink the security, steal someone's birthright. I don't think she does any of that. What she does is far more audacious: she risks the scorn of the religious elite.

This is the part I've seen many times: men and women with messy pasts, and very often messy presents, who risk the scorn, the sideways glances, the wary guardedness of the "good" people just to get close to Jesus. They come and they join the doctors and dentists and business owners and political leaders and high school teachers, and they often, in their sheer hunger and fervor for God, make the rest of us look stiff as mannequins. Some have tattoos embroidered on every part of their bodies. Some have parts of their flesh pierced and impaled with things that look like miniature replicas of medieval torture implements, like tiny copies of the hooked and spiraled and spiny and many-clawed things the English used to disembowel William Wallace. Some mingle, unconsciously, wildly colorful language with their everyday speech. Some have children who run amok during worship, terrorizing the guitarist and the accordion player, distracting half the congregation, while they lose themselves in prostrate devotion to God.

I've seen it often.

What I have never seen is what happens next in Luke's story: the woman gets unnervingly personal in her gratitude toward Jesus. She throws herself down before him, weeping, and begins stroking his feet, drenching them with her tears, sweeping her long loosed hair over them, taking each foot and wrapping it in the warm fold of her tresses to dry it. Her body heaves with the force of her sobbing.

And Jesus just sits there, unfazed, openly receiving this very physical act of her thanksgiving.

Simon, the party's host and house's owner, is appalled. Well, it's an awkward scene, and you or I might be likewise appalled: this woman, who not many nights ago was turning tricks for tanners and camel herders, who not many days back was a boardinghouse for demons, lacks all sense of decorum. She doesn't walk in wearing some elegant but modest evening dress, her clutch purse held demurely in front of her, uttering in measured tones a well-rehearsed speech: "Mr. Christ, I hope I have not caught you at an inopportune moment. Simon, I apologize for this impromptu visit. I know you are all terribly busy, and I promise I won't take up much of your time. But I did not want to be remiss in my duty to sufficiently thank you, Jesus, for the many kind things you've done for me. When we first met, I was going through a bit of a hard time, as you may recall. But your prompt and generous help has really made a difference. So I just wanted to take this opportunity to express my sincere appreciation, and let you know things are going much better. Well, thank you, and have a good day."

No. She emotes. She grandstands. She barges in. She blurts out. She holds nothing back. She is almost certainly improperly clad. The whole thing is scandalous. She does with Jesus a version of what she's done with most men in her life: shows affection through intimate touch.

I've wondered often about this. I've wondered how I'd have seen it, reacted to it, were I one of the "good" people over for lunch at Simon's house that day. Would I have "got it"? I doubt it. I likely would have been scandalized along with the rest. Likely I would have had thoughts similar to Simon's: "When the Pharisee who had invited him saw this, he said to himself, 'If this man were a prophet, he would know who is touching him and what kind of woman she is — that she is a sinner.' "[4]

That might be close to my own line of thought in the moment.

Sometimes, though, my wondering takes another turn. What if, I think, this happened to me? What if one Sunday a woman like this wanted to show to me publicly her gratitude, for some kindness or another I'd done, and in a way deeply familiar to her and distressingly awkward for me? What if one of the people I described above — pierced, tattooed, with a messy past — came up while I was preaching or worshiping or serving communion, and began doing something like what this woman does to Jesus? Lavishly, sensually, unabashedly, showing thankfulness in very physical terms?

I would flinch.

I would squirm.

Even if I submitted to it, which I doubt, I'm pretty sure I'd resort to wincing expressions and gestures of revulsion to signal to all the "good" people, *I'm not comfortable with any of this, you know that, right? I'm only enduring this so as not to embarrass the poor creature. I'll speak with her later to make sure nothing like this ever happens again. I'll let her know we're happy she's here, but this kind of behavior is not acceptable, not ever. In the meantime, let's just all humor her.*

This is decisively what Jesus does not do.

"Simon," Jesus says, knowing what Simon is thinking, "let me ask you a question."

And then Jesus cunningly draws Simon out. He tells him a story of indebtedness. Two people have debts, both sizable, but one much larger than the other. Both debts are forgiven. Jesus wants to know which debtor would love more. "I suppose the one who had the bigger debt forgiven," Simon answers.

"You have judged correctly," Jesus says.

And then he skewers Simon. "Do you see this woman?" The answer to that is a decisive no. Simon sees a label. A type. An example of moral warning. An offense to decency. He sees all that, but he doesn't see the woman. And so he's missed the most obvious thing: she loves much. She loves in a way that shows his love for what it is — a tepid, pallid, limping thing, a kind of allergy. Simon's love, such as it is, is expressed in what he doesn't do. It's rendered in acts of evasion and restraint. He's like the man who claims he loves his wife because he doesn't beat her.

But here's the thing to notice: Jesus measures love as hospitality. Love is rendered by how much we welcome the other. It's this failure of hospitality for which Jesus faults Simon, and the lavishness of hospitality for which he praises the woman. "I came into your house," Jesus says to Simon. "You did not give me any water for my feet, but she wet my feet with her tears and wiped them with her hair. You did not give me a kiss, but this woman, from the time I entered, has not stopped kissing my feet. You did not put oil on my head, but she has poured perfume on my feet. Therefore, I tell you, her many sins have been forgiven — as her great love has shown. But whoever has been forgiven little loves little."[5]

Love born of radical forgiveness expresses itself in radical hospitality. And the other way around: little forgiveness equals little love equals little welcome. It's worth noting that, in Jesus' story of two debtors, both actually needed the exact same amount of their debt forgiven: all of it. It's not that some people need only a little forgiveness, others a lot. We all need to be totally forgiven. We all need the whole debt canceled. That's what Simon doesn't get. He doesn't see himself as a great sinner. So he hasn't become a great lover. And the proof of it is that he's a terrible host.

Not only does this woman make up, and then some, for Simon's rude inhospitableness to Jesus; Jesus, likewise, makes up, and then some, for Simon's rude inhospitableness to her. In the center of a cold, cold room, in the midst of a cold, cold world, sit this woman and Jesus, one forgiven much and one forgiving much, kindling a warm fire called welcome.

This story presents us with two very different kinds of community: Simon's community, which is built on conventions of hospitality that bear striking resemblance to those that are widespread in most of North America; and Jesus' community, which embodies and distills God's radical welcome.

Let me boil it down to its starkest terms:

SIMON'S COMMUNITY	JESUS' COMMUNITY
Invites people we like, or who are like us, or who impress us, or whom we want to impress	Welcomes all who are thirsty
Judges (secretly) all who come	Blesses (openly) all who come
Conceals the true self	Discloses the true self
Withholds hospitality	Extends hospitality
Answers correctly	Lives worshipfully
Loves little	Loves much
Is proud	Is humble
Feels entitled	Feels gratitude
Labels the other	"Sees" the other
Creates tension and anxiety	Creates shalom
Traps us in our past	Releases us into our future

Given the choice, we'd never pick Simon's kind of community. But somehow, church after church after church, Christian after Christian after Christian, seems to end up with that anyhow.

Our safe churches aren't safe enough.

. . .

Several years ago, Wanda came to the church. She was thirsty for almost anything she could scrounge up—beer, port, rum, vanilla extract. She had only one way of paying for that: her well-worn body.

But she was desperate, and becoming thirsty for something else. She called the church one day, wondering if she could see a pastor, or two, or three, and now. Two of us met with her. She told us her story of woe. I told her the story of the woman at the well, whose life, like Wanda's, was in a tailspin. But Jesus offered her living water. I explained what that is—God's own presence within—and asked Wanda if she'd like to have that living water inside of her.

"Oh yeah!" she said.

We prayed. She confessed, repented, surrendered.

She arose joyful. The other pastor said, "Now, Wanda. This Sunday will be your first time in church. It's a big place and can be overwhelming. Don't feel you have to fit in right away. You can sit at the back if you like, come late, leave early. Whatever feels comfortable."

Wanda looked at him like he was plumb crazy.

"Why would I do that?" she said. "I've been waiting for this all my life."

That Sunday, Wanda was the first to arrive. She sat at the front and loudly agreed with everything I said. She was the last to leave. The next Sunday, same thing, except she brought a friend, one of *her* kind of people. I was preaching on servanthood. My main point: when you've tasted the love of Jesus, you want to serve. It was communion Sunday. In those days, we called our elders the Servant Leadership Team. I called them up to help with communion.

All Wanda heard was the word *servant*. And she had been listening intently to my sermon: if you've tasted the love of Jesus, you want to serve.

That day only two of our team of Servant Leaders were in church. They straggled to the front. Wanda was openly appalled. She stood, glared at the congregation, and then walked up to stand beside me and the other two servants.

Wanda was going to serve communion.

I flinched.

Then I remembered Luke 7. "Do you see this woman?" I saw that Wanda loved much. I leaned over to Wanda and said, "Since this is your very first time serving communion, do you mind if I help?"

So the two of us, she in her short skirt and spiky heels, went down the aisles, serving communion. The best part was looking at the faces of the people I love and lead and pray for and preach to. Not one of them flinched.

. . .

Psalm 84, by the sons of Korah, sums this up for me. "Better is one day in your courts," the psalm exudes, "than a thousand elsewhere" (v. 10). When our church sings those words, to Matt Redman's lovely melody, we do it with a passion somewhere between a swoon and a battle cry. We croon it like a love ballad. We belt it out like an anthem. It's a declaration and a plea.

Psalm 84 is a song about church, not heaven. It's a paean to the "house of the Lord," a testament to a wild and desperate longing: "My soul yearns, even faints, for the courts of the LORD" (v. 2). Which is wonderful, and very good, and as it should be. Because I'm a pastor, this pleases me very much. May the tribe increase.

But the sons of Korah, early in the psalm, make an observation that fills them with astonishment: "Even the sparrow has found a home, and the swallow a nest for herself, where she may have her young—a place near your altar" (v. 3). Swallows. Sparrows. Worthless birds, breeding in the thousands, common as stones. The offering of the poor. Creatures that fall along the roadside, unnoticed by all except God.

I sat once in a stone church in Kenya and watched and listened to the birds, not outside the building but within it. Because the church's windows had neither glass nor screen, the rafters were filled with chirping, fluttering birds which had made nests in the sharp inside corners of the roof trusses. They flitted and darted overhead and called to each other shrilly. I think perhaps they were swallows: light on the wing, blurringly fast, acrobatic, daring, precise. The pews and walls and floor,

I noticed, were streaked and flecked with their stool. Yet no one was bothered by them.

I realized, with a start of joy, that I was inside the skin of the sons of Korah. And I realized, with a jolt of pain, that I was far from their heart. In my church, we would try to schuss those birds out and, failing that, call in the exterminator. And then I realized, with a thunderclap of conviction, that the sons of Korah were not just talking about birds; they were talking about people. They were talking about those who, outside the courts of the Lord, except for the altar of God, have little value. They are considered worthless, expendable, a drain on resources. They're the welfare family whose "young" are unruly and disruptive. They're the ne'er-do-wells who use the church's benevolence fund like a personal bank account. They're the chronically unemployed. They're the hard-luck cases.

Even they have found a home here, a place near the altar.

They always will in any church worthy of being called that.

. . .

"Go in peace," Jesus says to the woman who anoints his feet. Go, and dwell in shalom. Taste it, bask in it, be healed by it, extend it. Know, inside out, the life God created you for.

Shalom.

A lovely benediction. But it makes you wonder: where will she go? Where can she, if shalom is to be her portion? Where does a scrawny sparrow like her, a woman with her reputation, socially awkward and ill mannered, find a place where she will not be scorned, not be judged, not be escorted to the door? In a world of Simons, it's hard to hold out hope that there is anywhere she can go in shalom.

Unless—well, here's an idea: can she come to your church?

CONCLUSION
THESE THAT TURN THE
WORLD ON ITS HEAD

"THESE THAT HAVE TURNED THE WORLD UPSIDE DOWN."[1]

That's what the men of Thessalonica accused Paul and Silas of doing: troublemaking, rabble-rousing, subverting. "These that have turned the world upside down are come hither also," is how the King James piquantly renders it. Their cry is alarmist but not entirely inaccurate. The phrase, literally, means here are those who have "raised up an insurrection." They've gone about overthrowing the existing order. They've supplanted what is with something altogether new. The men of Thessalonica, give them this: they know the kingdom of God when they see it rolling into town.

Which is almost ridiculous. Paul and Silas? Their physical appearance was hardly imposing. They were not embodiments of unstoppable menace. They were no specimens of fleshly intimidation, no incarnations of fierce invincibility. Paul, tradition says, was short, bald, stick-limbed. We know nothing of Silas's physical proportions, but even if he was a scowling knuckle-dragging hulk, ex-biker or bouncer, it was just him and Paul. There were perhaps also a few other "companions" — the text is not entirely clear who actually walked into town that day — but if so, in all likelihood the whole gang of them bore no resemblance to a band of vandals or berserkers. More like a chess club or lawn bowling team coming to town for a regional convention at the Super 8.

"These that have turned the world upside down."

What rumor were they working off of, these men of Thessalonica? What had they heard? What eyewitness testimonies had winged their way to their doorsteps, lathered them into this state of panic? What ghosts of things to come had mingled with the smoke of cook fires and threaded through their windows and troubled their sleep?

The answer: Philippi.

They must have heard about what happened in Philippi. That was the last place Paul and Silas were in, more or less. They "passed through" Amphipolis and Apollonia en route to Thessalonica, but there was no sojourning in those places. The last place they stayed was Philippi. The last place they caused a ruckus was Philippi.

And that's a story to be told.

Paul had never dreamed of going there. Or, more to the point, unless he *had* dreamed of going there, he never would have. He was bound in another direction. The opposite direction. But the Holy Spirit had other ideas and was blocking his path. (The whole book of Acts reorders contemporary notions of providence, but that's a whole other topic.) Then Paul had a dream. In it, a man from Macedonia — the province of which Philippi was the capital — stands and begs him to "come over to Macedonia and help us."

Paul concludes one thing from this: God is calling him and the others to "preach the gospel to them." They break camp and depart immediately to do so.

Full stop.

What does this mean, to "preach the gospel"? The usual answer is to explain, with clarity and brevity, the way of salvation: that Christ was crucified for our sin, that he died, was buried, was raised to life, ascended to heaven, and that we can receive eternal life through believing this. In fact, it's in Philippi that Paul gives the most succinct presentation of the gospel in this form. The jailer in Philippi asks Paul and Silas, "Sirs, what must I do to be saved?" To which they reply, "Believe in the Lord Jesus, and you will be saved — you and your household." The matter has rarely been stated so crisply.

Here's what intrigues me: how did the jailer know to ask that? This was the first time the gospel had ever shown up in Philippi. This man hadn't grown up in church. He was no lapsed Episcopalian or errant Baptist or wayward Pentecostal, someone who knew the basic "plan of salvation" and just needed a refresher. As an employee of Rome, he'd be a thoroughgoing pagan, offering sacrifices to the gods, hailing Caesar as Lord, *Kurios*, the term the church defiantly, exclusively, subversively reserved for Christ alone.

The question could have arisen only through his encounter with Paul and Silas. He must have known things about these men and observed things in these men that brought clarity and urgency to some deep intuition he held. I think for a long time he longed for his life to be otherwise. For a long time, he'd nursed deep suspicions about the potency of the gods and the divinity of Caesar. For a long time, he'd wondered why life could be so full of material and sensual abundance and so empty of meaning, so joyless and fruitless. For a long time, he'd worried that all his scrupulous adherence to the ways of Rome fell drastically short of what really truly mattered.

And then he caught a glimpse of all he longed for. He saw it, he heard it, in two men bleeding in the back room, bleeding and singing and praying.

. . .

Let me back up.

Paul and his companions conclude they are to travel to Macedonia to "preach the gospel." But what actually happens in Macedonia, in Philippi, is a series of interlocking events from which preaching is conspicuously absent. Maybe once, with a group of women, the team actually preaches, though what the text presents is more of a conversation between Paul, his companions, and these women. Otherwise, we don't see or hear a lot of classical preaching of the gospel. What we do see and hear is a vivid and winsome embodiment of the gospel. We see and hear a vibrant living out of the gospel.[2]

We see words becoming flesh and living among others.

And we watch this gospel, this three-dimensional, word-made-flesh gospel, turn lives inside out and the world upside down.

First, there's Lydia. She's a wealthy woman from Thyatira in the textile trade. She's in Philippi, we assume, to do business. On the morning she meets Paul and Silas, she seems to be doing breakfast with the local women's Rotary Club. Paul meets them when he's scouting a good place to pray, and doesn't miss the opportunity to "preach." Lydia is among those *listening*—a key word in the interlocking events of Philippi. She is already a "worshiper of God." But hearing Paul, "the Lord opened her heart to respond to Paul's message." Immediately, she is baptized, she and "members of her household," and she opens her home to the missions team.

So at the get-go, "preaching the gospel" affects livelihood. Now entire households are turned upside down. Now businesses also. The provisions of home and hearth and the resources of the marketplace are made to serve the work of the kingdom. Our private and our public worlds are disrupted and transformed by the gospel.

Then, there's the slave girl.

She meets Paul and Silas in the same place they met Lydia and her Rotary Club. The girl is well known in town: she has a spirit inhabiting her—her real owner, her real slaver—who allows her to cast fortunes. She's a soothsayer. Her owners make a pile of money off of her. It's unlikely she sees any of it.

But she's a local celebrity. She's sought far and wide to do her trick with tea leaves or tarot cards or goat innards, or whatever medium she employs. She must be good at what she does: a city full of repeat customers attests to that.

In fact, we have in this story from Acts clear evidence of just how good she is. She follows Paul and Silas around shouting a loud endorsement of them and their work. Here's her slogan, word for word: "These men are servants of the Most High God, who are telling you the way to be saved." These are those who have turned the world upside down.

Well, this is no small ad campaign. This girl, after all, is locally hailed and sought as a spiritual authority. She's a herald of the supernatural. People come to her, and pay big bucks to her slave owners, to give them insight into the world beyond the world. The deeper truths. The really real. Dispatches from the land not seen.

And she's nailed it. Not a word she speaks about Paul and Silas is anything but the truth, the whole truth, and nothing but the truth. The town's leading psychic gives them a robust endorsement. It's like the leading syndicated astrologer using everyone's weekend horoscope to promote a local evangelism crusade. For Gemini, for Leo, for Taurus, for all twelve zodiacs, she writes, "You've got to go hear Franklin Graham."

What evangelist would balk at that?

Paul. He puts up with it for several days, but "finally ... became so troubled that he turned around and said to the spirit, 'In the name of Jesus Christ I command you to come out of her!'

"At that moment, the spirit left her."

This is the gospel being "preached." This is the liberation from the bondage to decay. The gospel is, among other things, this trouble in our hearts at a world that would exploit a little girl for financial gain. It's this enlarging of our hearts that makes us care about the spiritual condition and social plight of a girl, a sparrow, no one else cares about, even knowing full well what it will cost us to intervene. What it costs Paul and Silas is a brutal scourging and an equally brutal imprisonment. Knowing that it would cost this, I'm guessing, held Paul back for many days from doing anything. Maybe, even, he was enjoying to some extent the notoriety the slave girl's advertisement was creating for the gospel.

But at some point the trouble in his heart got too heavy. He would not for one more minute benefit from her torment. He would not for one more moment flinch from the consequences of stepping in. He would, here and now, gladly be beaten and imprisoned in order to set her free. Paul — and Silas — exchange their freedom for hers. By their wounds, she is healed.

Chaim Potok, the Jewish novelist, grew up with one longing: to be a writer of stories. But his mother had other plans. She wanted him to be a doctor. "Chaim," she'd say. "Why be a writer? What do writers do? And they're poor. Be a doctor. You'll keep people from dying. And you'll make lots of money." This kept up for many years. One day, he'd had enough. He blew up at her. "Mother, I don't want to be a doctor. I don't care if I make lots of money. I don't want to keep people from dying. Mother, I want to be a writer. I want to show people how to live."[3]

Paul chose a vocation — actually, he was press-ganged by Jesus into one, but ever after he embraced it with all his heart — where he got to do both: keep people from dying *and* show them how to live.

And he pays dearly for it. Far from getting lots of money, he gets brutalized, here and on many other occasions. Here, the slave girl's liberation is a financial crisis for her owners. Her only value to them is wrapped up in her occultic powers, her voodoo ways. With this gone, she's just a mouth to feed. So they raise an alarm, and the city magistrate has Paul and Silas beaten in the Roman fashion—forty lashes minus one—and then tossed into the city jail, with instructions to the jailer to apply extra security measures. He puts them in the inner cell—the bowels of the prison—and shackles their hands and feet.

Do you see them? They're hard to recognize, disfigured as they are. Bruises bloom like dark magnolias on their flesh. Blood and pus shine darkly from the deepness of their open cuts, and blacken and harden the edges of their wounds.

Does the jailer puzzle over their crime? Does he know that they've been beaten like this, are now placed in his gruff care, because they set the captive free? As he leads his own captives stumbling down the stones, as he clamps cold metal on their torn flesh, does he reflect on the unfairness of that? He must know who that slave girl is. She's a local celebrity. He must have seen her often, plying her trade. Maybe his wife or son-in-law has employed her services. Maybe he has. Some journey he had to undertake, or some decision he had to reach, or some council he sought about a financial opportunity. Has he ever had a moment of wondering what a girl like that could be if this dark power within her was broken and bound and she walked free from her own prison? Or has his line of work, which is neither about keeping people from dying nor about showing them how to live, taught him to squelch such questions before they ever take shape?

We don't know what the jailer thinks, not about slave girls or about the men who set them free.

But what that jailer witnesses next does form a question in his mind, a question he finally asks. The question is pointed and urgent: "How can I be saved?"

Where did that come from? How on earth did he think to ask it?

Maybe he was thinking it all along. But my best guess, and the one that the story most clearly supports, is that his question arises from the way Paul and Silas respond to the beating, the imprisonment, the shackles.

They don't whine or curse or protest their innocence. They don't plead their case. They don't ask for a lawyer. They don't rage against the night.

They sing. They pray. They practice the sovereignty of God. They become living, breathing testimonies of what Paul later will write to the Romans:

For those who are led by the Spirit of God are the children of God. The Spirit you received does not make you slaves, so that you live in fear again; rather, the Spirit you received brought about your adoption to sonship. And by him we cry, *"Abba*, Father." The Spirit himself testifies with our spirit that we are God's children. Now if we are children, then we are heirs — heirs of God and co-heirs with Christ, if indeed we share in his sufferings in order that we may also share in his glory.

I consider that our present sufferings are not worth comparing with the glory that will be revealed in us. The creation waits in eager expectation for the children of God to be revealed. For the creation was subjected to frustration, not by its own choice, but by the will of the one who subjected it, in hope that the creation itself will be liberated from its bondage to decay and brought into the freedom and glory of the children of God.

We know that the whole creation has been groaning as in the pains of childbirth right up to the present time. Not only so, but we ourselves, who have the firstfruits of the Spirit, groan inwardly as we wait eagerly for our adoption, the redemption of our bodies. For in this hope we were saved. But hope that is seen is no hope at all. Who hopes for what they already have? But if we hope for what we do not yet have, we wait for it patiently.

In the same way, the Spirit helps us in our weakness. We do not know what we ought to pray for, but the Spirit himself intercedes for us through wordless groans. And he who searches our hearts knows the mind of the Spirit, because the Spirit intercedes for God's people in accordance with the will of God.

And we know that in all things God works for the good of those who love him, who have been called according to his purpose. For those God foreknew he also predestined to be conformed to the image of his Son, that he might be the firstborn among many brothers and sisters. And those he predestined, he also called; those he called, he also justified; those he justified, he also glorified.

What, then, shall we say in response to these things? If God is for us, who can be against us? He who did not spare his own Son, but gave him up for us all — how will he not also, along with him, graciously give us all things? Who will bring any charge against those whom God has chosen? It is God who justifies. Who then can condemn? No one. Christ Jesus who died — more than that, who was raised to life — is at the right hand of God and is also interceding for us. Who shall separate us from the love of Christ?

Shall trouble or hardship or persecution or famine or nakedness or danger or sword? As it is written:

"For your sake we face death all day long;
we are considered as sheep to be slaughtered."

No, in all these things we are more than conquerors through him who loved us. For I am convinced that neither death nor life, neither angels nor demons, neither the present nor the future, nor any powers, neither height nor depth, nor anything else in all creation, will be able to separate us from the love of God that is in Christ Jesus our Lord.[4]

Maybe it was this very night Paul composed in his heart these thoughts. Certainly, this very night he embodied them. Paul and Silas's hope in God's glory to be revealed through all things, their confidence in God's grace abounding in all things, their faith in God's power over all things—all this converges in the only act possible from men such as these under circumstances such as these: they sing; they pray. They must. They can do no other, for in all these things they are more than conquerors through him who loved them. Not even this pain, this mess, this loss, this prison, these chains, can separate them from the love of God that is in Christ Jesus.

The jailer sees that. He hears that. And now he's thinking. Now he's wondering. And he's not letting professional decorum or hard-bitten cynicism foreclose the question that arises.

Somewhere in the night, the jailer falls asleep. Maybe he's lulled by his prisoners' hymns and prayers. Around midnight, he's awakened, by an earthquake. It's so potent it shakes the doors of the prison cells open and shatters the chains of the prisoners. The jailer draws his sword. It's not to block anyone's escape. He believes either that they've already fled or, more likely, that there are too many for one man. So he draws his sword to impale himself. In good Roman fashion, he plans to commit ritual suicide to save Caesar the trouble of executing him, the punishment for letting prisoners under your watch escape, regardless of the circumstances under which it happened.

And then a voice. Loud. Urgent. A voice the jailer has come to know. Come to trust. "Don't harm yourself! We are all here!"

Keep people from dying.

Show them how to live.

One word in this story, an unlikely word, sums this entire thing up. Indeed, this one word refracts the whole splendor of the gospel: *we*. *We* are all here.

That prison held more prisoners than just Paul and Silas. Probably many more. We can safely guess that, unlike Paul and Silas, the majority of those other prisoners were there not for doing good deeds on behalf of slave girls but for actual crimes. They were the usual suspects, incarcerated for the obvious reasons: treachery, thievery, butchery. B and Es. Grand theft chariot. It was a house filled with brigands and assassins. The kind of men who have spent lifetimes taking advantage of the weaknesses of others. Men entirely self-concerned. Men willing to kill, steal, and destroy for what was in it for them.

Until now.

"*We* are all here."

What the jailer sees are two men who have, without even trying, orchestrated all this. He sees two men who can set captives free. Two men who can keep captives still. Two men who care about slave girls and criminals and jailers.[5] He sees two men who keep people from dying and then show them how to live.

And now his question becomes a fire in his bones. He can't hold it in any longer: "Sirs, what must I do to be saved?"

And by saved he must mean, "How do I get in on whatever it is you men have? How do I come to live the kind of life you're living, that can turn the whole world upside down?

. . .

So when Paul and Silas saunter into Thessalonica, and the hue and cry goes up, "These that have turned the world upside down are come hither also," the worry among the men of Thessalonica must be that as goes Philippi, so will go Thessalonica. Here are the men who don't just talk about their faith. They live it. They live it in dangerous, radical, subversive ways, in ways that leave no part of society untouched: rich people, slave girls, demoniacs, jailers, prisoners. The business community, the religious world, the judicial powers.

Nothing is left untouched. Nothing is as it was before. Once men like this get loose in your streets, no god, no demon, no bully, no system of oppression or corruption or seduction, no idolatry, no ideology, is safe again.

Beware the men and the women who turn the world upside down.

Better yet, become one.

ACKNOWLEDGMENTS

THIS IS MY SEVENTH BOOK. Writing seven books is, I imagine, like having seven children: you love each and all dearly, but can't always remember their names or their birth dates. I've written all my books, save one, *as I go*: in the hurly-burly of a thousand other demands, under the weight of a tumult of duties and distractions. Writing is my sideline. Books are what I glean from the edges of pastoring, a much larger field in which I labor. To make a book, it takes a lot of bending and grubbing among stubble, and even then it's just enough for a small loaf.

Thank God for all those who've bent and grubbed with me.

There's my ever-faithful agent, Ann Spangler. Between writing her own fine and bestselling books, representing a stable of other writers, and raising two lovely daughters, Ann makes herself readily available to me, to calm my worst fears and provoke my best creativity and scream and turn blue on my behalf. We've been arm in arm on all seven books, with no end in sight.

There are the good and wise people at Zondervan. Both Ryan Pazdur and Jordan Walters tied the first draft of this book to a chair and tortured many improvements out of it. Their toughness on my behalf — and yours — helped immensely.

There are those who read all or part of this manuscript, and whose comments and encouragements both kept me from quitting and spurred me on to do better: Rob Filgate, Susan Luscombe, Graham Bruce, Mindy Caliguire, Cheryl Buchanan. May all your tribes increase.

There's my church, New Life Community Baptist, who have put up with my antics and obsessions for more than sixteen years. They've been the crash-test dummies for many of the ideas in this book, and are my primary firsthand evidence that a church can more and more resemble the kingdom of God.

There are my children, Adam, Sarah, and Nicola, who are more than I deserve and exactly what I need.

There's my wife, Cheryl, who taught me how to pray, who believes in me beyond all good sense, who loves me, like God, extravagantly, and who remains my prized BMW: Beautiful Marvelous Wife.

And there's my Lord and Savior, Jesus Christ, by whom, through whom, and for whom all this be true. To the praise of his glorious name, now and forever. Amen.

—Mark Buchanan
March 2011

APPENDIX
THE A TO H SCALE

They devoted themselves to the apostles' teaching and to the fellowship, to the breaking of bread and to prayer (Acts 2:42).

Remember your leaders, who spoke the word of God to you. Consider the outcome of their way of life and imitate their faith (Heb. 13:7).

Do not be carried away by all kinds of strange teachings. It is good for our hearts to be strengthened by grace, not by ceremonial foods, which are of no value to those who eat them (Heb. 13:9).

Obey your leaders and submit to their authority. They keep watch over you as men who must give an account. Obey them so that their work will be a joy, not a burden, for that would be of no advantage to you (Heb. 13:17).

. . .

Everyone was filled with awe, and many wonders and miraculous signs were done by the apostles (Acts 2:43).

Therefore, since we are receiving a kingdom that cannot be shaken, let us be thankful, and so worship God acceptably with reverence and awe, for our "God is a consuming fire" (Heb. 12:28–29).

All the believers were together and had everything in common. Selling their possessions and goods, they gave to anyone as he had need (Acts 2:44–45).

Keep your lives free from the love of money and be content with what you have, because God has said, "Never will I leave you; never will I forsake you" (Heb. 13:5).

Remember those earlier days after you had received the light.... You ... joyfully accepted the confiscation of your property, because you knew that you yourselves had better and lasting possessions (Heb. 10:32, 34).

·   ·   ·

Every day they continued to meet together in the temple courts. They broke bread in their homes and ate together with glad and sincere hearts, praising God and enjoying the favor of all the people. And the Lord added to their number daily those who were being saved (Acts 2:46–47).

Let us not give up meeting together, as some are in the habit of doing, but let us encourage one another—and all the more as you see the Day approaching (Heb. 10:25).

See to it that no one misses the grace of God and that no bitter root grows up to cause trouble and defile many (Heb. 12:15).

Keep on loving each other as brothers. Do not forget to entertain strangers, for by so doing some people have entertained angels without knowing it (Heb. 13:1–2).

NOTES

INTRODUCTION

1. Mark 9:1.
2. 2 Peter 1:16–18.
3. Heb. 1:1–2.
4. Mark 9:6.
5. See Heb. 12:22–29.

CHAPTER ONE

1. For example: N. T. Wright, *Bringing the Church to the World*; Kevin DeYoung and Ted Kluck, *Why We Love the Church: In Praise of Institutions and Organized Religion* and *Why We Are Not Emergent: By Two Guys Who Should Be*; Marva Dawn, *Reaching Out without Dumbing Down*; almost anything by Brian McLaren. And many, many more.
2. John 17:24, emphasis mine.
3. John 15:9–17.
4. John 17:23–26.
5. Eph. 3:16–19.
6. 1 Cor. 13:1–3.
7. 1 John 3:1.
8. Zeph. 3:14–17 TNIV.
9. Rom. 5:5 KJV.

10. This woman is, according to John's gospel, the first person to whom Jesus reveals his messianic identity. Jesus chooses to tell a woman, a Samaritan, and a "sinner" this before he even tells his disciples—men, Jews, semi-well-behaved personages.

CHAPTER TWO

1. James 1:19–20 TNIV.
2. Mark 3:14.
3. Mark 3:16–19 TNIV.
4. Luke 9:51–56 TNIV.
5. Ps. 2:12 KJV.
6. Mark 10:33–34 TNIV.
7. See Matt. 16:22.
8. Mark 10:35–38.
9. 2 Cor. 3:18.
10. Eph. 5:25.
11. Col. 1:24.
12. 2 Cor. 4:8–9.
13. 2 Cor. 4:16.
14. See Matt. 26:53.
15. Matt. 5:43–48, emphasis mine.
16. Story cited in A. J. Conyers, *The Eclipse of Heaven: The Loss of Transcendence and Its Effect on Modern Life* (Downers Grove, Ill.: InterVarsity, 1992), 165.

CHAPTER THREE

1. Lauren F. Winner, "Suffer the Children: Inner-City Gradeschoolers Reawakened Author Jonathan Kozol's Dormant Faith," *Christianity Today*, June 12, 2000, 94–95.
2. *Rez* is Native slang for an Indian reservation.
3. Amos 4:1.
4. Jonah 1:3, 10.
5. Jonah 3:2, 4–5.
6. Prov. 29:1 TNIV.
7. Jonah 1:2; 3:2–3; 4:11.
8. See Paul's sequence of thought in 2 Corinthians 4 and 5.
9. Jonah 4:1–11.
10. Luke 15:25–32.

Chapter Four

1. Matt. 25:14–30 TNIV.

Chapter Five

1. Daniel J. Boortsin, *Hidden History* (New York: Harper and Row, 1987), 297–98.
2. Acts 2:44.
3. Phil. 2:3.
4. I'm referring here to the first disciples and to the abolitionist movement under William Wilberforce.
5. This scene is not part of the book.

Chapter Six

1. *Synoptics* is the academic term for the first three gospels. It means "same eye" or, more naturally, "to see together," a term meant to capture the broad similarities in style, content, perspective, and structure among Mathew, Mark, and Luke, and in contrast to John.
2. John 6:5.
3. John 6:26.
4. *Johanine* is the academic term to describe the apostle John's unique style, form, content, and theology.
5. John 6:53–58.
6. John 6:66.
7. John 6:67.
8. John 6:68–69.
9. Jesus right after makes a comment that one of the Twelve, Judas, is a devil. So even among this core group, conviction wanes.
10. Acts 8:26–40.
11. Acts 9:1–19, 26–30; 7:54–8:1.
12. John 14:11, emphasis mine.
13. See Matt. 7:24–27.
14. James 1:22.
15. 1 Cor. 2:1, 4.
16. Col. 3:17.
17. Phil. 4:9.
18. 1 Peter 2:12, emphasis mine.

19. 1 John 4:2–3.
20. 1 John 3:18.
21. Rev. 2:2, 19; 3:1, 8, 15.
22. John 20:21.
23. Phil. 2:6.
24. Heb. 1:3.
25. Col. 1:15–17, 19.
26. Eph. 3:10–11, emphasis mine.
27. Col. 1:24–27, emphasis mine.

CHAPTER SEVEN

1. Zech. 8:23.
2. *Gossip* derives from the phrase *God's sibling*, which referred to a close, confidential relationship. In time, this was shortened to *God's sib*, then *Godsib*. When it morphed into *gossip*, not only the word but the meaning shifted; it now refers to the betraying of secrets, where once it meant the confiding of them. At our church, we have a regular practice on Sunday mornings of *Godsib*, where anyone in the body can share what God is doing in or around them.
3. Zech. 8:20–21.
4. Ps. 22:30–31.
5. Gen. 17:19.
6. Deut. 6:7.
7. Compare 1 Kings 3:1–15 with 11:1–13.
8. 1 Kings 12:7.
9. 1 Kings 12:8, emphasis mine.
10. 1 Kings 12:10–11.
11. Zech. 8:7–8.
12. Eph. 4:3.
13. 1 Peter 2:9.
14. 1 John 1:7.
15. Zech. 8:9–13.
16. Jared Diamond, *Collapse: How Societies Choose to Fail or Succeed* (New York: Viking, 2005). Diamond distills the causes of societal collapse to five factors: environmental damage, climate change, hostile neighbors, friendly (or unfriendly) trade partners, and the society's response to its environmental problems (pp. 10–15). Most

of the book documents this fifth factor, and it's here that themes of corrupt or rigid religion, corrupt or greed-driven business, and land degradation and exploitation play significant and recurring roles.

17. Zech. 8:14–17.

18. An experience I enjoy, and sometimes endure, more and more frequently as I travel internationally.

19. Residential Schools were a collaborative effort between Canada's federal government and three church denominations (Roman Catholic, Anglican, and United Church) to carry out federal policy to educate and assimilate Indigenous children. The first schools were begun in the 1840s and the last closed in 1996. Many of the schoolchildren were forcibly separated from their families, systematically stripped of their language and heritage, and sexually, physically, and emotionally abused. There is strong but inconclusive evidence that in some of the schools, children were deliberately infected with tuberculosis. There were very high rates of sickness and mortality in many of the schools, mostly because of sordid living conditions, malnourishment, poor sanitation, and inadequate medical treatment. The social fallout of these schools is vast.

20. John 10:10.

21. Zech. 8:19.

22. All of these images and phrases have been gleaned from Heb. 12:1–11.

23. Matt. 6:16–18.

24. Zech. 8:20–23.

25. Rom. 11:13–14.

Chapter Eight

1. Acts 18:10.

2. Gen. 18:1–8.

3. I don't want to read too much into this, but it's hard not to see this as a Trinitarian theophany; the melding of three-in-one and one-in-three is built into the very grammatical structure of this story.

4. Gen. 12:2–3.

5. Ps. 32:4.

6. John 4.

7. Luke 10:1–9.

8. Cf. 1 Corinthians 8 and 10:14–31, and Romans 14.

CHAPTER TEN

1. For the full list of Scriptures, consult the appendix.
2. Acts 2:42 – 47; 4:32 – 35 TNIV.

CHAPTER ELEVEN

1. See Heb. 1:3.
2. Leon Morris, *The Gospel according to John*, rev. ed., New International Commentary on the New Testament (Grand Rapids, Mich.: Eerdmans, 1995), 65.
3. John 17:24, emphasis mine.
4. 1 Peter 1:18 – 21, emphasis mine.
5. Eph. 1:3 – 5, emphasis mine.
6. See John 3:2 for the Nicodemus reference, 2:23 – 25 for the crowd reference.
7. Isa. 53:2 – 3.

CHAPTER TWELVE

1. John 5:19.
2. This is the only place in the Gospels where the word *justified* is used in the Pauline sense of the word.
3. Luke 18:14.
4. Gal. 6:1 – 5 TNIV.
5. John 1:14, 16 – 18 TNIV.
6. I've not space here for a discussion of the New Testament's recasting of the Mosaic law, other than what follows under my discussion of conviction 5. In brief, the New Testament recognizes both the enduring power of the law to reveal God's standards and yet its complete impotency to help us live according to those standards. So Jesus fulfills the law for us. What this means in practice is a full canceling of the Mosaic law in some instances (what you wear, what you eat, etc.) and an impartation of the Spirit's power to live according to the law in other instances (primarily, the Decalogue, or Ten Commandments). But, again, this is a topic for another time and place.
7. Lev. 15:31.
8. Luke 9:35 (emphasis added), the chapter right after the one we're examining in this section.
9. Luke 8:42 – 48.

10. Lev. 15:28–30.
11. Matt. 8:1–4 TNIV.
12. Lev. 13:45–46 TNIV.

Chapter Thirteen

1. 1 Thess. 5:19.
2. Eph. 4:30.
3. Screwtape was C. S. Lewis's name for the devil in his famous *The Screwtape Letters*.
4. Linda Blair played Regan, a demon-possessed teenager, in the notorious 1973 movie *The Exorcist*.
5. There is, I think, a fourth spirit: a wounded spirit. But it's unlike the other three. It is drawn to Jesus, but wary of him. Though Jesus often seeks out people with this spirit, people with it rarely seek him out. When he shows up, it tries to slip into the shadows. I'm thinking of the Samaritan woman whom Jesus meets at a well. I'm thinking of the invalid by the pool at Bethsaida whom Jesus tracks down. I'm thinking of, perhaps, the woman with the flow of blood who, hesitantly, risks touching Jesus but then quickly tries to dodge him. The distinctive thing about a wounded spirit is its deep sense of shame and, sometimes, self-pity. It wants what Jesus has but feels unworthy of receiving it, or lacks the faith that it would make any difference.

   I have a theory: that a wounded spirit, left untreated, is most susceptible to a religious spirit. A religious spirit is the armor that a wounded spirit wears to protect itself. And, as I say about the religious spirit, it is most susceptible to an evil spirit.
6. See 2 Tim. 2:23–26.
7. See John 7:14–52; 8:12–59; 9:13–41; 10:22–39; 11:45–57; 12:9–11, 37–43. John 12:37 sums it up: "Even after Jesus had done all these miraculous signs in their presence, they still would not believe in him."
8. Luke 6:6–11.
9. John 11:53.
10. John 11:48 TNIV.
11. Fyodor Dostoyevsky, *The Brothers Karamazov*, trans. Andrew H. MacAndrew (1880; Toronto: Bantam, 1970), 299.
12. Ibid., 307ff.
13. Ibid., 314.

CHAPTER FOURTEEN

1. Mark 2:2–12.
2. Mark 2:6–7.
3. Mark 2:8–12 TNIV.
4. See John 1:12–13.
5. 2 Tim. 2:26.
6. See Judg. 6:25–26.
7. Rom. 12:1–2.

CHAPTER FIFTEEN

1. Ps. 133:1.
2. James 1:17.
3. Eph. 4:1–7, 11–16 TNIV.
4. Eph. 2:13–18 TNIV.
5. Eph. 2:12 TNIV.
6. 2 Cor. 5:18–20.
7. The phrase comes from Philip Yancey, *What's So Amazing about Grace?* (Grand Rapids, Mich.: Zondervan, 2002), 161–75.
8. 2 Cor. 5:16, 19 TNIV.
9. 2 Cor. 5:19.
10. John 17:20–23 TNIV, emphasis mine.
11. Vv. 14, 25.
12. 1 John 4:20 TNIV.
13. See Phil. 4:2–3.
14. Eph. 4:4–6.
15. Eph. 1:18 TNIV.

CHAPTER SIXTEEN

1. Mark 7:1–5 TNIV.
2. Mark 6:53–56, emphasis mine.
3. See Mal. 4:2—the "healing in its wings" is linked to the "sun of righteousness" rising, a messianic image. The image is associated with judgment and punishment of "every evildoer" and "the wicked." Malachi raises the question whether deep healing of wounds inflicted by the malice of others can happen without retributive justice.
4. I first heard this story from my friend Carolyn Arends (whose music and writing you should get to know, if you don't already), who heard

it first from her friend Steve Bell (ditto regarding music). After which, I researched to verify the story and gather further details.

5. Part of our story has been documented in various places: Christianity Today International's DVD curriculum *Intersect Culture* (2007), later repackaged as *Where Faith and Culture Meet*; Karen Stiller's book, *Going Missional: Conversations with Thirteen Churches Who Have Embraced Missional Life*; Charlene De Haan's article "A Church You Should Know About," in *Faith Today* (Sept. – Oct. 2009); Willow Creek Association's Canadian version of 2011 Global Leadership Summit; my article "The People and the Black Book," in *Leadership* (Summer 2010); Jeremy Bell's *News and Notes with Jeremy Bell* (December 2010) on the Canadian Baptists of Western Canada website.

6. Neh. 1:3; interestingly, the situation of exile for the Jewish people had existed for around a hundred and fifty years, approximately the number of years the Cowichans have been under some kind of colonial rule.

7. John 14:12.

8. John 9:1 – 4.

9. I was alerted to this textual variation by Gary M. Burge, *The NIV Application Commentary: John* (Grand Rapids, Mich.: Zondervan, 2000), 272.

10. Matt. 9:22; Mark 10:52; Luke 17:19; etc.

11. Dan. 3:16 – 18.

CHAPTER SEVENTEEN

1. Josh. 5:1 – 2; Gibeath Haaraloth means "hill of foreskins," which, as my teenage daughters like to say, is too much information.

2. Both James 2:25 and Heb. 11:31 describe her as *raab hē pornē*, Rahab the prostitute, or as we might put it, Rahab the porn star. There's no ambiguity in this rendering.

3. 2 Cor. 10:2 – 6.

4. Heb. 11:1.

5. Heb. 11:6.

6. See Neh. 1:1 – 2:10.

7. Cited in Richard John Neuhaus, *Death on a Friday Afternoon: Meditations on the Last Words of Jesus from the Cross* (New York: Basic, 2001), 253. No source given.

8. Mark and Luke have one blind man, Matthew two. Only Mark gives the man's name. I am basing my retelling of this on Mark's gospel. For the story of James and John, see Mark 10:35–45. For the story of Bartimaeus, see Mark 10:46–52.
9. Luke 18:39, emphasis mine.
10. Mark 10:42–45; Jesus' rebuke to James and John and the other disciples comes immediately before the encounter with Bartimaeus.
11. Neh. 2:5, 7–8.
12. The title of a landmark book by Elizabeth O'Connor on her remarkable church in Washington, DC, circa 1970.
13. Heb. 4:14–16.

Chapter Eighteen

1. 2 Cor. 9:11.
2. 1 Tim. 6:17.
3. 1 Tim. 6:17–19.
4. Luke 7:39.
5. Luke 7:44b–47 TNIV.

Conclusion

1. Acts 17:6 KJV.
2. This story is in Acts 16:16–40.
3. Told in Eugene Peterson, *Under the Unpredictable Plant: An Exploration in Vocational Holiness* (Grand Rapids, Mich.: Eerdmans, 1992), 46–47.
4. Rom. 8:14–39 TNIV.
5. I wonder if part of Paul and Silas's motivation in saving the jailer's life was the story of Peter's miraculous escape from prison, recorded in Acts 12. That story would have been well known in the early church. The story ends with this grim comment: "After Herod had a thorough search made for [Peter] and did not find him, he cross-examined the guards *and ordered that they be executed*" (v. 19). I speculate that the death of those guards was a heartache for the early church, and that a resolve took hold that, if ever God provided one of his servants with another such miraculous escape, the greater miracle would be to "live such good lives among the pagans that, though they accuse you of doing wrong, they may see your good deeds and glorify God on the day he visits us" (1 Peter 2:12).